Autonomy and Interdependence

AUTONOMY

AND

INTERDEPENDENCE

U.S.–Western European Monetary
and Trade Relations, 1958–1984

THOMAS L. ILGEN

Brandeis University

ROWMAN & ALLANHELD
PUBLISHERS

ROWMAN & ALLANHELD

Published in the United States of America in 1985
by Rowman & Allanheld, Publishers
(a division of Littlefield, Adams & Company)
81 Adams Drive, Totowa, New Jersey 07512

Library of Congress Cataloging in Publication Data

Ilgen, Thomas L.
  Autonomy and interdependence.

  Bibliography: p.
  Includes index.
  1. United States—Foreign economic relations—Europe.
2. Europe—Foreign economic relations—United States.
3. International economic relations. 4. International
finance. 5. Economic history—1945-   I. Title.
HF1456.5.E8147 1985   337.4073   84-27557
ISBN 0-8476-7413-4

85 86 87 / 10 9 8 7 6 5 4 3 2 1
Printed in the United States of America

To my father,
Joe S. Ilgen

Table of Contents

Preface and Acknowledgments

The initial research for this book was undertaken in 1974–1975 when relatively little attention had been directed to economic problems in the Atlantic Alliance and university courses in international relations were only beginning to consider the dilemmas posed by issues of political economy. My purpose at that time was to explore the economic side of the Western alliance to complement the analyses of political and military-strategic relations in works such as Robert Osgood's *NATO: The Entangling Alliance* and Henry Kissinger's *The Troubled Partnership: A Re-Appraisal of the Atlantic Alliance*. I was struck from the first by the asymmetry of influence in Atlantic political and strategic relations, how Washington prevailed on all the issues that really mattered, and by the problems that this asymmetry generated within the alliance over time. Close inspection of economic relations revealed a similar asymmetry in negotiations over the trade and monetary rules by which all agreed to play, which in turn bred similar alliance difficulties and resentment in Europe. What, for me, seemed most interesting and most perplexing was that American power over Atlantic economic relations appeared not to have declined, as many were beginning to argue in the early 1970s, but to have been sustained through more vigorous action such as Nixon's decision to cut convertibility between the dollar and gold, the push toward flexible exchange rates in 1973, and a determination to secure trade benefits through new measures such as voluntary export restraints. Nevertheless, while this negotiating influence was sustained, American economic fortunes steadily declined; the dollar came under repeated attack, trade surpluses disappeared, and one American industry after another came under serious competitive challenge from abroad. In the past decade of Western trade and monetary relations, American power and economic decline have existed side by side, and it is this peculiar legacy that this book seeks to explain. The explanation offered draws upon the rich literature of international political economy of the past ten years, literature that has benefited from the work of both international relations scholars and students of domestic and comparative politics.

In the course of writing this book, I have learned much from others. Wolfram Hanrieder introduced me to the study of comparative foreign policy and pushed me to explore its neglected economic dimensions. Every young scholar should have such a supportive mentor and loyal friend. While others helped in numerous ways, the following colleagues and associates read the entire manuscript and provided invaluable guidance and criticisms: Robert Art, Seyom Brown, Robert Gilpin, Michael Gordon, Peter Katzenstein, Robert Keohane, Peter Merkl, and Richard Rosecrance. While they did not always agree with me, they deepened my understanding of substantive and theoretical issues and helped to clarify and refine my arguments. For the weaknesses and errors that remain, I alone am responsible.

I wish to thank also the John Parker Compton Fellowship Program at the Center of International Studies at Princeton University for supporting my work durng the 1976–1977 academic year. Brandeis University and Cornell University, the institutions at which I have taught since 1977, also provided research support and assistance in the preparation of the manuscript.

My biggest debt is to my wife, Chris, who read carefully the many versions of the manuscript and whose belief in my idea never wavered. I have dedicated this book to my father, who died unexpectedly when work on it was just beginning.

1

Autonomy and Interdependence

American economic performance at home and abroad deteriorated significantly in the 1970s. The domestic expansion and full employment of the
1960s gave way to double-digit inflation, sluggish growth, and high
unemployment. The comfortable trade surpluses of the 1950s and 1960s
became worrisome deficits in the last decade as oil imports grew and industrial competitiveness lagged. The dollar, which had been the linchpin
of the postwar monetary order, suffered repeatedly under speculative attack. While the United States was not alone among industrialized states
in experiencing economic difficulties, the problems were particularly difficult to accept in a country that had dominated the international
economy for two decades after the war. Moreover, some countries, notably West Germany and Japan, maintained high levels of economic performance in the face of these adverse conditions in the international
economy. The search for the roots of this American economic malaise and
the secret of its competitors' successes have captured the attention of
scholars and policy-makers alike.[1]

While there are many explanations for American difficulties, the most
widely accepted can be grouped into three general categories. The first,
which derives from what has come to be known as the hegemony thesis
and is persuasive among students of international politics, stresses the
importance of the distribution of global power and the econmic structures
that evolve from it.[2] The "hegemonic stability" thesis argues that an effective and efficient international economy requires the leadership of a dominant power, such as Britain in the 19th century or the United States in the
early years after World War II. The hegemon prefers a liberal and open international economy and benefits most from these trade and monetary arrangements, which in turn explains its willingness to assume a leadership
role.[3] While the United States took the lead in organizing the postwar international economy, it also assisted postwar reconstruction in Europe
and Japan, promoted European integration, opened its markets to foreign goods, and encouraged the free flow of capital and investment,
which together ensured vigorous economic competition over the long
term. Inevitably, European recovery diminished the unchallenged U.S.

dominance of the world economy. The relative decline of American economic strength, coupled with political and military-strategic developments in Atlantic relations that made the Europeans less reluctant to challenge American leadership, contributed to an overall loss of U.S. power.[4] Most significant about this power shift, according to the argument, has been Washington's inability to structure unilaterally the principles and procedures of international economic relations, the international economic "regime," in the way it formulated the GATT–Bretton Woods regime after World War II.[5] The hegemonic order of the 1940s and 1950s became in the 1960s and 1970s, a negotiated system of rules and procedures that grew out of a pluralistic division of power among the leading states.

For some, pluralism represented a more-equitable way to structure economic relations, a means to reduce interstate frictions by quieting those who claimed that the rules unfairly benefit the powerful.[6] For others, efficiency conceded too much to equity in a pluralist scheme, and a more-even division of power yielded only stalemate and unworkable compromise in the negotiation over new rules.[7] Regardless of how one viewed it, pluralism brought a loss of American political control over the structure of the international economy that had served it so well after the war. Faced with new competition and without the ability to define the rules to suit its interests, American economic leaders have been unable to reverse a steady economic decline.

An assessment of this argument requires a careful definition of the often-elusive concept of economic power.[8] In this analysis, economic power will be defined narrowly as the ability of states to structure or restructure the principles and procedures of the international economic "regime" in which they participate. Economic *power* is distinguished here from economic *strength* or wealth, which is measured by both the economic resources that a state has at its disposal—land, labor, minerals and energy, financial strength, technology, and managerial know-how—and the standard indicators of economic performance—gross national product, per capita income, trade competitiveness, and currency stability. As Robert Gilpin argues, power is a relative concept, meaningful only when weighed against the power of others.[9] Increasing the power of one state necessarily diminishes the power of others. Wealth or economic strength is absolute, measured against common standards—currency units, tons of steel, acres of land, numbers of workers, etc. The increased wealth of one state need not diminish the wealth of others, although in some circumstances it may.

The relationship between economic power and wealth or economic strength is a complex one. State wealth may, and frequently does, augment state economic power. Yet, states of considerable wealth may possess little economic power; moreover, a state that enjoys considerable economic power may rank low relative to other states in terms of wealth. These circumstances arise because the concept of economic power includes much more than raw measures of wealth, such as noneconomic resources—military strength or political-diplomatic leverage—and a state's *willingness* to use its resources in the service of its economic objectives.[10] It is generally believed that economic power serves to enhance wealth or economic strength, but this analysis will show that the exercise of economic power for noneconomic purposes or other reasons may actually diminish economic strength or undermine a state's capacity to increase its wealth.

A second explanation, what might be labeled the "shifting international division of labor" argument, focuses not on the distribution of power among states, but rather on the inevitable ramifications of an effectively operating liberal international economy.[11] This view, often favored by liberal economists, argues that liberal trade and monetary arrangements designed by Washington in the early postwar years have, ironically, had significant negative consequences for American economic performance. The key features of this liberal regime are free trade and the free convertibility of currencies, which together have fostered both a new international division of labor less favorable to traditional American exports and an internationalization of capital markets that has facilitated outflows of direct foreign investment. Liberal rules gave economic initiative to the private sector and in the postwar era to large multinational firms. As economic opportunities declined with the maturing of the postwar American economy, liberal rules encouraged large firms to seek new opportunities in more rapidly growing economies abroad. Such firms found it easy to bring capital, technology, entrepreneurial skills, and jobs to new foreign settings, steadily eroding the relative advantage enjoyed by the American marketplace after the war.[12] Moreover, liberal rules also enabled newly competitive foreign products, some produced by U.S. firms abroad, to enter American markets and grab a growing share of the market from domestic producers. The challenge to domestic industry came, first, in labor-intensive sectors such as textiles and electronics, and has spread rapidly to steel, automobiles, and more technology-intensive industries. In short, this global marketplace has resulted in rapid shifts in the international division of labor with no clear and identifiable American superiority in any industry or group of industries.[13]

The mobility and flexibility of the private sector under a liberal regime have also reduced the effectiveness of policy instruments, incrementally diminishing government influence on domestic economic performance.[14] Raising interest rates to slow domestic expansion and fight inflation invites capital inflows that put money in the hands of entrepreneurs and inflate the money supply. Lower rates encourage capital outflows and undermine efforts to stimulate domestic growth. Increasing taxes, designing new regulations, or imposing minimum wage restrictions may succeed only in convincing domestic firms to relocate where public policies are more favorable. Finally, by facilitating the integration of trade and capital markets, liberal rules have made successful economic performance at home dependent upon successful performance abroad. Countries must maintain competitive export sectors, and domestic industries must be able to hold their own against the rising tide of imports. For the United States, which had long regarded its economy immune from overseas economic developments, this reality was not easily accepted or understood.

In summary, liberal rules encouraged the transfer of economic resources from the United States to others, undermined the effectiveness of domestic policy instruments to make the necessary adjustments, and ensured that prosperity at home would be increasingly tied to the vagaries of the international economy. It is not surprising that some liberal economists and Marxists seized upon these developments as evidence of the demise of the modern state as an economic actor and the emergence of the multinational firm as its more-efficient (or -oppressive) replacement.[15] While these views undoubtedly overstate its influence, the postwar liberal economy has set in motion a changing international division of labor that has proven to be particularly troublesome for the United States.

A third view, advanced largely by scholars trained in comparative politics, has located the origins of American economic troubles not in international political or economic arrangements, but in the relationships among public and private domestic economic actors responsible for the elaboration and execution of foreign economic policy.[16] In this age of interdependence, foreign policy and domestic policy have become so intertwined that one can no longer be distinguished from the other. Economic issues have been the driving force behind the "domestication" of foreign policy-making and, not surprisingly, domestic institutional relationships among pertinent actors decisively shape policy outcomes.[17]

The authors of works on advanced industrialized countries have concluded that some states are better able than others to cope with the complexities of interdependence and to formulate and execute effective foreign economic policies. Generally, countries which have experienced a long tradition of close and cooperative relations between state and society, government and citizen, have enjoyed an advantage in policy-making. Japan, France, and several small European states are held up as the models of success; Britain and the United States are cited as examples of failure. West Germany occupies a middle position.

The liberal pluralist tradition of American politics is particularly ill-suited to the formation of foreign economic strategy. A strong liberal tradition has resulted in continuing public distrust of government involvement in economic affairs and ongoing suspicion of any policy initiatives taken in the name of the public interest. The pluralist tradition of adversarial relations between government and business and between business and labor regularly yields stalemate and mixed signals, rather than direction and movement.[18] Economic organization and social history are at odds with effective economic policy-making. With close collaboration between government and business, harmonious labor relations, and a strong leadership role granted to the state in foreign economic affairs, Japan offers a striking contrast to the American domestic setting.[19] Collaboration between banks and big business since the early days of industrialization and a postwar history of good labor relations have given similar foreign economic advantages to West Germany.[20] The central role of the state in the modernization and rationalization of the French economy after World War II was a major factor in France's assuming a position of international economic rank in the 1960s.[21]

In sum, comparative analysis argues that success and failure in the international economy depends principally on the institutions and structures adopted by countries to address economic problems that penetrate their borders. Such responses are not randomly chosen, but derive from patterns of domestic political and economic relations that stretch back to the political formation of national units and the unique experiences with industrialization.[22] The American historical legacy is frequently at odds with the requirements of economic policy-making in an age of international interdependence. American successes after the war were possible only as long as European recovery remained incomplete. Once European domestic structures were restored, the weakness of American arrangements became apparent.

Each of the three explanations calls attention to factors critical to any country's performance in the international economy. The international power argument reminds us that the structure of international economic relations, the rules and procedures of international exchange, are never neutral in their impact on participating states. Different norms and guidelines affect different countries differently, which assures that decisions regarding such rules will always precipitate international debate. The distribution of power among states will be an important factor in determining the outcome of such debate. A change in the distribution of power may well be accompanied by a change in the rules. Those who have focused on the shifting international division of labor show us the ramifications of a particular set of international rules. They reveal that an international economy governed by liberal guidelines diminishes the influence of states over national economic performance, both by creating more mobility and flexiblity in the private sector and by reducing the effectiveness of domestic policies. Comparative analysis teaches us that even among states with relatively similar political, social, and economic backgrounds, domestic arrangements to cope with economic problems vary widely. Even when confronting similar external pressures, these domestic structures may yield very different policy outcomes.

Each of these explanations contributes to an understanding of American difficulties in the international economy, but each employs a logic that, when applied to the postwar context, frequently results in overstatement and misinterpretation. Seldom do supporters of a particular view draw upon the contributions of competing views. Supporters of the hegemony position, with eyes fixed on the distribution of state power, fail to acknowledge that rule changes in the international economy and the economic fortunes of the leading state may result from forces other than changes in the balance of power.[23] For example, the consequences of the workings of a liberal economy as explored by liberal analysts of the evolving international division of labor may lead a hegemonic state, whose economic strength may be declining but whose relative power resources have not changed at all, to design and implement new rules to shore up flagging commercial fortunes. A single-minded focus on power can lead to the often-faulty conclusion that changes in international norms and rules are preceded by shifts in the distribution of power among states. As the following chapters will show, this is the mistake of the hegemony argument when applied to postwar Atlantic economic relations. Those who have observed changes in the GATT–Bretton Woods regime have too quickly assumed that those changes have followed a decline in American power and the emergence of powerful industrial rivals. A closer look reveals that, while American economic strength has declined relative to Europe and Japan, U.S. economic power, as measured by the ability to control the shape and direction of rule change in the international economy, has held up remarkably well.

Students of the shifting international division of labor, whether liberal economists or Marxists, provide useful analyses of the economic consequences of a liberal global economy, such as the internationalization of production and finance; but they overstate the political impact such developments have on the modern nation-state and its ability to respond to the ramifications of economic interdependence. As the comparativists have shown, the state is far from obsolete as a player in the international economy; adjustment strategies to cope with the changing international division of labor have demonstrated the vitality of modern governments and their societies to cope with rapid economic and technological change. New arrangements in advanced and developing countries to guard against the disruptive activities of multinationals and other private-sector actors indicate a continuing determination to exercise political control over commercial and financial developments.

The comparativists, who have focused on domestic sources of economic strength and weakness in the global economy and have identified significant differences among the industrialized countries, generally assume that the structure of the international economy and the processes it sets in motion affect these states in similar ways. Little attention is directed to the relationship between the evolution of domestic structures and the constraints imposed on or opportunities created for different participants in the international economy.[24] National economic performance that is heavily dependent on success abroad and seriously disadvantaged by international rules-of-the-game may demand domestic arrangements carefully tailored to external conditions. A state with a largely self-sufficient economy or one which enjoys special privileges under international rules by virtue of its leadership role may enjoy greater flexibility in establishment of domestic economic structures. As others have noted, states feel the pull of economic interdependence in different ways and with different levels of intensity.[25] The domestic explanation is incomplete without an accounting of the external political and economic forces that affect individual countries very differently.

The argument of this book is eclectic: I attempt to draw upon the major strengths of each of these important contributions to our understanding of the workings of the international political economy and to combine them in a way that offers a fuller accounting of American economic troubles. Each of the three prospectives provides crucial assumptions on which the argument rests. First, I share with those who focus on the distribution of global power the belief that the norms and rules that shape the international economy are vitally important to participating countries and that such rules are politically determined. Crucial to that political determination will be the interstate distribution of economic power.

Second, I believe, as do the economic liberals and Marxists who point to changes in the international marketplace, that the postwar liberal economic order has fostered an economic interdependence that both grants greater mobility and flexibility to the private sector and complicates the management of domestic economies by making traditional economic policy instruments less effective. I stop short of those who see political power eventually passing from the state to the private firm.

Finally, I accept the comparativists' claim that domestic structures influence economic performance abroad, but go further to suggest that those institutions and relationships are shaped not only by internal political and industrial development, but also by the unique configuration of external circumstances encountered by each country.

Building on these assumptions, the argument can be summarized as follows: after World War II, the United States enjoyed an economic strength unmatched by any country and the economic power to shape the postwar international monetary and trading systems as it saw fit. Or, as others have put it, the United States enjoyed the role of hegemonic power in the postwar economy. This power was exercised in the service of two attractive objectives. The first was to promote a network of economic *interdependence* that would offer foreign trade and investment opportunities for the domestic economy and would complement American political and strategic objectives. Such interdependence was to be fostered by economic liberalism—the unhindered flow of goods, services, and capital across national borders—from which all would benefit. To be interdependent was to be able to trade freely, to invest without constraints, and to raise capital in international money markets, but at the same time to know that domestic economic management had to conform increasingly to the vagaries of the global marketplace. By drawing European states into this network of interdependence, American officials could effectively bind together Atlantic allies in a way that complemented the strategic interdependence institutionalized through NATO. It is worth emphasizing that the strategy to promote economic interdependence by installing a regime of liberal rules that would foster the internationalization of commercial and financial markets was aimed not at interdependence of a bilateral sort, one state depending upon another, but at a multilateral dependence on the successful functioning of the international economy as a whole for each state's own prosperity.[26] The political consequences of this economic interdependence are that domestic and foreign economic policies must be made compatible, a difficult task to achieve when domestic demands clash with international requirements. This problem is drawn in sharp relief in the many developing countries' struggles to balance the domestic needs for growth and development with the burdens of repaying foreign debts.

The second objective of economic leaders in Washington was to ensure autonomy in the management of the American domestic economy. External trade and capital accounts should not affect decisions about economic policy at home.[27] Autonomy was less a new strategy than a well-engrained pattern of policy-making. With an abundance of natural resources and a huge domestic market, American officials had never paid much attention to external accounts that regularly comprised only a very small percentage of national economic activity. With its strong and largely self-sufficient economy after World War II, the United States had little reason to expect that national policy should be made to conform with international requirements. Autonomy is also a strategy preferred by politicians, since external problems such as trade deficits or currency weakness can impose unpopular domestic correctives resulting in economic slowdown and high unemployment. Autonomous management was also particularly attractive to Atlantic postwar governments as they intervened regularly in their domestic economies. The growth of the modern welfare state with its commitment to full employment and new social services required that governments expand policy alternatives, not narrow them by international obligations.[28]

While the appeal of promoting interdependence and simultaneously maintaining autonomy in the management of a state's domestic economy is understandable, the basic contradiction between the two objectives cannot be avoided. An unfolding economic interdependence weaves together the commercial and financial fortunes of participating states, increasing the need for policy coordination and narrowing the opportunities for autonomous national action. The insistence on autonomy implies the capacity for self-sufficiency and self-reliance and the reduction or elimination of external economic constraints. The average industrialized country could not expect to pursue such contradictory strategies for long without experiencing some serious economic difficulties both at home and abroad. By trying to sustain its role as an economic leader in the postwar liberal economy and to realize its welfare state objectives, Britain confronted the consequences of this contradiction in the 1960s.[29] But the United States was not an ordinary country after World War II, and remains extraordinary even in the 1980s.[30] It has used its economic power to shape the rules-of-the-game in money and trade as a vehicle to overcome the contradiction between autonomy and interdependence from the mid-1940s to the present. The irony is that in sustaining its economic power and in using that power to achieve these competing objectives, Washington has steadily undermined its economic strength. In other words, the power to set the rules has not declined significantly, as most students of American foreign economic policy have argued; instead that power has become a growing liability for American economic interests and the competitiveness of the national economy.

The West Europeans, in contrast, lacked the economic power enjoyed by the Americans, and while they, too, would have been attracted to the benefits of interdependence while retaining autonomy at home, their weaker position demanded that domestic policies be tailored to the growing constraints of the international marketplace. Here, too, there is irony. The requirement that domestic and foreign economic policies be made compatible encouraged European economies to adapt to life in the global economy and, while they resented the privileges of American power in the short term, they positioned their economies to compete more effectively in the long haul. As the following chapters will show, some European states adapted more successfully than others. In short, as the Americans found economic power to be a growing liability, the Europeans came to benefit from their inability to mobilize such power resources for themselves.

To promote *interdependence,* the Americans pressed for a liberal regime in money and trade. Some of these norms and rules were made explicit by treaty; others were a product of informal understandings. This GATT–Bretton Woods system, as it came to be called, outlined procedures by which trade barriers could be eliminated and capital could flow freely across national borders. The market, rather than the hand of government, would guide the evolution of the postwar economy, and the beggar-thy-neighbor policies of the 1930s would be avoided. As the most-efficient and -productive economy after the war, the United States would surely benefit from a scheme that paid dividends to the most competitive. As the most self-reliant, the American economy would be constrained least by the dependencies that grew from the market system.

A market-oriented regime that required little government involvement was also appealing at a time when Washington was already undertaking unprecedented political and strategic commitments abroad and when American leaders were uneasy about entering into any Atlantic economic arrangements that might increase international burdens. It was hoped that liberal rules would depoliticize economic relations and move commercial and financial affairs out of the policy spotlight.

The rules of the monetary system were negotiated in 1944 at Bretton Woods, and three basic principles emerged to give the regime its liberal character.[31] First, member states committed themselves to fixed exchange rates with the intent of encouraging stability and predictability in monetary affairs, which, in turn, would facilitate the expansion of trade and investment. Recognizing that economies grow and inflate at different rates and that temporary payments imbalances were inevitable, the agreement included procedures to permit exchange-rate adjustments. On a daily basis, currencies were allowed to fluctuate within "trading bands," 1 percent margins on either side of the pegged rate. For more serious difficulties, states could intervene to devalue or revalue their currencies by larger margins as long as they first consulted with other states.

The second principle of Bretton Woods, implicitly accepted by all but never stated explicitly in the written agreements, was a commitment to free convertibility among Western currencies. Free convertibility argued for the elimination of national restrictions on capital flows and opened opportunities for international investment. The weakness of European currencies made convertibility impractical after the war, but the elimination of restrictions on capital flows was a high priority of the recovered European economies in the late 1950s.

The third leg of the Bretton Woods triad was the central role to be played by the American dollar. The dollar was linked to gold through a legal commitment on the part of the United States to convert any foreign-held dollars into gold at a fixed rate. In the early postwar years, the gold-exchange system became the lubricant of the recovery process in Europe and the currency of interdependence as the allies eagerly sought dollars to underwrite their economic recoveries and finance the growth of Atlantic trade.

The Atlantic trade regime took its norms and rules from the 1947 General Agreement on Tariffs and Trade (GATT), following unsuccessful efforts to establish a more-ambitious International Trade Organization along lines that would complement the Bretton Woods Agreement and the International Monetary Fund.[32] These rules followed closely the Ricardian free-trade tradition supervised by the British through the 19th and early 20th centuries. Two guidelines are worth noting for their contribution to the expansion of trade and the growth of commercial interdependence. First, member states were required to grant most-favored-nation (MFN) status to all other signatories of the GATT. MFN status discourages discrimination among trading partners by requiring that all members receive the most-favorable tariff and non-tariff treatment accorded to any individual state. This principle of nondiscrimination in commerce eased access to new markets and encouraged the development of new trading relationships. The second guideline, not articulated through formal agreement, was the principle of reciprocity in trade negotiations. States agreed that concessions extended by one member, such as the reduction of tariffs or quotas, should be met by equivalent concessions from other members as the basis for liberalizing trade relations. Unilateral concessions or preferential agreements were discouraged.

While some of these rules and procedures were altered in the 1970s and numerous temporary exceptions in both money and trade have been granted along the way, the United States has never rejected the two core norms of these regimes, free trade and the free convertibility of currencies, which together constitute the strongest evidence of a continuing commitment to economic interdependence.

To assure *autonomy* in the management of the domestic economy, the United States used its position as the leading power in the GATT–Bretton Woods regime to structure and restructure the rules-of-the-game in ways that would guarantee flexibility at home. In other words, when external accounts threatened to impose constraints on the domestic economy, the rules were altered and others were made to shoulder the burdens of adjustment. This analysis does not explore the politics of domestic policies or judge the merits of particular policy decisions. Rather, it takes such policies as given and focuses on how American officials were able to manipulate regime rules and procedures to assure that external pressures did not interfere with domestic objectives.[33] By manipulating the common rules to its advantage, Washington effectively shielded the domestic economy from the growing constraints of interdependence.

After World War II, when American economic strength was overwhelming and levels of interdependence were low, the task of assuring autonomy was an easy one. As European recovery progressed and the bonds of interdependence grew stronger, the job became steadily more difficult. American leaders employed three successive strategies to tailor regime rules in ways that would guarantee continuing flexibility at home. Each is elaborated in succeeding chapters, but is briefly described here. A strategy of generosity and reward was employed from the mid-1940s to the late 1950s and was predicated on the role of the dollar and the competitive edge enjoyed by American exports. The failure of the Bretton Woods system to provide sufficient liquidity in the form of gold or other reserve assets to finance postwar recovery led Western states to turn to the dollar to fill the liquidity gap.[34] The dollar rapidly acquired the status of a reserve currency and was soon regarded "as good as gold." One way to meet the growing international demand for dollars was for the United States to run deficits in its balance of payments. By eagerly accepting dollars, countries abroad effectively financed American deficits. This deficit financing simultaneously permitted leaders in Washington to address domestic economic needs with the knowledge that their policy choices would not be affected by balance-of-payments constraints.

This flexibility was also guaranteed by the dominance of American goods in international markets, which assured comfortable trade surpluses regardless of how rapidly the economy expanded at home. The dominance of the American economy in the first decade after the war and pressing security concerns encouraged policy-makers to be generous with Atlantic allies. With autonomy unchallenged, the strategy was to assist those states whose recovery was essential if the alliance was to survive and interdependence was to grow. Exemptions to the trade and monetary rules laid down at Bretton Woods and by the GATT fostered this recovery.[35] In commerce, the Europeans were permitted temporary tariffs and quotas designed to exclude dollar goods. Washington also gave support to a discriminating common market, which facilitated integration and interdependence among European economies but also erected common barriers to American products. In monetary affairs, Washington accepted the postponement of free currency convertibility and permitted elaborate exchange restrictions to safeguard vulnerable European currencies. The extension of Marshall Plan aid completed this package of American assistance. It was a time of considerable harmony in Atlantic economic relations. As Benjamin Cohen described it, a bargain was struck that enjoyed strong support on both sides of the Atlantic.[36]

Europe was spared the strictures of a competitive liberal economy during its process of recovery, and the United States enjoyed considerable flexibility at home and abroad, bolstered by the strength of its trade position and the new reserve status accorded the dollar.

It is regrettable, but perhaps inevitable, that economic interests diverged and the era of good feelings came to an end in the late 1950s, the point of departure for the chapters that follow. Evidence of both the successful containment of communism in Western Europe and strong economic recovery diminished Washington's feelings of generosity toward its Atlantic partners. American leaders pressed for currency convertibility and the end to trade discrimination as European goods more frequently challenged American products in international markets. With economic recovery well under way in this era of declining cold war tensions, West European nations were less dependent upon American goodwill. A narrowing of the liquidity gap made them even less eager to finance continuing balance-of-payments deficits.

Economically, the time was ripe to implement fully the postwar liberal trade and monetary rules that had been put aside in the late 1940s. The success with limited currency convertibility in France, Britain, and West Germany at the end of 1958 and the takeoff of the European Common Market provided sufficient evidence of European recovery. International reserves fed by dollar deficits had reached adequate levels, and American payments could be safely brought back into equilibrium with little fear of disrupting global recovery. Politically, however, the efforts to eliminate the "temporary" arrangements that had become "normal" behavior in the postwar years met stubborn resistance from states who benefited from different aspects of the existing pattern of relations. The Europeans, who had come to depend on discriminatory trade advantages, were reluctant to surrender those advantages to the principle of free trade. The Americans, who had become accustomed to payments deficits and the flexiblity they granted both to domestic economic management and to the financing of global commitments, were not enthusiastic about pursuing internal deflationary measures or cutting back on external commitments. Each side pressed the other to make the needed adjustments. The Americans wanted to talk about trade and European discrimination; the Europeans preferred to discuss money and persistent American deficits.[37]

The new American strategy, practiced from the late 1950s through 1967, was to seek European cooperation in advancing trade liberalization and in devising new schemes for balance-of-payments financing to assure that external accounts did not interfere with the expansion of the American economy in the 1960s. The Dillon and Kennedy Rounds of trade negotiations were the means to greater trade liberalism. Ad hoc arrangements such as the London gold pool, the foreign sale of medium-term treasury bonds, currency swaps, technical drawings from the International Monetary Fund (IMF), and the creation of Special Drawing Rights were measures designed to prop up the dollar and to encourage Western allies to go on financing payments deficits. While the American strategy worked and autonomy was preserved, success came with greater difficulty in the 1960s. European leaders, most notably Charles de Gaulle, understood that Washington was seeking to enjoy the benefits of international exchange without assuming the domestic obligations that such exchange normally entails, and they were less and less willing to go along.

Autonomy was also more difficult to sustain because Washington's simultaneous promotion of economic interdependence was beginning to bear fruit. The removal of major trade barriers and the convertibility of Western currencies set in motion a rapid internationalization of the Atlantic marketplace in the 1960s.[38] The expansion of foreign direct investment by multinational firms, the growth of the so-called "Euro-dollar" market beyond the reach of national financial institutions, and the rapid international movement of capital in response to changing interest rates or the calculations of currency speculators combined to reduce the effectiveness of domestic economic policies by granting greater freedom of movement to the private sector.[39] While Washington may have succeeded politically in assuring that foreign economic partners did not dictate domestic policy decisions, the flowering of interdependence ensured that policies of its own making would be less effective economically.

But the emerging interdependence also had the salutory effect for American foreign economic policy-makers of limiting the extent to which the Europeans were willing to challenge American adjustments to the liberal rules. European recovery and subsequent progress toward EEC integration had been sustained by a rapid expansion of foreign trade, access to foreign capital, and the acceptance and use of American dollars. Europe, too, had tied its economic fortunes to the liberal regime; to upset that regime simply because it offered some advantages to the United States made neither economic nor political sense. Europe's acceptance of the basic rules-of-the-game meant that negotiations were limited to debates over how to make those rules function more effectively.

Reliance on trade liberalization and patchwork monetary reform concluded in 1967 with the completion of the Kennedy round of trade negotiations and the agreement to create new international reserve assets, Special Drawing Rights. Instead of enlisting the aid and cooperation of their allies, the U.S. officials chose initially to ignore those partners altogether by employing a strategy of "benign neglect," and later decided upon tough unilateral action in rewriting the rules to suit American purposes. Amid persistent payments deficits and a deteriorating trade balance, Washington refused to accept the need for domestic correctives and blamed these problems on undervalued European and Japanese currencies and lingering trade discrimination. Instead of seeking cooperative ways to finance the dollar deficits, the U.S. officials, by use of "benign neglect," proclaimed that such outflows were Europe's problem that could be easily corrected by currency revaluations. Washington would concentrate on the sound management of its domestic economy; international accounts would take care of themselves. With the world on a de facto dollar standard by the late 1960s, European states had to go on accepting dollars, revalue their currencies, or bring down the system. Washington knew that Europe, with no acceptable alternative reserve asset, could not seriously consider the last option. By requiring that others make the adjustments, the United States again assured that domestic economic policy could be made autonomously.

The shift from negotiation and cooperation to "benign neglect" followed several developments. First, the United States had largely exhausted the political capital it had acquired as alliance leader after the war. As the reluctance to challenge American leadership declined, the cooperative mode required more time and patience and yielded less-productive results. The protracted negotiations over trade liberalization and monetary reform in the mid-1960s left few nations eager to launch new negotiations. The rejection of politically negotiated remedies was reinforced by Nixon's economic advisors, who supported "benign neglect" by arguing that markets, not governments, should restore balance in money and trade.[40]

The policy of "benign neglect" and recourse to market solutions gained ever-wider support as the patchwork monetary solutions of the 1960s were repeatedly overwhelmed by the volume and pace of international capital movements. Moreover, marginal tariff reductions were of declining importance in the face of major commercial shifts in the international division of labor. Developments in the private sector simply moved more quickly than multilateral negotiating channels' ability to respond. Interdependence was in full flower in the late 1960s and early 1970s, and all found it increasingly difficult to manage and control. "Benign neglect" was, to some extent, an acknowledgment by Washington of this loss of control and a willingness to let others or the market cope with the excesses of the internationalization of trade and money.

Extraordinary speculative pressure against the dollar in 1971 and the anticipation of the first postwar trade deficit convinced American leaders to forego temporarily the strategy of "benign neglect" and to take tough unilateral action. In August 1971, Washington formally cut convertibility between the dollar and gold, demanded currency revaluations from its partners, and imposed a 10 percent surcharge on American imports to secure what it believed to be the necessary currency adjustments. The adoption of domestic deflationary measures that would improve external accounts met strong resistance at home, particularly in the year prior to a presidential election.[41] If adjustments were required, other countries must make them. Unilateral action was again employed in early 1973 to nudge Western economic partners to a system of flexible exchange rates, a logical extension of the reasoning that the market should be the arbiter of currency values. With the dollar firmly in place as the sole reserve asset, flexible exchange rates once again prevented external interference in domestic economic management, and Washington could comfortably resume the posture of "benign neglect." And while the Europeans were irritated first by American neglect and then by tough-minded tactics, there was little to be done. Their continuing dependence on the dollar and on the successful performance of the Atlantic economy for their own well-being ensured that efforts to develop an alternative through a European economic union would make little headway.

The changes initiated by the United States in the early 1970s protected the flexibility in domestic policy-making and sustained the belief that autonomy and interdependence could be made compatible a while longer. Many were quick to proclaim the death of Bretton Woods and a new era of protectionism, but a closer look reveals that the norms of free trade and free currency convertibility, the central building blocks of economic interdependence, survived the buffeting of the early years of the decade.

Nevertheless, in the late 1960s and early 1970s indications began to appear that the effective use of American economic power to ensure success in achieving the contradictory objectives of autonomy and interdependence was undermining American economic strength. The steady deterioration of the trade account from a record surplus in 1965 to deficit in 1971 could be attributed in part to an overvalued dollar, but there were also more-worrisome signs of diminished competitiveness: an aging industrial base, less attention to research and development, and marginal gains in labor productivity. With increasing frequency, large American firms chose to locate new investments abroad where labor costs were lower, productivity was rising rapidly, and governments were more inclined to promote rather than regulate new enterprises. American weakness in international markets was also encouraged by the absence of balance-of-payments constraints, which in turn encouraged expensive government commitments, such as the Vietnam War, and fueled domestic inflation.

The U.S. weakness was made even more apparent by the new strength of others. In an interdependent economy, the Europeans and the Japanese won growing market shares in industries which the Americans formerly dominated. Not only did shares of foreign markets decline in vulnerable industries, but industrial competitors took on American producers in their own home market. The rise of imports, not only of manufactured goods but also of natural resources such as oil, steadily pulled the American economy into the web of interdependence. Trade came to occupy a growing percentage of GNP, foreign direct investment became an integral part of American corporate strategy, and financial institutions rapidly expanded lending activities abroad.[42] At a time when those concerned with domestic economic policy should have sought ways to cope with these consequences of interdependence, American power preserved the illusion of autonomy.

As the following chapters show, the Europeans were seldom willing accomplices of American efforts to restructure the rules. DeGaulle and the French resented the privileges accorded the dollar and argued for a return to the gold standard. Awash with deficit dollars, the Germans repeatedly called for greater discipline in Washington's management of external payments. At the height of their frustrations, European Community members sought monetary union and a common currency. Nonetheless, national differences exposed by EC negotiations proved more salient than common opposition to American maneuvers. These unsuccessful challenges taught some member states early that successful adaptation to the Atlantic economic regime was likely to produce better returns than repeated efforts to change it. Adaptation was the sensible strategy of the politically weak, and tailoring the management of the domestic economy to the constraints of interdependence was the most-viable route to prosperity. Knowing full well that its postwar political and economic recovery depended upon international acceptance, the West Germans were the first to adopt export-led growth and to tie their future to European integration. Bonn quickly understood that domestic sacrifice and adaptation to life in the international marketplace was crucial for both economic and political recovery.[43]

As victorious powers, Britain and France enjoyed greater political influence after World War II and were less constrained by foreign powers in their economic recoveries. Moreover, national populations were eager to share the benefits of recovery and less willing than the Germans, the Dutch, or the Swiss to make domestic sacrifices for the sake of international competitiveness. Even the French, in the late fifties and again in the late sixties, and the British, in the mid-1960s and again in the mid-1970s, endured the unpleasant domestic correctives that were required following a deterioration in external accounts. Such experiences Washington successfully avoided; by so doing Washington also missed the lessons about how to renew and restore competitiveness in the international marketplace. The bonds of interdependence provided guidelines for industrial change for liberal economies. Freedom from such bonds ironically deprived the United States of this guidance.

Not until the quadrupling of oil prices in 1973–1974 did Washington begin to realize the impact that the world economy could have on domestic economic performance. The oil crisis brought the contradiction between autonomy and interdependence into full relief and demonstrated how ill-prepared the United States was for life in the competitive international marketplace. It also demonstrated the extent to which other states had adapted their domestic institutions and policy-making procedures to cope with the consequences of international economic change. Countries much more dependent on imported oil than the United States, such as Japan and West Germany, made the appropriate domestic adjustments more rapidly and were able to avoid high inflation to restore moderate levels of economic growth and to rebuild surpluses in their external accounts.

In the decade since the oil crisis, Washington has shown indications of appreciating the importance of structuring domestic policies to conform with global economic realities.[44] Yet, policy-makers have been extremely reluctant to give up old ways. Efforts to curb inflation and restore moderate levels of growth in the domestic economy after the oil crisis convinced most American officials of the dangers of ignoring international commercial and financial consequences. Unilateral U.S. expansion in the late 1970s not only triggered a deterioration in the trade account, but also put downward pressure on the American dollar, which raised the costs of imports and rekindled domestic inflation. A sinking dollar also meant declining revenues for oil producers, who sought to cut their losses by raising prices, which further fueled the fires of American inflation. Even so, the Federal Reserve did not intervene in currency markets on behalf of the dollar until 1979. Such experiences affirmed the views of those who argued for the coordination of the economic policies of industrialized states, those who have supported informal cooperation through economic summits.[45] Coordination argues for a better balancing of internal needs and external demands and for a recognition that unilateral action rapidly becomes counterproductive for all. While Washington has regularly paid lip service to the need for industrial adaptation to the global marketplace and to the benefits of coordination, there remains a strong countertendency, bolstered by abundant oil, a strong dollar, and a president convinced of the merits of market solutions, that argues for the United States to once again chart a course informed primarily by circumstances at home.

The purpose of this introductory chapter has been to offer a brief overview of a fuller explanation of American economic troubles in the 1970s and 1980s by drawing upon and integrating the contributions and lessons of three other persuasive views—the power or hegemony thesis, the international division of labor argument, and the comparativists' claims about domestic institutions and structures. I agreed with students of international politics that the power to shape and reshape the norms and rules of international monetary and trade regimes can be a valuable tool for modern states in the quest for economic well-being and that the loss of such power can result in rule changes detrimental to a state's economic interests. Yet I also argue that under certain circumstances such power, while permitting politically attractive options in the short term, can encourage states to pursue strategies that have damaging economic consequences in the long term. This latter scenario best accounts for American economic difficulties over the last decade. While American power to shape the rules did not decline appreciably through the mid-1970s, as many have argued, it is ironic that the U.S. ability to sustain its position of influence contributed to its economic weakness. This counterintuitive conclusion follows from the particular ends to which such power was put; namely, the promotion of interdependence through liberal monetary and trade arrangements and the insistence on autonomous management of the domestic economy.

As liberal economists predicted, the successful implementation of rules guaranteeing free trade and free movements of capital resulted in an internationalization of the marketplace, an economic interdependence that granted greatest national successes to countries able to respond quickly and efficiently to shifts in the international division of labor. Here the argument of the comparativists becomes most compelling, for in a condition of advanced global market integration, the ability of a state to coordinate and make compatible its domestic and foreign economic policy becomes the crucial ingredient for economic welfare. American insistence on autonomy both disguised the impact that interdependence was having on economic performance and reduced incentives to tailor domestic institutions and structures in ways that would ensure international competitiveness. Moreover, a legacy of liberal pluralism in American politics fostered national divisiveness and uncertainty, rather than unity and coherence, in government efforts to confront changes in the marketplace. And as time has passed, American power to shape the rules became less useful as a tool to redress emerging economic problems. The deepening bonds of interdependence made all Western nations increasingly reliant on the effective functioning of the global economy for their continued prosperity. Each individual state, even the most powerful, has grown steadily more reluctant to advance major rule changes, particularly those that would bring greater protectionism and unravel this network of relationships.[46] While some talk of a "new protectionism," American leaders remain fundamentally wedded to the norm of free trade while recognizing the need to accommodate certain domestic interests with "temporary" and "voluntary" protectionist schemes.

American power played a decisive role in the establishment of the postwar interdependent international economy, with the result that Americans eventually had trouble competing in the regime of their own making. In contrast, most rivals in Europe have been "blessed" with weakness, enjoying neither the ability to define the rules nor the luxury of ignoring external pressures in setting domestic policy. Instead they gained valuable experience in adjusting to life in a rapidly changing and unforgiving international marketplace, experience that American officials are only beginning to acquire.

The following chapters examine why the United States chose to exercise its power in the pursuit of these twin objectives of autonomy and interdependence and how it managed to realize these goals well into the 1970s. To understand the former choice, one needs a complete overview of the domestic environment in which American national and international economic policy was made, and each chapter attempts to provide the pertinent background. To explain the latter, the chapters focus on monetary and trade negotiations between the United States and Westen Europe. It was with Europe, primarily, and particularly with the largest European states—Britain, France, and West Germany—that the battles over changes in trade and monetary rules were waged. The Japanese became more active in the early 1970s, but most American leverage was exerted against the Europeans. As such, the dynamics of intra-European relations became important in understanding Washington's success in getting its way. Without agreement among leaders in London, Paris, and Bonn, European resistance to American pressures was greatly weakened. American power was therefore not only a function of the effectiveness of the diplomacy practiced by U.S. diplomats, but also of the extent of European disharmony.

The analysis proceeds chronologically, beginning in the late 1950s when European recovery was largely complete, when frictions emerged in Atlantic economic relations after more than a decade of relative harmony, and when American power was first tested. Chapter 2 examines the debates over major rule changes in these years—the restoration of free convertibility in European currencies, the shape of a European economic community, and the launching of the Dillon round of trade negotiations. The years 1961–1967, discussed in Chapter 3, were the years of patchwork reform in both money and trade when the United States actively sought European cooperation to remedy monetary troubles and to move closer to the norm of free trade. The conclusion of the Kennedy Round of trade negotiations and the agreement to create Special Drawing Rights in 1967 marked the end of this era of cooperation.

Chapter 4 treats the years 1968–1973, the time of crisis in Atlantic economic relations. The United States experienced a steady deterioration in its trade balance and protectionist impulses grew, the major currencies endured speculative attack, and the monetary system appeared on the verge of collapse. "Benign neglect" and tough unilateral action were the Nixon adminstration's responses to these troubled times. The existing regimes required major rule changes if autonomy was to be maintained and if interdependence was to survive.

The fifth chapter focuses on the years 1974–1984, giving special attention to Atlantic responses to the ramifications of the oil crisis. The rise in petroleum prices and the embargo clearly demonstrated the extent of American reliance on the international economy and the futility and dangers of attempting to insulate domestic policy formulation from external economic developments. But the chapter reveals that American leaders made only limited progress in promoting compatibility between domestic and foreign economic policy and in coordinating American efforts with those of other leading states as the age of interdependence requires. Chapter 6 offers some general conclusions from these two decades of economic relations.

Old Habits and New Problems: 1958–1960

In the first decade after the war, Washington's desire to foster economic interdependence among Western states and at the same time to maintain autonomy in the formulation of domestic economic policy was never seriously challenged at home or abroad. Indeed, foreign partners, consumed with the tasks of reconstruction, were happy if Washington's imprudent economic management resulted in payments deficits, since their own dollar reserves were in short supply. Moreover, U.S. domestic economic interests were not bothered by the trade advantages extended to rebuilding European economies while American goods remained highly competitive and comfortably in surplus. This compatibility in economic relations permitted policy-makers to concentrate on what they regarded as the most-pressing problem in international affairs, the containment of the Soviet Union.

By the late 1950s, conditions had changed. Dollars were now abundant in Europe and American trade surpluses were no longer so comfortable. The economic arrangements that had been designed to promote European recovery and assist American containment efforts now tended to irritate rather than facilitate monetary and trade relations. Washington complained that European trade discrimination was cutting into American surpluses; Europe responded that American payments deficits were flooding European money supplies and eroding confidence in the dollar, the system's primary reserve asset. The attempts to resolve these frictions, the subject of this chapter, also reveal the beginnings of a growing incompatibility between American objectives of autonomy and interdependence.

Both the United States and Western Europe were shielded from the full consequences of a liberal interdependent economy after the war. Europe had imposed exchange restrictions on its currency and trade barriers against dollar goods; Washington had been permitted a flexibility in its balance-of-payments management by virtue of the role of the dollar. The realities of reconstruction and containment required both. In the late

1950s Washington and Western Europe pressured each other to surrender postwar privileges and to undertake the full obligations in a liberal economic order. Both were strongly committed to this liberal system: the United States had been its chief architect in the 1940s and Europe had premised recovery on its realization in the 1950s, but neither was eager to give up old ways. Removing the barriers to American exports threatened newly recovered European industries and jeopardized the prospects for intra-European trade in the new Common Market. Loss of payments flexibility for Washington meant that domestic management would have to be more carefully tailored to trends in external accounts.

As this chapter shows, the United States focused attention on European trade discrimination and took advantage of European dependence on the dollar to side-step criticism of its payments policy and calls for monetary reform. This strategy effectively preserved the flexibility of American payments policy and ensured the autonomy of domestic economic management. The Europeans, reluctant to challenge American economic leadership and unable to forge a common strategy among themselves, succumbed to American pressures for trade liberalization and failed to extract greater discipline in American balance-of-payments management. American successes on trade issues were aided by deep divisions among the principle European powers regarding the commercial shape of the European Economic Community. The French were determined to keep the community small, an arrangement that would allow them to play a more-decisive leadership role and would discriminate against non-members by means of a common external tariff. The British preferred a less-discriminatory free-trade arrangement that would provide access for their Commmonwealth partners and other North Atlantic countries, including the United States. Economically, the West Germans were attracted to broader trade opportunities for their newly competitive industries offered by a free trade area, but politically they recognized the importance of facilitating political reconciliation with France to enhance German credibility in the European movement.

The late 1950s also reveal how the American position of power enabled it to pursue both domestic economic objectices (recovery from recession) and other foreign policy objectives (those related to containment) without the constraints imposed by external accounts. The Europeans, by contrast, had to tailor domestic policy to life in the international economy. Those who did so most successfully, such as West Germany and to a lesser extent France, began to show considerable economic promise compared to those who did not, such as Great Britain. The first section of this chapter briefly treats these varying national approaches. The second and third sections examine the legacy of monetary and trade negotiations. The theme that runs throughout is that Washington successfully focused

Atlantic attention on trade relations as a means to remedy growing balance-of-payments problems. While this strategy shifted the burden of economic adjustment to the Europeans, it also meant that monetary problems, rooted in the Bretton Woods regime, would continue to worsen in the 1960s.

THE DETERMINANTS OF FOREIGN ECONOMIC POLICY

The United States

The contradictions between foreign and domestic economic policy became problematic in the last years of the Eisenhower administration. American trade and payments balances deteriorated significantly between 1958 and 1960, owing in large measure to the restored competitiveness of European products in world markets and to the return of currency convertibility, which was followed by an outflow of American investment capital. Moreover, persistent domestic recession in the late 1950s drew demands for government action and interest rate and tax relief, policies likely to aggravate rather than improve the status of external accounts.

In some respects, Eisenhower can be credited for minimizing the contradiction between domestic and foreign economic policy toward the end of his second term, action seldom taken by American presidents in the 1960s. Unquestionably, he gave greater attention to the domestic recession than to deteriorating trade and payments balances, but his fear of inflation, reluctance to approve a fiscal stimulus, and determination to balance the budget contributed to considerable caution in addressing the problems of economic slowdown.[1] His unwillingness to support a tax cut in 1958, amid strong domestic pressure for action, and his push for budget surpluses in 1959 and 1960 were informed by a logic of how the domestic economy should be managed, but they were also consistent with efforts to slow the deterioration in American accounts abroad.[2] There are some indications that Eisenhower did become concerned with the health of the dollar in 1959 and 1960. In his memoirs, he drew a somewhat erroneous connection between domestic budget surpluses and a strong dollar.[3] Elsewhere he noted the connection between policies to fight inflation at home and economic well-being abroad:

> Without this firm display of fiscal prudence we could not hope to achieve price stability, and without reasonable price stability and freedom from pernicious effects of inflation, we could not avoid a reduction in our exports or continue to enjoy the confidence required by our role as banker for the world.[4]

The pressures of the contradiction between internal and external policy also faced Federal Reserve Board Chairman William M. Martin, who bowed to domestic imperatives. As one analyst put it:

> If he did not ease pressure on credit, a severe recession could be the result. If he eased the pressure and the interest rates fell, that would stimulate the flight of the investment dollars to Europe where nations, at grips with inflation, had further reason to maintain their higher rates. As the least of several evils, Chairman Martin chose the latter.[5]

In November 1960, with the balance-of-payments deficit standing at $3.8 billion and foreigners continuing to draw down the stock of American gold, Eisenhower ordered a cut of $1 billion in foreign expenditures and argued that continuing American leadership was dependent upon responsible monetary policies that would bolster confidence in the dollar.[6] Eisenhower's concern for foreign accounts was not shared by Kennedy and the Democrats in 1961, who were elected with a mandate to move America ahead at home. Under both Kennedy and Johnson, full employment and social welfare programs assumed high priorities and were pursued through deficit spending and easier money policies, with less attention paid to the consequences for the dollar and American monetary policy abroad.

Most attention of American foreign economic policy-makers in the late 1950s was directed toward trade. After an extraordinary commercial surplus of $6.5 billion in 1957, the surplus slippped to $5.8 billion in 1958 and then dropped precipitously to $1 billion in 1959 before rebounding to $5.5 billion in 1960.[7] For the first time since the war, trade came under pressure from foreign competition and serious domestic pressure urged protectionist relief. Existing American trade legislation expired in June 1958, and the battle over new legislation provided the opportunity to air these commercial concerns and to devise ways to ensure redress from Europe.

In his proposal for new trade legislation, Eisenhower reaffirmed his commitment to free trade and commercial interdependence while at the same time conceding the need to consider the claims of domestic interests. The underlying premise was that American surpluses could be rebuilt and enlarged if pressure was applied to American trading partners to remove postwar quotas and high tariffs. Both bilateral arm-twisting and multilateral negotiations were viewed as appropriate ways to secure the necessary concessions. The protectionist case received special administration attention because 1958 was an election year. Worried by the troublesome recession, American Congressmen were particularly sensitive to constituency complaints about unemployment and struggling local industries. The trade legislation passed in August 1958 was a victory for the administration and for free trade. Its four-year provisions empow-

ered the President to cut existing tariffs 20 percent through the GATT reciprocal negotiating process, provided that no tariffs were reduced more
than 10 percent in one year.

The Eisenhower leadership also sought assistance for the flagging U.S.
trade balance by applying bilateral pressure to trading partners and providing new incentives to American exporters. Officials argued first for the
elimination of quotas on imports of dollar goods, and received generally
favorable responses from European nations by mid-1960. Treasury Secretary Robert Anderson pressed for larger foreign aid and defense contributions from allies in Europe and, in October 1959, launched a "Buy
American" policy, which required that recipients of aid purchase only
U.S. products. The intent of the latter policy was less to increase U.S.
sales abroad than to encourage the Europeans to enlarge their own aid
programs. Through the 1950s, the Europeans boosted their own trade
balances by selling goods to developing countries who financed their purchases with American funds. Anderson also lobbied the Atlantic allies for
greater contributions to the escalating costs of Western defense. In a mis-
sion to Europe in November 1960, the treasury secretary sought an additional $650 million from Bonn to offset the costs of maintaining American
troops in Germany. To aid U.S. exporters, the administration expanded
financing available through the Export-Import Bank, doubled the number of commercial attachés abroad, increased the number of Commerce
Department personnel assigned to export promotion services at home
and, for the first time, offered Export-Import Bank guarantees against foreign political risks on short-term export credits granted by private banks.

The attention directed to getting Western Europe to share the burdens
of foreign assistance and to promoting exports was expected to resolve
monetary problems. As is well known, the dollar gap became a dollar glut
in the late 1950s with payments deficits growing, confidence in the dollar
declining, and foreign countries beginning to convert their growing reserves of dollars into American gold.[8] After years of very modest outflows, $2.3 billion in bullion left the United States in 1958, $1 billion in
1959, and $1.7 billion in 1960. By mid-1960 the decline in American gold
stocks had become a sensitive political issue in the presidential campaign.
Amid general nervousness about the gold outflow and a rumor that John
Kennedy, if elected President, would suspend dollar conversions into
gold and raise the gold price, speculators rushed into the London gold
market in October, pushing the price of gold above the official $35 ceiling
to $40 an ounce. Assurances that convertibility and the $35 price would be
maintained were required by the U.S. Treasury and by the Democratic
candidate before speculation declined.

While the U.S. officials argued that balance-of-payments deficits could
be remedied by more attention to trade, full implementation of Bretton

Woods rules following European recovery in the late 1950s, and the manifestations of economic interdependence that followed, made the American task more difficult. Two sets of problems were unleashed when major West European currencies were made convertible at the end of 1958. The first was an unprecedented expansion of American direct foreign investment. Lingering domestic recession offered few opportunities for American business at home in the late 1950s, and large firms were attracted to the boom underway in Western European economies. These short-term responses were reinforced by long-term projections that an integrated West European market offered lucrative opportunities for efficient, large-scale American firms. The prospect that a common external tariff might limit access to the Common Market reinforced the attractiveness of producing within the market rather than exporting to it. The net outflow of private long-term capital stood at $2.5 billion in 1958, $1.5 billion in 1959, $2.1 in 1960, and would continue to grow in the 1960s. Although the assumption was that this dollar outflow would one day be more than offset by an inflow of repatriated earnings, this early exist of investment funds became a steady drain on the U.S. balance of payments.

The second and more-direct ramification of convertibility was the beginning of the internationalization of major capital markets, very rapidly sensitizing short-term money flows to changes in national interest rates. As already noted, this interest rate sensitivity became particularly troublesome for the Eisenhower administration as it sought to cope with recession during the late 1950s. "Out of phase" with expanding European economies, a reduction in U.S. interest rates to stimulate domestic expansion encouraged the flow of funds to Europe, where higher rates were supposed to moderate expansion and curb inflation. The higher American priority accorded to domestic objectives almost assured aggravation of the balance of payments. It is important to note that this internationalization of capital markets also undermined the effectiveness of the monetary instruments in both the United States and Europe.

The management of capital markets was further complicated by the piling up of unwanted dollars in West European banks, prompting some foreign dollar holders to begin lending them in European capital markets at competitive rates of interest. This Euro-dollar market, the origins of which can be traced to the mid-1950s, operated largely without the normal lending controls, such as reserve requirements or interest rate regulations.[9] From an estimated volume of $1 billion in 1960, the market grew rapidly through the 1960s, fed by continuing U.S. balance-of-payments deficits and its own money-generating powers. The lack of both national and international controls on lending assured that this multibillion dollar pool would inevitably aggravate the already troublesome management of capital flows.

American economic policy in the late 1950s must also be placed in the changing context of the Cold War. The confrontation between the United States and the Soviet Union both shaped American economic objectives abroad and provided useful leverage to secure those objectives. The growing belief that the Soviet threat had been successfully contained in Western Europe once political and economic recovery took hold permitted Washington to phase out its economic assistance to the region and address its own economic interests more directly. In the late 1950s, European leaders generally responded favorably to new American requests, but as Cold War tensions continued to decline they, too, looked to their own economic interests and showed less reluctance to challenge the alliance leader.

American policy also responded to growing Soviet overtures in the Third World. Military-strategic and ideological competition in Europe gradually gave way to economic and technological competition between the superpowers in the late 1950s, much of which focused on the newly independent developing countries. Washington's expanded foreign aid policy contributed to balance-of-payments deficits and was the reason for efforts to secure greater levels of assistance from less-eager European partners. Finally, the continuing Soviet threat must also be viewed as reaffirming the American commitment to economic interdependence at a time when its virtues were beginning to be questioned at home. Free trade and a liberal investment policy were viewed as the best means of linking market economies and resisting the appeal of state-controlled communist economic systems. A U.S. retreat to protectionism would have sacrificed one of the strongest instruments tying the Western alliance together. Such thinking was particularly evident in domestic debates over trade legislation in 1958, and its broad appeal is an important reason why cries for protectionist relief failed to generate more than minimal election-year attention.

Western Europe

The late 1950s were years of hope and promise in European economies. The take-off of the European Common Market in 1958, marred only by the absence of Britain, proved that European exports could once again compete successfully in world markets. Successful implementation of currency convertibility at the end of 1958 affirmed European monetary recovery. Nevertheless, the breadth and depth of economic recovery varied appreciably among the leading economies. So, too, did the political purposes of foreign economic policy. As a consequence, important divisions among these European states emerged, slowing the thrust toward European unity and complicating designs to achieve equal status with the United States. Moreover, as this section reveals, each of the three major European countries lacked the flexibility in balance-of-payments management enjoyed by the United States. As a consequence, each was required to address the early ramifications of economic interdependence in constructing domestic economic policy. Their varied records of success frequently deepened the divisions among them.

France achieved the most-remarkable reversal of national economic fortunes in the late 1950s. Foreign economic accounts deteriorated rapidly in the last years of the Fourth Republic following the exhausting involvement in Algeria, the 1956 Suez crisis, and the harsh winter of 1956. Balance-of-payments crises in 1956 and 1957 required the Fourth Republic to seek foreign financial assistance, and negotiations completed in January 1958 produced contributions worth $655 million from the United States, the European Payments Union, and the International Monetary Fund. Premier Felix Gaillard claimed that he had not agreed to "political" conditions in exchange for the aid, but the government did announce domestic economic programs to curb inflation and limit domestic spending and plans to eliminate temporary import and export quotas by the end of the year. Domestic policies were clearly designed to assist the recovery of French external accounts.

By mid-1958, it was clear that even more action was required if France was to meet its foreign economic obligations, particularly those imposed by Common Market membership. In June, these tasks were entrusted to the new Fifth French Republic, which granted wide-ranging economic authority to its new president, Charles de Gaulle. De Gaulle vividly described the economic conditions he faced when taking office:

> No sooner was I installed at Matignon than Antoine Pinay outlined the situation to me. On every single score we were on the verge of disaster. The 1958 budget was to reveal a deficit of one billion two hundred million francs. Our foreign debt exceeded three thousand million dollars, of which half was repayable within a year. As regards our trade balance, receipts amounted to barely seventy-five percent of outgoings in spite of the *de facto* devaluation, known as "Operation 20%," which the Felix Gaillard government had put into effect in 1957. By way of reserves, on June 1 we had no more than six hundred and thirty million dollars' worth of gold and foreign currency, the equivalent of five weeks' imports, and all the external sources of credit, relentlessly drawn on by the previous regime, had now completely dried up. Nothing remained of the last line of credit we had been able to raise—some five hundred million dollars—which had been reluctantly granted to Jean Monnet's begging mission at the beginning of the year by the International Monetary Fund and the American banks. . . . All in all it was a choice between a miracle or bankruptcy.[10]

Virtually all of the policies of the new French president were aimed at returning France to a position of rank in international affairs.[11] Weakness in external accounts had to be eliminated, and foreign economic policy was to become a vehicle to French prestige and prosperity.[12] The reversal in external accounts required bold action. In talks with other Werstern leaders, de Gaulle secured an additional $450 million in foreign loans and an international consensus on a 17 percent devaluation of the franc. In return, he agreed to make the franc convertible in January 1959 and to remove quota restrictions on 75 percent of trade with Western Europe and on 50 percent of the imports from the United States. The program's success, however, can in large part be explained by de Gaulle's insistence that it be augmented by unpopular corrections in the domestic economy—$600 million in new taxes and a reduction in agricultural subsidies. In a televised address to the nation in December 1958, the French president claimed that such domestic sacrifice was required for national salvation and eventual greatness. Without it, France would remain "a country in tow, swinging perpetually between drama and mediocrity."[13] Workers' and farmers' groups denounced the government measures, but his secure political position kept de Gaulle immune from such criticism.

By April 1959, improvements began to appear. For the first time in thirty years a devaluation of the franc did not set off an inflationary spiral. The trade balance also improved, as the devaluation made exports more competitive and the domestic slowdown reduced demand for imports. In May, the first month's trade surplus was achieved since 1955. At year-end, French reserves stood at a comfortable $1.7 billion. Steady improvement in the trade balance and growing confidence in the franc resulted in trade and payments surpluses in 1960. Only two years after flirting with international bankruptcy, France was well on the way to commercial and financial recovery.

External recovery was crucial for de Gaulle's foreign policy designs in the 1960s. Economics was to be the handmaiden of political influence.[14] Foreign economic policy would enhance the rank and prestige of the French nation within Europe, vis-à-vis the United States and throughout the world. As is discussed in the next chapter, de Gaulle made the most of trade surpluses and a vigorous franc to advance French political objectives in the 1960s. It can be argued, however, paraphrasing an old adage about de Gaulle, that this strategy gave too much attention to the international rank and prestige of France and too little to the economic welfare of the French.[15] The rapid recovery in external accounts came from the devaluation of the franc and from the willingness of Frenchmen to endure austerity measures, foregoing wage gains to keep French products competitive and postponing consumption of foreign goods to slow the growth of imports.[16] With time, the credibility of political leadership was

likely to be measured by its commitment to reward those who made sacrifices, particularly when economic recovery was robust. De Gaulle's
single-minded pursuit of French independence and grandeur and distrust of anyone who acted to undermine these objectives made him unwilling to consider the appropriate concessions to domestic groups. By
ignoring the internal constraints of interdependence, de Gaulle, by the
late 1960s, had undermined his domestic political basis of support. Such
concern for independence also narrowed the terms under which he
would embrace cooperation with other European states.

While the Americans gave primary attention to domestic economic
welfare and the French acted decisively to rebuild external accounts, the
British sought a more-balanced response to internal and external demands. Operating an economy long tied to the commercial and financial
vagaries of the world economy and at the same time often finding itself
constrained by powerful political groups at home, the British government
faced more directly than any other Atlantic country the contradictions between the objectives of the welfare state and the consequences of liberal
interdependence.[17] London's response was to alternate between policies
that encouraged economic growth and met social welfare demands, but
precipitated a deterioration in external accounts, and those that improved
trade and payments balances but did so at the expense of economic activity and employment at home. This stop-go cycle plagued British economic prospects through most of the 1950s and 1960s.[18]

The late 1950s were years of steady improvement in British trade and
payments accounts and, in some respects, created a misleading sense of
well-being for the architects of foreign economic policy. Responding to
the deterioration of foreign accounts following the Suez crisis, the Conservative government resorted to austerity measures in the last quarter of
1957. By early 1958, external accounts already showed new vigor, aided
by declining international commodity prices that figured prominently in
U.K. imports and, following the move to convertibility, by capital inflows
responding to higher British interest rates and declining confidence in the
dollar. Performance on trade and payments accounts remained encouraging in 1958 and 1959. When they began to show weakness early in 1960,
the Bank of England further increased interest rates, which had a positive
effect on the balance of payments by attracting short-term capital from
abroad. Such measures were particularly irksome in Washington, since
capital flows undermined efforts to stimulate the domestic economy and
contributed to even larger balance-of-payments deficits. Moreover, they
merely papered over problems in the British trade balance, which continued to decline through 1960. Resort to short-term policy adjustments suggested by the conditions of the moment rather than confronting the need
for more fundamental structural change in the British economy was a ra-

tional political strategy for a country caught between internal and external demands. Nevertheless, it was a recipe for continuing economic troubles. By reducing the external pressures on British policy-makers, temporary improvements in trade and payments accounts in the late 1950s discouraged London from making the tough but necessary foreign policy choices that would have redefined Britain as a regional rather than a global power. Most important was the decision to retain close commercial ties with the Commonwealth and the United States at the expense of participation in the European Community.[19]

Britain's historical role as an international financial power also discouraged this adaptation to a country of middle rank. London was reluctant to give up its role as a center of international finance, the role that accompanied sterling's rise to the status of reserve currency but that also served, with time, to funnel British capital away from the domestic base to more-lucrative opportunities overseas.[20] With sterling continuing to serve as a reserve currency for former colonies with continuing economic ties to Britain, monetary officials were reluctant to diminish sterling's role or engage in exchange-rate changes of the sort orchestrated by de Gaulle.[21] As a result, sterling became chronically overvalued in the 1960s, further eroding the prospects for trade.

In short, the United Kingdom began to feel the pinch of interdependence in the late 1950s but was able to employ short-term remedies to achieve necessary adjustments. Nevertheless, the legacies of British power, acquired in an earlier era, and the unwillingness of domestic groups to forego for long the promise of the welfare state suggested tougher times in the decade ahead.

External constraints and the domestic fear of inflation figured prominently in the shape of West German economic recovery, often dubbed the German "economic miracle."[22] The Allied Control Commission, which participated actively in the affairs of the Federal Republic until 1955, encouraged individual initiative, the free play of market forces, and the decartelization of German industry. The Federal Republic, under the direction of Economics Minister Ludwig Erhard, combined his liberal market orientation with a strong commitment to social welfare objectives to yield a strategy known as *Soziale Markwirtschaft* (capitalism with a conscience).[23] Erhard followed a cautious domestic economic course designed to avoid the dreaded inflation of the interwar period and to assure the competitiveness of German exports.[24] This deflationary policy resulted in slack domestic demand and short-term unemployment, but also in rapidly expanding export sales. Domestic growth was therefore dependent on the foreign demand for German goods, or export-led, and domestic policy was from the beginning tailored to the requirements of exporters and the vagaries of the world economy. Bonn's weakened political position in international affairs no doubt contributed to this unique policy mix. As demand for German goods grew, unemployment declined and the federal government moved to meet its social welfare commitments.

The payoffs from this early austerity were regular trade and payments surpluses that soon became the envy of Atlantic partners. Between 1950 and 1957, the German share of world exports rose from 3.8 percent to 8.7 percent and imports were up from 4.6 to 7.1 percent, and between 1958 and 1960 trade and payments surpluses were sustained. The Federal Republic enjoyed a $1.5 billion surplus in 1958; in the first half of 1959, German exports ($3.99 billion) surpassed British foreign sales ($3.89 billion) for the first time, more than doubled French exports ($1.93 billion), and did not lag far behind the United States ($4.85 billion). By the end of 1960, German foreign exchange reserves totaled $8 billion. The launching of the Common Market and the liberalization of international trade in the late 1950s, the commercial manifestations of interdependence that were often regarded as challenges and burdens to the French and the British, were regarded as opportunities for the Germans.

Nevertheless, continuing German political weakness and strategic dependence on its NATO allies diminished the usefulness of this newfound economic strength and at times turned it into a liability. With ample trade surpluses, the Federal Republic was a natural target of U.S. efforts to secure greater European contributions to the costs of Western defense and growing foreign aid programs. Within the European movement where the Germans needed French political support, de Gaulle insisted that Bonn pay for political acceptance with economic concessions. In other words, German economic strength was not easily translated into political power.[25]

Political and economic interests were frequently at odds in German foreign policy in these years, and their clash often had the effect of casting Bonn in the role of mediator in negotiations over Atlantic regime changes. On trade issues, the German political objective was to reach accommodation with France in the Common Market, which often meant agreeing to discriminatory and protectionist measures; the German economic objectives were to provide opportunities for German exporters that were consistent with American preferences for more-liberal trade. On monetary issues, the Federal Republic's political ties to the United States pushed them to endorse American financing remedies for balance-of-payments disequilibria, while economic interests fell closer to the French, who advocated greater discipline in American monetary policies.

Each of these European countries responded differently to the pull of economic interdependence in the late 1950s, but none could afford to ignore it. Among other factors, their responses reflected various configura-

tions of domestic politics, the peculiarities of national economic
circumstances, and their power or lack of it in international affairs. As the
following sections discuss, these different European responses complicated the task of responding to American trade and monetary initiatives
and of insisting that Washington play by the rules that it provided for
others.

ATLANTIC ECONOMIC RELATIONS IN THE LATE 1950s: THE PRIMACY OF TRADE

A desire of each country to preserve the "temporary" advantages it was
permitted as part of the postwar bargain and a determination to remove
the privileges of others and to move toward the full implementation of the
GATT–Bretton Woods regime define American and European
negotiating positions in these years. Washington sought to protect its
flexibility in balance-of-payments management by arguing for removal of
discriminatory European trading practices and for advancing the Atlantic
commitment to free trade through the GATT. Free trade would result in
larger trade surpluses, balance-of-payments equilibrium, and restored
confidence in the dollar. In short, regime changes in trade would remedy
monetary problems as well. If trade improvements proved insufficient,
payments difficulties could also be assisted by a better distribution of defense and foreign aid costs among members of the Western alliance.
Washington refused to accept the view that the emerging consequences
of interdependence might require domestic adjustments; adjustments
were to be made by others.

The view from Europe was that troubles could be minimized if
Washington accepted the obligations assumed by other Bretton Woods
participants to take the appropriate domestic action to maintain equilibrium in its balance of payments. And it was wishful thinking in a world of
many trading powers to believe growing trade surpluses could be guaranteed to cover expanding payments deficits. Without eliminating the
American habit and privilege of balance-of-payments flexiblity and imposing some discipline on the management of the domestic economy, Atlantic economic harmony would remain elusive. Negotiations should
focus on the monetary regime; alleged discrimination in trade was not the
root of the problem. Subsequent history confirms that the European analysis was probably closer to the mark, but the actual conduct of negotiations reveals that the American view and American power more often
dictated the course of regime change by focusing attention on trade. This
American power derived first from a greater willingness to protect economic interests as Cold War tensions declined. Vocal domestic groups,
challenged by new foreign competitors, increasingly put pressure on

Washington to argue strenuously for the removal of discriminatory practices abroad. In the power calculus, this new American resolve was aug-
mented by European divisions. European economic recovery brought
potential power approaching that of the Americans, but it also brought a
revival of national economic claims in individual European states that repeatedly prevented these nations from acting together.

The evidence of American power is found in several sets of negotiations, each of which are treated briefly in the final section of this chapter.
The issues that divide European states and often permit Washington to
play one off against another are shown both by the debates between
Britain and the Continent over the size and intent of the European movement and by Franco-German negotiations over the pace and direction of
movement toward a European common market. The American resolve to
eliminate discrimination in trade is evident in the larger context of Atlantic commercial relations in the creation of the Organization for Economic
Cooperation and Development (OECD), in GATT multilateral negotiations, and in American-initiated bilateral talks to eliminate postwar discriminatory practices in Europe. This final section also looks briefly at the
lesser role of monetary relations, the American strategy to minimize monetary reform, and the European reluctance to press the issue.

Commercial Divisions in Europe

As a result of different historical circumstances and economic conditions,
leading European states had varying interests and concerns regarding
European and international trade. The six signatories of the Treaty of
Rome considered trade with one another as the heart of their commercial
future and committed themselves to the establishment of a common market that would facilitate such trade and establish common tariffs with
non-member states. This affirmation of common interests, however,
masked important differences among them, most important those between West Germany and France. The French saw the European Economic Community (EEC), with its limited membership, as a means to
exert French political and economic leadership on the Continent. It would
also assure some control over the pace at which nervous French industries were exposed to international competition and would provide lucrative markets for French agricultural interests that would be denied to
non-European producers.[26] For the French, uncertain and insecure about
their commercial prospects, the Europe-of-the-Six was an acceptable half-
way house between protectionism and international liberalism.

The West Germans saw recovering European economies as important
to their strategy of export-led growth, and the competitiveness of their exports ensured that German goods would win sizable market shares of the

common market. Yet the EEC was also important to Bonn as a means to political acceptability and legitimacy in Europe and the West.[27] Becoming a trusted and responsible member of a European coalition was an objective of West German Chancellor Conrad Adenauer, and the crucial test of acceptance was political reconciliation with France. Unconstrained by these political considerations, Bonn's commercial interests mandated a broader-reaching and less-discriminatory trading regime, which explained quiet support for the free trade area proposed by Britain and open enthusiasm for the multilateral reductions through the GATT, both of which sought to minimize potential discrimination between Europe and the larger Atlantic region.[28] As an industrial power dependent upon agricultural imports, the Germans also resisted French efforts to gain agreement for a common agricultural policy that would deny Germany access to cheaper farm products from the United States and elsewhere. While the need for political acceptance in Europe and reconciliation with France remained Bonn's top priorities in the late 1950s, the Germans never fully accepted the limited French economic vision for Europe and frequently showed quiet support for British and American commercial positions.

The most-crucial European split on trade matters came after Britain's decision not to become a signatory to the Treaty of Rome and its last-minute efforts in 1958 to convince other European members to forego the Common Market and embrace a free trade area (FTA).[29] The British strategy was to use the existing seventeen-member Organization for European Economic Cooperation (OEEC) as the framework for a North Atlantic Free Trade Area. Both an FTA and a common market would eliminate tariffs among member states, but a common market would go further by specifying the creation of a common external tariff (CET) against non-member states. In other words, an FTA was compatible with London's reluctance to give up trade opportunities in the Commonwealth and with the United States and to tie its commercial future more closely to Europe. This reluctance was part of the larger painful process of adjusting to a reduced global role. Ironically, the temporary strength in British external accounts in the late 1950s mistakenly led some to believe that economic competitiveness and commercial influence could be restored.

British insistence on the FTA and its unwillingness to consider an alternative scheme that might have yielded an accommodation with the six can be explained, in part, by a misreading of the French ability and determination to exert leadership over these European negotiations and the German and American unwillingness to support the British position. The miscalculation of French influence followed from an assessment of the French political and economic position prior to the return of de Gaulle. Early in 1958, there was serious question whether French commerce would be able to survive the tariff cuts scheduled for January 1959.[30] With the French economy on the brink of bankruptcy in June, London expected weak resistance from Paris for the FTA proposal and growing support in Washington and Bonn, where economic interests were more compatible with the British scheme. The British plan was dealt a final blow when political calculations led the Germans and the Americans to give tacit support to de Gaulle and the French. The German position on the FTA was ambiguous from the start. Prior to de Gaulle's return in June 1958, it was reported that Economic Minister Ludwig Erhard gave his support for the FTA in discussions with the British negotiator Reginald Maudling. Nonetheless, de Gaulle made Franco-German political reconciliation conditional on German support for the smaller common market and won Chancellor Adenauer's support by late in the year. U.S. trading interests stood to gain more from a free-trade arrangement than from a discriminatory trading bloc, but larger American political and security objectives were better served by political and economic integration in Western Europe. Caught uncomfortably between allies, the Americans attempted to remain aloof from the European talks, supporting the general thrust of the French position only when pressed.

The failure to reach a compromise between the British and EEC positions resulted in the launching of the Common Market in January 1959 and the beginnings of serious commercial divisions in Europe.[31] London was critical of the lack of American support and threatened retaliation against Common Market members. In late 1959, the British also organized the seven-member European Free Trade Association made up of European countries that did not join the EEC. These so-called "outer-seven" proved of little value to British trading fortunes and served to irritate further relations with the United States. Washington regarded EFTA as divisive of European unity both politically and economically and was openly critical of the British efforts.[32]

The failures of British policy were evident in 1960. The take-off of the Common Market, the weakening of British external accounts, and the irritations brought about by EFTA brought reassessment. By mid-year, Prime Minister Harold Macmillan was seeking acceptable terms from the EEC for belated British membership.[33] While the Germans showed interest, de Gaulle's firm grip on the European movement dictated tougher terms for British entry.

Once the EEC was under way in January 1959, the differences in commercial interests between France and West Germany further divided the principal European states. Fearful of losing access to lucrative non-Common Market trade, the German strategy on internal tariff cuts and the establishment of the common external tariff was to coordinate them with tariff negotiations undertaken by the GATT and promoted by the

United States.[34] The French strategy was to speed up the schedule of tariff cuts and hasten the implementation of the common external tariff to give European producers special advantage in European markets. A temporary accommodation was reached through the so-called Luxembourg Compromise, which accelerated tariff cuts but not as rapidly as the French would have preferred and permitted agricultural tariffs to lag behind industrial cuts as a concession to German farmers.

Atlantic Trade Negotiations

European commercial differences in the late 1950s assisted the pursuit of American trade objectives. Nevertheless, American bargaining successes were probably more limited than they might have been had it not been for continuing political and strategic priorities that required European unity. As suggested above, ongoing support for a discriminatory regional trading bloc remained in tension with Washington's principal commercial objective, the liberalization of Atlantic trade through the General Agreement on Tariffs and Trade.

The Americans sought to reverse flagging fortunes by promoting free trade in three ways. First, pressure was applied both bilaterally and through the GATT to get the E.E.C. to remove unilaterally quotas and other dollar restrictions permitted during postwar recovery. Deputy Assistant Secretary of State for Economic Affairs W. T. Beale made the American case at the opening of the GATT meeting in May 1959:

> Old arguments about the dollar shortage and the unique export position of U.S. goods have lost their relevance . . . as inconvertibility has given way to convertibility, so discrimination and bilateralism should now give way to non-discrimination and multilateralism.[35]

The major assault on restricted American goods came in Tokyo at the fall 1959 GATT session. During these meetings, trade negotiator Douglas Dillon argued forcefully that trade barriers against dollar goods were largely responsible for the growing U.S. balance-of-payments deficits and demanded that other nations take immediate steps to eliminate them. American toughness brought quick results. Shortly after the meetings, the British Board of Trade removed the bulk of its quotas, including such important products as cars, machinery and industrial equipment, and textiles. The French, too, agreed to remove about one-fourth, or 200, of their remaining quotas, including items such as textiles, clothing, tools, and agricultural equipment. Paris also promised to lift all quota restrictions on European and U.S. goods within two years. By the early 1960s, European quotas ceased to be a major obstacle to American exports.

The second and most-important American initiative was to seek the reciprocal reduction of Atlantic tariff barriers through multilateral negotiations. Armed with the enabling legislation passed by Congress in 1958,
the Eisenhower administration pushed for a round of tariff bargaining
through the GATT.[36] The multilateral effort was seen in Washington and
also in Bonn as a useful way to ensure that the gap between tariff levels
negotiated by the EEC countries and those achieved by the broader GATT
membership did not become a major barrier to trade. The negotiations
that yielded agreement on the format of the meetings reflected the equity
problem between the six and the larger Atlantic region. The GATT talks
were to proceed in two stages. The first, to be conducted between the
EEC and the other GATT members, was to address the problem of
compensating non-EEC countries for commercial injuries incurred from
the EEC's new common external tariff. The second stage, to begin in January 1961, was to be a general tariff-reducing bargaining session that
would aim for 20 percent reduction in overall tariff levels.

Preliminary meetings in May 1960 produced the ground rules for subsequent discussions. Lists of products eligible for tariff reductions were exchanged, and the laborious process of negotiating cuts item by item was
adopted. Discussions that began in September and made little progress
by year's end demonstrated that forward movement would not come easily. With American trade balances slipping for a third consecutive year,
the United States adopted a hard line in seeking significant concessions.
Buttressed by the new confidence generated by their economic successes,
the Europeans grew more determined not to bow easily to American
pressures. This Dillon Round of trade negotiations, the results of which
are discussed more fully in the next chapter, was not completed until 1962
and produced slightly less than the hoped-for 20 percent reduction in
tariffs. Nevertheless, it set the stage for a more-ambitious American attack on trade barriers in the 1960s and demonstrated Washington's ability
to move the Europeans to follow its thinking.

Finally, Washington's growing uneasiness with the commercial divisions in Europe, represented most clearly by the split between the EEC
and EFTA, and diminished direct American influence over such affairs
as the work of the Organization of European Economic Cooperation
(OEEC), generated interest in a new multilateral institution. Such an institution would give the United States a voice in the commercial and
broader economic developments of all industrialized states. At a meeting
in Paris to decide the fate of the OECC in January 1960, the Americans advanced a proposal to create a body for more-regular trade consultations.
The idea was viewed with suspicion by both the British and the French,
but they did agree to establish a committee of "Four Wise Men" to study
the proposal. The committee report, which appeared in April 1960, rec-

ommended the formation of a trans-Atlantic economic body, the Organization for Economic Cooperation and Development (OECD), with powers of decision by unanimous vote. The draft of the organization's Charter downplayed the importance of current trade issues and emphasized instead the need for economic cooperation among industrialized states and assistance to developing countries. The final version of the Charter, which was adopted by nineteen states in November 1960, identified two principal tasks for the new organization. Nations were to undertake close cooperation on general economic and business cycle policy to maximize economic growth and prosperity for all; and development assistance, a high priority of American foreign policy-makers, was to be expanded under OECD direction. The OECD was approved by the U.S. Congress in 1961 and became another tool of U.S. involvement in European trade affairs in the 1960s.

Atlantic Monetary Relations

The U.S. view that frictions in Atlantic economic relations could be solved by reducing European barriers to trade to permit the expansion of American trade surpluses argued implicitly that adjustments in the monetary system were unnecessary. The single exception to this line of reasoning was that European restrictions on capital movements, permitted during postwar recovery when their currencies were weak, should be removed and national currencies should be made fully convertible, which in turn would mark the full implementation of the Bretton Woods agreements. Negotiations were undertaken to achieve this move to convertibility in 1958 parallel to American pressure to rid the trading system of quotas on dollar goods.[37] The strong market position of all three European currencies by the end of the year made the transition painless. Another important building block of Atlantic interdependence was put in place.

Negotiations surrounding convertibility were the only significant discussions of change in the monetary system in the late 1950s, but convertibility itself introduced some problems of monetary management that would require attention in the 1960s. As discussed above, convertibility greatly facilitated the movement of direct foreign investment from the United States to Western Europe and elsewhere, opening up lucrative new business opportunities for American firms but also depriving the domestic economy of investment funds and contributing to larger balance-of-payments deficits. Convertibility also sensitized short-term capital markets to national interest rates and undermined domestic monetary policy. An increase in rates, designed to slow the domestic economy, pulled in funds from abroad, further expanding the money supply. A reduction in rates, used to bring an economy out of recession, could trigger an outflow of funds and slow the process of recovery. Countries such as Britain also learned that interest rate adjustments could be used as a quick-fix for balance-of-payments problems, avoiding more politically difficult domestic adjustments. Convertibility also made currency speculation an attractive option in world money markets, a feature that came to have serious consequences for the system of fixed exchange rates. Speculation against the dollar occurred first in late 1960, driving up the price of gold. Speculation often raised the costs of having a currency in strong demand, as the Germans learned. The speculators' desire to hold Deutsche marks as confidence in the dollar declined brought inflows of dollars into the Bundesbank, expanding the size of the German money supply at a time when Bonn officials were struggling hard to prevent inflation. More than any other factor, convertibility internationalized economic activity and made necessary the careful coordination of foreign and domestic economic policy. The smaller and more internationally involved economies in Western Europe felt these consequences of convertibility sooner and with greater impact than did the much larger and relatively insular American economy. Such effects would not be fully felt across the Atlantic until the late 1960s and early 1970s.

Even though the seeds of Atlantic discord were sown in the late 1950s, and early efforts to address further problems would have undoubtedly made later monetary management easier, these issues were kept off the agendas of economic negotiations, as Washington preferred. While the Europeans began to sense that action was required on these matters and on lingering American payments deficits, they were reluctant to speak out. Vigorous alliance debate continued to be muted by Cold War tensions, but there was also a reluctance to challenge Washington's policies when the American economy was in the throes of recession. Efforts to reduce American payments deficits through deflationary policies could easily widen and deepen the slowdown, pulling European economies into a downswing that would jeopardize their recovery. Moreover, individual European leaders were too deeply involved with their own domestic economic fortunes to worry much about the U.S. monetary misfortunes that affected them only indirectly. The French, who had come uncomfortably close to exhausting their international reserves in mid-1958, were caught up in the implementation of policies to rebuild their reserve position and the strength of the franc. Dollar outflows aided this French reserve accumulation. Not until foreign accounts were under control could de Gaulle launch a major assault on U.S. monetary abuses and the privileged position of the dollar.

The British also enjoyed considerable benefit from the early stages of dollar weakness. In the new context of free convertibility, speculative attention that might have been directed against sterling turned against the

American dollar instead. Moreover, as already noted, the British took advantage of American easy-money policies by raising interest rates and drawing in short-term capital to rebuild reserves of foreign exchange. American policies actually helped the British to avoid monetary weaknesses of their own. When the U.S. position improved in the early and middle 1960s, the temporary shelter provided by the dollar was lost and the pound came under serious speculative attack.

In West Germany, where repeated payments surpluses and a strong mark provided the best economic foundation for criticizing American monetary management, there were strong political incentives to speak softly with the principal alliance leader and guarantor of German security. Instead, pressures were applied from Washington to make the Germans pay for their prosperity and sound economic policies through larger military offset payments, increased foreign aid, and a revaluation of the mark. Although Adenauer stubbornly resisted these American pressures, he was clearly on the defensive and could not hope to offer a major initiative that would challenge the privileges of the dollar or call for monetary reform.

CONCLUSION

The late 1950s were years of transition in Atlantic relations. Postwar objectives of European economic recovery and containment of the Soviet Union in Europe were largely achieved at a time when deepening conflicts of interest were beginning to aggravate relations among Atlantic states. American policy justifications invoked the old Cold War rhetoric urging the Western allies to team with the United States to do economic battle with the forces of communism, but it was less enthusiastically received by European partners more involved with managing the return to prosperity. Moreover, an uneasiness was growing in Washington from the economic challenge mounted by trusted allies and friends. European pronouncements continued to be full of praise for American postwar recovery assistance and ongoing strategic protection but at the same time hinted at a new resentment of American economic arm-twisting. This odd mixture of old harmonies and new tensions shaped the pattern of economic relations and regime changes in the late 1950s.

The lesson of these years is that Washington drew upon the old harmonies to secure the cooperation of its European partners in meeting the new tensions. The elimination of quotas and other restrictions on dollar goods, the beginnings of a major multilateral round of tariff negotiations, and the successful achievement of currency convertibility together pushed the Western world closer to the realization of a truly liberal economic order and to the American objective of economic interdependence.

It was the Europeans who were persuaded to give up hold habits in an effort to address some problems while Washington preserved its balance-of-payments flexibility, which in turn permitted autonomy in the management of the domestic economy. Yet, while autonomy was sustained, its compatiblity with the emerging consequences of interdependence was seriously questioned for the first time. The growing tension between autonomy and interdependence affected not only the United States in the late 1950s, but the three European states as well. Indeed, it was this need for each European country to cope with its own peculiar problems imposed by interdependence that regularly stood in the way of European unity and a common bargaining position vis-à-vis the United States. But in facing these challenges head on, the stronger European states were better prepared to cope with the economic changes in the 1960s.

3

The Years of Patchwork Reform, 1961–1967

By reducing barriers to trade and achieving currency convertibility, the Atlantic countries came closer to implementing fully the liberal rules that had been adopted in the 1940s. Unfortunately, this liberal push and the economic interdependence that it promoted did little to slow the growth of economic frictions between Western Europe and the United States. Trade problems, the object of primary concern in the late 1950s, continued to draw attention in the new decade as progress toward a common market threatened to raise new barriers to American exports. Moreover, troubles that had been confined to trade affairs now spread to monetary issues as ongoing American payments deficits drew new challenges from abroad, requiring corrective actions. Currency convertibility was followed by the rapid movement of money across national borders, demanding new measures to manage capital flows and discourage speculation against national currencies. For the United States, this meant devising procedures that would address international developments without interfering with the management of the domestic economy.

Chapter 3 demonstates how the Americans negotiated such monetary adjustments and at the same time sought expanded trade surpluses through a major new liberalization initiative in the GATT. Continued balance-of-payments flexibility placed few constraints on the most-vigorous economic expansion of the postwar period, the rapid growth of social welfare programs, and growing foreign policy commitments, most notably in Vietnam. Washington's efforts were made easier by the willingness of all European partners, with the exception of France, to continue to follow the American lead.

The U.S. ability to sustain the push for free trade and orchestrate frequent but marginal changes in the monetary rules-of-the-game is still testimony to its role as alliance backer in an era of Cold War tensions. And credit must also go to the economic leaders who devised an ingenious collection of short-term palliatives, particularly in the monetary sphere, that made dollar abuses relatively painless for European economies. The patchwork measures were also attractive as the tightening screws of interdependence deepened the divisions among the major West European states and prevented agreement on more-fundamental rule change. Britain's sterling difficulties throughout these years gave London more in common with the plight of U.S. dollar interests than with the monetary interests of France and West Germany. Strains in Franco-German relations prompted by DeGaulle's quest for independence and growing German economic strength also narrowed the range of common European action. This chapter first treats briefly the specific constraints and opportunities that the early 1960s presented to each of the four countries and then looks at trade and monetary relations in greater detail.

THE DETERMINANTS OF FOREIGN ECONOMIC POLICY

The United States

John Kennedy took office in 1961 amid growing domestic impatience with the lingering recession. The Democrats were eager to see him meet his campaign commitment to increase American economic growth from 2 or 3 percent to 5 percent and to reduce unemployment from an unacceptable 7 percent. Yet the new President, reluctant to employ measures that would result in budget deficits and charges of fiscal irresponsibility, made a cautious beginning.[1] He also rejected a proposed tax cut in 1961 in favor of a program of limited welfare relief that reduced the burdens of recession but offered little to economic growth. While Kennedy's caution primarily reflected domestic political realities and a need to gain support from fiscal moderates and conservatives in Congress, it also followed to a lesser extent from external economic worries, particularly the sagging confidence in the dollar that had precipitated a speculative rush into gold in the months before he took office. The declining trade surplus in 1960 also gave little comfort.

In spite of this caution, it became clear that the new administration firmly believed that foreign and domestic policy did not have to work at cross-purposes, and that growth at home and balances on external accounts could be achieved simultaneously. Kennedy appointed Walter Heller, a liberal economics professor, to be Chairman of the Council of Economic Advisors and gave him the task of rejuvenating the domestic economy. He named Douglas Dillon, a moderate investment banker from the Eisenhower administration, as Secretary of the Treasury and gave him the assignment of bringing order to external accounts.[2] As time went on, it was clear that domestic policy was the administration's chief concern. After rejecting the tax cut option in 1961, continuing economic stagnation brought a reassessment by mid-1962. By June, a decision was made to seek the "revolutionary" fiscal action; and while Congressional approval was not forthcoming until February 1964, the commitment to economic growth was seldom questioned for the remainder of the Kennedy presidency, nor was it challenged through most of the Johnson years.

The passage of the tax cut of 1964 became the policy instrument that triggered one of the largest and most-vigorous expansions in American economic history. These were heady days for Keynesian economists who made policy in Washington, and the view took hold that an activist administration armed with a variety of Keynesian tools could fine-tune American economic performance, sustain a steady level of growth, and avoid the painful downturns of the business cycle.[3] Such thinking and an era of prosperity tempted Lyndon Johnson and the Democrats to think more ambitiously about expanding social programs, eliminating poverty, and creating the "Great Society." When the growing costs of the Vietnam involvement were added, a recipe for overheating and inflation was the result.

The success of these policies of expansion, and there were few who did not regard them as successful at the time, had important consequences both at home and abroad. Many who had been fiscal conservatives and had applauded Eisenhower's determination to balance the budget became converts to the benefits of deficit spending. Congress, which had moved cautiously to pass the tax cut in 1964, soon took credit for its results but was then reluctant to take the required contrary fiscal measures once full employment was achieved and inflation appeared. Almost inevitably, success led to excess. More important for our purposes here, the attention directed to and euphoria surrounding this sustained era of growth increased the politicians' determination that external accounts should not interfere with domestic developments. In the late 1950s, Eisenhower's concern for balanced budgets may have left behind a legacy of recession and slow growth, but it also exercised a braking function on the deterioration in external accounts. Domestic policies of the 1960s required more creative efforts to boost trade surpluses and finance payments deficits. With the home economy riding a wave of expansion, others would have to bear the costs of adjustment. More important, prosperity at home yielded a forgiving economy, one that permitted many inefficient firms to survive and gave imports a larger share without seriously threatening domestic producers. In other words, prosperity tended to mask a deterioration in the competitive position of American industries which, when coupled with inflation in the late 1960s, resulted in the steady deterioration of the trade account. The "advantages" of being able to design economic policy with little regard for its impact on external accounts and the success of that policy in generating an era of unprecedented prosperity would begin to undermine the strength of the American economy by the end of the decade.

After claiming that domestic and foreign economic policy did not have to work at cross-purposes, the record indicates that this was so only to the extent that the latter was made to conform with the former. Kennedy's trade policy did not differ markedly from Eisenhower's. Its first objective was to attract more American producers to export markets through a package of incentives. Export credit and insurance schemes were upgraded to match those of competitors, a White House Conference on Export Expansion was created, the use of trade fairs and commercial missions was expanded, and E-for-Export letters were awarded to businesses that expanded sales abroad. Export surpluses did improve in the early 1960s, standing at $5.42 billion in 1961, $4.39 billion in 1962, and $5.06 billion in 1963.

Like Eisenhower before him, and confident of the competitiveness of American goods and services, Kennedy's principal efforts were directed at lowering international barriers to trade through the GATT. Inheriting the congressional authority to reduce tariffs by 20 percent through June 1962, Kennedy first sought a successful conclusion of the Dillon Round begun in the late 1950s. But he also set loftier goals when he submitted ambitious new trade legislation to Congress in 1962. In his 1962 State of the Union message, the President asked for passage of the Trade Expansion Act, which would grant authority for five years to the Chief Executive to negotiate the gradual elimination of tariffs on any goods where the United States and Europe controlled 80 percent of world trade and a 50 percent across-the-board reduction in tariffs on all other items.[4] The administration gave this legislation high priority in 1962, and Congress, despite some protectionist rumblings, preserved its key features and gave it overwhelming support in September. The Trade Expansion Act became the vehicle for addressing emerging trade discrimination in the EEC and provided the framework for the so-called "Kennedy Round" of trade negotiations between 1962 and 1967.

While the liberals controlled American commercial policy in the early 1960s and achieved sizable reductions in tariffs through multilateral bargaining, the administration also found it necessary to accommodate some early signs of trouble among American exporters before it could be assured of congressional support for tariff-cutting authority. In his call for new legislation, Kennedy appealed to the protectionists by saying that he would resort to instruments such as the "peril point," the "escape clause," and a national security amendment to assist struggling industries. Moreover, he called for federal adjustment assistance, often referred to by unions as burial insurance, to aid workers hurt by growing imports. The textile industry was the first major sector to make its case for protectionist relief, charging that low-cost producers in the Far East were winning an alarming share of the American market. To ignore the pleas of so important an industry in the South would have been an imprudent beginning for the new administration. To win the region's support for his larger trade initiatives, Kennedy sent Under Secretary of State George Ball to convince low-wage textile-producing countries to limit "voluntarily" their exports of textile products to the United States. Ball successfully negotiated a one-year agreement in October 1961, which was followed by a new five-year restraint program in February 1962 that controlled 90 percent of the free world trade in cotton products.[5]

This pattern of American arm-twisting and the use of voluntary restraint agreements were employed repeatedly beginning in the late 1960s, as one after another American industry was subject to vigorous competition from abroad. American leverage, usually in the form of threatening ever more restrictive legislative action, often convinced the foreign producers to agree to the "voluntary" scheme, but, as David Yoffie has shown, the measures seldom provided the assistance that American firms claimed they would and, ironically, often enhanced the competitiveness of the firms and industries they were trying to exclude.[6] In other words, just as liberal trade policy was designed to expand American surpluses by getting others to reduce their trade barriers at times when it was believed that U.S. firms were most competitive, this emerging pattern of protectionism attempted to shift the costs of declining competitiveness to foreign producers. In neither case was very much attention directed to ways to sustain the competitiveness of American firms in the first instance or to restore it in the second. It was easier and more politically acceptable to exercise power over others than to devise corrective measures at home; i.e., to avoid the consequences of interdependence rather than to adapt to them.

Kennedy's untimely death produced few immediate changes in trade strategy. Lyndon Johnson's faithful execution of the powers provided by the Trade Expansion Act brought the lengthy Kennedy Round negotiations to a successful conclusion in 1967. Yet the steady rise in trade surpluses that began in 1961 and peaked at $6.5 billion in 1964 was reversed in 1965 and was followed by a steady erosion of American trade strength through the remainder of the decade. Decline logically followed domestic expansion, inflation, and an overvalued dollar. More important, the Johnson administration failed to sustain the liberal momentum in American trade policy after 1967. The President offered no new liberal trade legislation, in effect surrendering the initiative to a growing group of protectionists.

The breakup of the liberal trade coalition was due to the convergence of a number of factors. The Kennedy Round's successes in tariff reductions made further multilateral efforts of dubious value, removing an important rallying point for export promoters. The growth of American direct foreign investment diminished the relative importance of trade as a part of foreign economic activity, and the perception among unions that multinationals were exporting jobs steadily pushed American labor into the protectionist camp.[7] Others pointed to the changing strengths of the domestic economy from the production of goods to the sale of services, further diminishing the importance of merchandise trade.[8]

Most important, protectionism began to appear in a discrete number of industrial sectors—textiles, footwear, electronics, and later steel and automobiles—where state- or multinational-assisted development of these industries in foreign countries, often with lower-priced labor, was resulting in shifting comparative advantages away from American producers. This shifting international division of labor fostered by the liberal trade and monetary arrangements put in place at the beginning of the decade required careful attention to changes in the global marketplace, attention it seldom got from American firms or domestic policy-makers.

It is important to stress that this "new protectionism" was selective, targeted at particular distressed industries. It never consumed American commercial policy as a whole and as such coexisted somewhat uncomfortably with a commitment to free trade and commercial interdependence. In some respects, this mix of selective protection and free trade produced the worst of both worlds. As David Yoffie argues, by limiting protection to certain industries or parts of those industries and by maintaining an otherwise liberal posture, the United States encouraged some competitors to diversify and upgrade their exports to avoid protectionist measures.[9] Not only did the United States take pains to avoid the adjustments necessary to ensure its own competitiveness, its actions gave such incentives to others.

Domestic growth, increased government spending at home, and the deepening involvement in southeast Asia almost ensured growing monetary problems in the 1960s. Moreover, the internationalization of capital markets made money flows even more difficult to control. Resulting payments deficits and the growing reluctance in Europe to go on building dollar reserves required more concerted action from Washington. Robert Roosa, Kennedy's Under Secretary of the Treasury for Monetary Affairs, became the chief architect of international monetary policy. The tasks of Roosa and his associates included slowing short- and long-term capital outflows, finding new ways to finance American balance-of-payments deficits, and discouraging conversions of foreign-held dollars for gold, all without interfering with the commitment to domestic expansion.

The reductions in domestic rates to spur expansion in the early 1960s had the negative effect of increasing capital outflows, both because domestic investors looked for higher returns abroad and because foreign borrowers went to American markets for cheaper sources of funds. Speculation against the weakened dollar also produced intermittent outflows. To control short-term capital movements, the administration experimented first with split interest rates, pegging short-term rates higher than long-term rates, in effect discouraging short-term movements while keeping long-term funds available for domestic expansion. In 1963, Kennedy proposed the Interest Equalization Tax, designed to increase the interest costs to foreigners seeking to raise capital in the United States. The tax was aimed at stock purchases and debt securities, not commercial bank loans and direct investments made by U.S. companies. In effect, the IET reduced interest rate differentials between the United States and Western Europe without tampering with domestic rates. The tax was not passed until 1964, but the threat of retroactive application and the uncertainty over final terms did serve to slow capital outflows prior to its passage.

To strengthen its hand against speculators, Washington devised several measures. Following an international operation to rescue the British pound in 1961, the Federal Reserve launched a network of bilateral currency "swaps" through which one central bank loaned foreign exchange to another whose currency was under attack. As Robert Stevens noted, "this plan provides a system of 'instant liquidity' for meeting large and sudden losses of reserves, since each can be activated in a few minutes by a single telephone call."[10] When the speculative wave was broken and funds moved back into the state which had suffered the capital outflow, the lending country could be repaid. Swap lines were established with eleven countries in 1961, and their success in managing the financial nervousness surrounding the Cuban Missile Crisis in 1962 and the Kennedy assassination in 1963 led to an enlargement of the "swap" amounts in 1963.[11] A second means to combat speculation was the expansion of the financial resources of international institutions like the IMF and a new currency-pooling scheme among industrialized states called the General Arrangements to Borrow (GAB). Drawing rights permitted countries with currencies under attack to make use of the sizable pool of foreign exchange.

The efforts to manage short-term capital flows were far more effective than those to control long-term movements. Kennedy proposed to tax nonrepatriated foreign earnings of American companies to slow the pace of foreign direct investment, but the measure failed to gain congressional approval. More than 1400 American companies established operations in Western Europe between 1958 and 1962, 456 in the last half of 1961 alone.

Action to finance American deficits and protect the gold stock was the last component of the monetary strategy. Measures were needed both to deter speculators from creating instability in gold prices and to discourage European central bankers from converting unwanted dollars into American gold. The first speculative rush into gold occurred in the fall of 1960, and national officials cooperated to restore order to gold markets. European central banks refrained from buying gold on the London market, and Britain and the United States contributed ample quantities of official gold for use in holding down prices and diffusing speculative demand. Encouraged by this cooperation, Washington urged creation of the London gold pool, into which members contributed a portion of their gold reserves to be used in the London gold market to counter speculation.[12] Any profits and losses were divided according to the weight of individual contributions. While not eliminating speculation in gold altogether, the gold pool served to stabilize the private market until the late 1960s.

Protecting the U.S. gold stock from European dollar conversions required even greater ingenuity. Secretary of the Treasury Robert Roosa proposed that foreign central banks purchase medium-term treasury bills, or "Roosa bonds," with unwanted dollars that those banks had intended to convert into gold. The bonds were offered in the holder's own currency to protect against a possible dollar devaluation, were highly liquid, and paid a high rate of interest. A second tactic was for the United States to offer foreign currencies instead of gold to those who wished to unload excess dollars. In 1963, states were unable to pay debts to the IMF with dollars because IMF dollar holdings were already at their limit. To prevent these countries from exchanging their dollars for gold that could then be paid to the IMF, the United States used its automatic borrowing rights in the Fund to withdraw foreign currencies. These currencies were then exchanged for dollars with those nations who, in turn, used these currencies to repay the IMF. This strategy worked through the mid-1960s until the United States began to approach the limits of its own automatic drawing rights. A final means to limit dollar conversion, and by far the most difficult to document, was simply for American officials to pressure European allies to continue to hold dollars. Undoubtedly, the Germans were often the targets of such arm-twisting.

As in trade, there was considerable continuity in American monetary policies from Kennedy to Johnson. In 1964 and 1965 a belief grew that American payments deficits might soon disappear altogether. In 1965, Johnson introduced a program of "voluntary" foreign investment restraints through which banks and corporations were expected to reduce the capital they exported by 15 to 20 percent.[13] Compliance was unusually high since all anticipated that a poor performance would bring mandatory controls (which indeed were imposed in 1968). By mid-1965, some Europeans expressed concern about a new dollar gap, and the expectation of imminent payments surpluses convinced the administration of the need to consider creation of a new international reserve asset to supplement the American currency in the absence of dollar deficits.

Parallel to commercial affairs, the optimism prevailing in 1964 and 1965 that external monetary difficulties could be managed by American "adhocery" and that balance-of-payments deficits would be steadily reduced was replaced in 1966 and thereafter by a growing pessimism regarding monetary management.[14] The galloping domestic expansion and the escalation of the Vietnam War all but eliminated hopes of closing the irksome payments gap. In the words of Treasury Secretary Fowler: "The multiple costs of Vietnam have made the task more difficult, and it may be that we will have to settle for an interim objective of equilibrium exclusive of the costs of Vietnam."[15]

The last years of the Johnson administration also revealed the inadequacies of earlier temporary correctives as the consequences of American domestic policies and the ramifications of monetary interdependence became evident. The London gold pool that had worked effectively in the early 1960s required attention in 1967, only to be overwhelmed by speculation in 1968. Washington's policies to discourage gold conversions became less workable as confidence in the dollar continued to decline. Currency reserves and "swap" lines proved unable to cope with the speculative pressures that hit foreign exchange markets in the late 1960s. The time had come for more direct American action.

In sum, Washington's focus on domestic expansion and economic growth in the early and mid-1960s complicated the management of external accounts. In the early years, trade liberalization and temporary monetary palliatives were attractive policies for a leadership unlikely to listen sympathetically to talk of the need to make domestic adjustments for the sake of external accounts. But such policies, which permitted Washington to ignore what was happening in the world economy rather than encouraging adaptation to global changes, were likely to be successful only in the short term.

Western Europe

Washington's efforts to promote trade liberalization with the EEC and to sell temporary adjustment in monetary arrangements were aided by growing divisions in Europe and the American ability to define common interests with London on money matters and with Bonn on trade. De Gaulle's largely unilateral challenge to American economic privileges proved an unsuccessful strategy to diminish American power. Widening differences in national political and economic circumstances contributed importantly to these deepening divisions in Europe.

French foreign economic policy in the early 1960s was shaped by the remarkable economic turnaround of the late 1950s. The growing strength of external accounts permitted de Gaulle to use trade and monetary policy as part of a larger strategy to enhance France's role as a global power.[16] Because de Gaulle's designs frequently contradicted the economic interests of important domestic groups, their effectiveness was limited to a time-frame within which the political influence of such groups could be contained. That de Gaulle's quest for French independence was as often directed against his European partners as against the United States undermined common efforts to create useful alternatives to American initiatives.

Between 1961 and 1964, the French president focused on sustaining improvements in trade and payments balances and managing the domestic austerity program that made them possible. Foreign exchange holdings reached $2.8 billion by the end of 1962, with a trade surplus of $523 million. In March 1963, domestic opposition was registered by striking coal miners and by French farmers looking for price increases on meat and dairy products. Modest government concessions combined with other inflationary forces affecting much of domestic industry made necessary a new stabilization program in the fall. Credit was tightened, tariffs were lowered to encourage price-cutting competition between foreign and domestic goods, and price ceilings were imposed on selected products and services. Continued inflationary pressures brought further austerity measures in early 1964. Domestic restraint and high interest rates pushed French reserves to $5 billion by mid-1964.

While high interest rates had the beneficial effect of pulling in capital from abroad and building reserves of foreign exchange, rapid inflows of the magnitude that accompanied an easing of monetary policy in the United States in these same years and speculative pressure against the British pound also had the effect of inflating the French economy, which in turn required even harsher austerity measures. Such inflows became particularly irksome to de Gaulle in late 1964; the costs of restoring order to external accounts were increased unacceptably by the policies of domestic expansion and the absence of balance-of-payments discipline abroad.

De Gaulle's unhappiness was revealed in a memorable news conference in February 1965, during which he was openly critical of the dollar's privileged position and the payments flexibility it granted to American policy-makers.[17] His preferred remedy, following the advice of French economist Jacques Rueff, was to return to the gold standard, under which all countries would be subject to the same balance-of-payments constraints.[18] To challenge the role of the dollar and show his support for gold, de Gaulle began monthly conversions of French dollar holdings for American gold. De Gaulle was also concerned that payments flexibility and an overvalued dollar were permitting American multinationals to buy into and control an unacceptable number of French companies. In March 1965, Finance Minister Giscard d'Estaing announced measures to screen and restrict the flows of direct foreign investment into France.[19]

De Gaulle's use of foreign economic policy to serve national interests and to assert French independence was directed also at EEC members, particularly the West Germans whose economic strength and declining reluctance to assert their own interests were of growing concern in Paris. French opposition to a European Commission proposal to move the EEC closer to the goal of political unity culminated in a French boycott of all EEC activities during the last six months of 1965.[20] De Gaulle also vetoed British applications for EEC membership in 1963 and again in 1967.

De Gaulle's success in building external accounts permitted some moderation in the austerity program and the limited encouragement of domestic economic expansion. Lower interest rates and accelerated growth not only proved popular for the president, who won re-election at the end of the year, but also slowed the inflow of foreign exchange and moderated trade and payments surpluses. Economic strength peaked both at home and abroad in the first six months of 1966. Domestic policies yielded moderate growth and low inflation; payments surpluses and a strong franc pushed French reserves to almost $6 billion, 86 percent of which were held in gold.

In the second half of the year, weaknesses began to appear. French reserves, which had shown steady monthly increases, fell repeatedly after July, prompting a discontinuation of dollar-for-gold conversions in October. The balance-of-payments surplus, which stood at $1.1 billion in 1965, dwindled to $344 million in 1966 and was projected to record its first deficit in a decade in 1967. De Gaulle's hard line on limiting foreign investment in France also softened in 1966. Applications from Ford, Motorola, Revlon, and General Motors that had generated no official action in 1965 were all quickly approved in 1966. As external surpluses declined, so too did confidence in French competitiveness.[21] American technology and managerial know-how, readily available to France's European competitors, were viewed as of increasing importance as progress was made toward a fully operational Common Market. Moreover, foreign investment provided a short-term remedy for a deteriorating balance of payments.

De Gaulle's prospects for reclaiming the initiative on foreign economic matters were further clouded by pressures from unions and workers for wage increases and expanded social welfare benefits. (Their expectations had been raised by the moderate expansion of 1965, after they had shouldered the costs of stabilization and austerity since the late 1950s.) Unwilling to make such concessions, de Gaulle continued his verbal attacks on the dollar and denied for a second time British membership in the EEC, although he did so on a steadily eroding domestic base. That erosion was complete when students and workers took to the streets of Paris in the spring of 1968.

In strengthening the French trade position and restoring confidence to the franc, de Gaulle provided a glimpse of the influence France could have on trade and money matters with the United States and Europe. But his quest for French independence and rank was inappropriate in two respects. First, its focus on France gave too little attention to the economic needs of the French, and de Gaulle learned too late that power abroad depends upon strength and support at home. Equally important, however, independence was ill-suited to circumstances emerging in the international economy in the 1960s. Isolation was the darker side of independence, and de Gaulle's policy frequently distanced France from her economic partners in Europe and the United States, a strategy that actually diminished French influence in an interdependent Atlantic world.

More than any other country, Britain was caught between internal demands and external constraints in the 1960s, and the legacy of the years 1961 to 1967 failed to address either set of problems satisfactorily. Unlike the French, who were seeking to recapture a position of rank and were convinced to make short-term domestic sacrifices to improve their prospects, the British found themselves burdened with the obligations and responsibilities of a global power, but with neither the resources to fulfill them nor a domestic population willing to sacrifice for the sake of external economic strength.[22] Britain's most-troublesome burden was the felt need to defend sterling's role as an international reserve currency and to avoid any change in its value.[23] Without the option of a major devaluation of the sort achieved by de Gaulle in 1958, policy-makers in London found themselves alternatively fighting off the speculators with international bailouts and domestic austerity packages and coping with domestic resistance to rising unemployment and economic slowdown when austerity measures took hold. The dynamics of the "stop-go" cycle were in full swing.

The deterioration in British external accounts that began in 1960 accelerated in 1961 and required corrective action by mid-year.[24] The Conservative government negotiated a $1.5 billion aid package through the IMF to replenish British reserves and then raised taxes, increased the bank rate from 5 to 7 percent, reduced foreign aid, and imposed a "pause" on wage increases. While the actions produced the desired turnaround in external accounts, they also pushed unemployment to the highest levels since 1947.

In early 1963 unemployed workers battled London police outside Parliament in what were described as the worst riots since the 1930s. Domestic discontent and the prospect of domestic elections in 1964 prompted the Conservatives to relax their grip on the economy in 1963. Interest rates declined and taxes were cut to provide domestic relief, but with them came renewed inflation, the inevitable deterioration in external accounts, and speculation against the pound. But with elections approaching, the government was unwilling to reimpose unpopular domestic measures. By early 1964, Britain was on the verge of a payments crisis, but still the government refused to take decisive action at home. Labour leader James Callaghan termed it a "dreadful race" between the election date and the date by which critical economic decisions had to be made if the British economy hoped to recover.[25]

The election of a Labour government was followed in late November 1964 by heavy speculation against sterling. Unwilling to consider devaluation, which had been their undoing in the late 1940s, Labour leaders imposed a 15 percent surcharge on imports and raised the bank rate from 5 to 7 percent. They also secured $3 billion in assistance from eleven Western nations to maintain the value of the pound. Recovery was anything but smooth in 1965, with additional international assistance required and stiffer austerity measures introduced in April and again in the summer. By year-end, more than $5 billion had been mobilized to defend the pound.

Optimism in early 1966, following Labour's victory in March and hopes that the pound had been stabilized, faded rapidly after a maritime strike immobilized the British shipping industry in May, triggering another run on sterling. New troubles required another multilateral aid package and brought the strictest austerity measures to date. Among other measures, taxes were raised $500 million, terms of domestic installment buying were stiffened, a six-month wage freeze was imposed, and voluntary guidelines were established to hold down prices and dividends. Defense commitments in Europe could be maintained only if the West Germans agreed to pay the full cost.[26] And for the first time, the British Cabinet gave serious consideration to devaluation.

Sterling made a steady recovery through the second half of 1966 and the first months of 1967, and by late spring Labour was back in the old bind. Each monthly improvement in sterling balances made it more difficult for the government to justify a continuation of the domestic squeeze. Unemployment reached a twenty-seven-year high in July.

Attacks on sterling late in the year made it appear as if all the domestic belt-tightening had been in vain. A rapid deterioration in the trade account in October prompted a heavy attack on the pound in the following month. After losing between $300 million and $1 billion in reserves on

November 17, Labour was faced with the prospect of imposing the severest of austerity measures or devaluing the pound. The following day sterling was devalued by 14.3 percent, and the Bank of England raised bank rates to 8 percent, the highest in fifty-three years. To make the devaluation work, Britain also counted on monetary assistance from abroad. A loan of $1.4 billion was arranged through the IMF, and an additional $1.6 billion was supplied by the Group of Ten. French participation in the second loan was conditional on London's willingness to implement tough new austerity measures: a steep increase in taxes, a freeze in the size of the money supply, and defense-spending reductions of $240 million.

The inability to make internal welfare compatible with external trade and payments stability was a dilemma that tormented British leaders throughout the 1960s, and the November 1967 devaluation was the climax of that frustration. The legacies of these years were marginal growth at home and diminishing economic influence within the Atlantic Community.[27]

The West Germans were the most successful of the three European states in balancing noninflationary growth at home with healthy trade and capital accounts abroad. Erhardt's insistence on domestic austerity in the 1950s and the Allies' surveillance of Germany's external economic performance yielded, in the 1960s, an economy structured to maintain compatiblity between internal policy and foreign accounts. Continuing political weakness abroad both aided and complicated Bonn's efforts to achieve this compatibility. The Federal Republic's need to prove itself a reliable Atlantic partner limited the economic claims of domestic groups and contributed to consensus building in industrial relations, a marked contrast to the pattern in Britain. But political weakness also made West Germany the target of efforts by other Atlantic states to shift abroad the costs and burdens of their own mismanagement. Some of these costs were translated automatically by the rules of the liberal economy. Attacks on foreign currencies led speculators to take refuge in the strong Deutsche mark, producing upward pressure on the currency and inflating the German money supply. Imprudent domestic policies abroad also triggered capital inflows as foreigners were attracted to higher German interest rates and German firms went abroad to raise money. But pressures were also applied more directly—requests for foreign aid, increased defense contributions, or a revaluation of the mark. Several times during monetary crises when economic partners refused to devalue, the Germans were faced with three costly alternatives: continuing to accept inflating speculative inflows, providing substantial assistance to the currency in crisis, or revaluing the mark and jeopardizing the competitiveness of its vital export sector.

In the early 1960s, Bonn relied principally on monetary policy to walk the fine line between domestic needs and external demands. The objective was to fix interest rates at a point high enough to control domestic inflation but not so high as to attract capital from abroad, a strategy that worked reasonably well as long as currency speculation remained under control. But when the dollar and sterling came under attack in late 1960 and 1961, more direct German action was required. After experimenting with interest rate reductions, the government finally succumbed to pressures for a 5 percent revaluation of the mark, which moderated the chronic surpluses in German external accounts.[28]

In the middle 1960s, domestic policy-makers sought to consolidate the gains of the "economic miracle" achieved in the 1950s. Attempts focused on slowing economic growth as labor shortages appeared and industrial plants operated near full capacity. To avoid inflation, interest rates were raised twice in 1964, but the higher rates also made Germany an attractive refuge for funds leaving inflation-ridden Italy and Britain, where the pound came under attack. In an effort to slow the inflow without adjusting the interest rate, the government increased reserve ratios on foreign liabilities, halted interest payments on foreign deposits, devised a 25 percent tax on interest paid to foreign holders of fixed interest stock market securities, and exempted Germans taking capital abroad from the existing 2.5 percent turnover tax on securities.

Inflationary pressures continued to plague the German economy in 1965 and 1966, and the government relied on tight money to slow the economy even further. That policy was undermined repeatedly by capital inflows following successive attacks on sterling and by the American policies of domestic expansion. Such influences made necessary even-higher domestic rates to prevent inflation bringing on a domestic recession and contributing to the fall of the government of Ludwig Erhard. While the policies of the new Grand Coalition government reduced interest rates and experimented with fiscal policy instruments and deficit spending, recovery was again complicated by speculative crises and the strength of the mark in 1968 and 1969.

Throughout these years, German economic leaders benefited from considerable consensus at home that domestic policy must be made compatible with the vagaries of the international economy, consensus that never emerged in France or Britain. Nevertheless, they also faced inflationary pressures for the first time since postwar recovery and found how difficult it was to address this problem in an era of easy capital movement and growing speculation. The German task was made no easier by a continuing reluctance to challenge economically less-prudent postwar allies. "Success" in defeating inflation, much of which was unwillingly imported, was achieved when recession took hold.

The difficult economic fortunes of France, Britain, and West Germany during the early and middle 1960s made it increasingly unlikely that European states could define their commercial and financial interests in common. De Gaulle's successful restoration of French external accounts made an effective platform for articulating a French vision of a new Atlantic economic order less dominated by the Americans, but it was a platform that neither the British nor the West Germans were willing or able to share. Britain's failure to escape the contradictions between a stagnating domestic economy and deteriorating trade and payments accounts not only muffled the British voice in European circles, but also brought London's interests more closely in line with those in Washington. German leaders may have sympathized with some of de Gaulle's economic reasoning, but they could not yet risk the political consequences of direct confrontation with the United States. De Gaulle's own ability to challenge effectively American hegemony was premised on the acquiescence of French domestic interests, a less-reliable assumption after 1967.

THE POLITICS OF PIECEMEAL CHANGE

American success in persuading Europe to go along with the move toward more-liberal trade arrangements and with making temporary adjustments in the international monetary system is best demonstrated by examining the actual conduct of negotiations. American success is explained both by the influence and ingenuity of United States policymakers and by the failure of the Europeans to agree on alternatives. American successes encouraged the growth of interdependence but also ensured that Washington could respond to domestic economic claims with little regard for the international consequences. And as noted above, this period provides preliminary evidence that the contradiction between interdependence and autonomy is beginning to take its toll on American economic strength.

We will look first at Atlantic trade relations, examining both the breadth of European commercial differences and disagreements and the conduct of multilateral negotiations during the Dillon and Kennedy Rounds. That discussion is followed by the politics of monetary reform, with special attention to the negotiations leading to the creation of the Special Drawing Rights in 1967.

Commercial Divisions in Europe

Declining domestic economic fortunes and the take-off of trade in Europe convinced the Conservative government of Harold Macmillan in 1961 to seek membership in the EEC.[29] And while the new administration in

Washington was enthusiastic about the prospects, viewing greater European unity consistent with its political objectives and British membership a vehicle for better representing American commercial interests, its enthusiasm was not shared by all in Europe. De Gaulle and the French were the most-vigorous opponents of British membership; and although much has been made of the political challenge the French president feared from London, important differences in commercial interests between the two countries were at least as important in French thinking. As a producer and exporter of manufactured goods and an importer of foodstuffs, Britain was eager to expand sales of industrial products in the lucrative European market. At the same time, however, London was reluctant to give up access to low-cost agricultural products from the Commonwealth in exchange for high-priced European foodstuffs that would be supported by the Common Agricultural Policy. As an agricultural economy with insecurities about its industrial competitiveness, Paris was both unwilling to make agricultural concessions to the British, which would penalize its own farmers, and wary of British industrial prowess. And while German economic interests continued to parallel those of the British in the early 1960s, these were the years of closest political ties between Adenauer and de Gaulle.

With such fundamental differences guiding British and French leaders, it is not surprising that negotiations concluded unsuccessfully. De Gaulle and Macmillan met three times between November 1961 and December 1962, with each meeting raising new objections on both sides. Early differences continued on agricultural issues, but the final meeting in December 1962 brought economic and strategic issues together and preceded by one week Macmillan's meeting with Kennedy in Nassau, which sealed Britain's strategic dependence on the United States. De Gaulle vetoed British membership in the following month.[30]

The Labour government again raised the issue of membership following the Common Market crisis of 1965.[31] Deteriorating relations between France and West Germany seemed to offer the prospect that Bonn might more openly support the British case. Moreover, France's growing wariness of German economic power led some to believe that Britain might come to be viewed in Paris as a useful counterweight to the Federal Republic. The French resistance to European steps toward political unity, a major reason for the 1965 French boycott, also seemed to indicate a growing determination to preserve national sovereignty in a confederated European structure, an arrangement more in keeping with British interests. And the state of British industries in the mid-1960s presented a less-serious challenge to their French rivals.

Efforts to woo the French made little impression on de Gaulle however. In an interesting shift in logic, he showed concern not for London's economic strength and old ties to the United States, but rather for the weaknesses of British accounts and the economic burden that membership would likely impose on France and the others. Flagging trade fortunes and a faltering pound suggested that Britain would be unable to pay its way. When the Council of Ministers met in December 1967 to discuss the question of opening talks on British entry, de Gaulle once again vetoed the move.

The inability of France and Britain to resolve outstanding differences on the issue of British membership perpetuated European commercial divisions and the EEC's weakened bargaining position vis-à-vis the United States. That position was further undermined by emerging Franco-German economic disagreements that followed the era of political reconciliation, which was capped by the signing of a bilateral Treaty of Friendship in 1963.[32] At a general level, de Gaulle's quest for an independent and global role for France clashed with the more-limited objective of an integrated regional community pursued by the West Germans. De Gaulle spoke of a larger Europe, from the "Atlantic to the Urals," and of French leadership over a confederation of independent nation-states that would define interests and foreign policy objectives separate from those of the United States and the Soviet Union.[33] Unity among the six narrowed this vision and threatened French sovereignty. Threats to sovereignty were taken more seriously once the Germans had achieved political respectability among Common Market partners and showed a new assertiveness in the defense of their economic interests. The retirement of Adenauer in 1963 and his replacement by Ludwig Erhard, long an advocate of German economic interests, increased French worries. Unlike the close personal relations between de Gaulle and Adenauer, relations between de Gaulle and Erhard remained cool.[34]

The principal EEC issues that divided the two countries in the 1960s were the establishment of a common agricultural policy (CAP), the timetable for eliminating internal EEC tariffs, and an initiative by the European Commission to take a first step toward political unity. In 1961, de Gaulle made continuing reductions on internal tariffs conditional upon European commitment to the CAP. In 1963, progress toward the CAP, pushed by the French, was linked to agreement on a liberal common European position in the Kennedy Round negotiations, important to the Germans. The French wanted further movement toward a common farm policy for fear that GATT negotiations with the Americans would dilute French agricultural advantages in the Common Market.[35] The Germans wanted a liberal European tariff position in Kennedy Round negotiations to assure German industry access to non-European markets.[36]

Further, disagreement arose over the timetable for eliminating internal Community tariffs. The French, more for political than economic reasons, had encouraged the rapid reduction of internal tariffs in the early 1960s as a means to distance Europe commercially from Britain and the United States. The Germans, who actually benefited more from such internal tariff cuts, attempted to impede the pace of reductions to minimize the adjustments necessary to accommodate British membership and to coordinate them with anticipated GATT reductions. The veto of British membership in 1963 prompted a reversal of the two nations' positions. The Germans proposed to accelerate the completion of the customs union, while the French agreed to go along only if the Germans made concessions on agricultural policy. The June 1965 compromise provided that in exchange for the early elimination of all internal tariffs, the Germans would accede to the French demand for a fully implemented Common Agricultural Policy by 1 July 1967.

The most-telling Franco-German disagreement occurred in July 1965 when de Gaulle decided to boycott all European Community activities to show his opposition to a proposal granting increased authority to the European Commission.[37] The action came at the peak of de Gaulle's determination to demonstrate French independence. The withdrawal from NATO, conversions of dollars for gold, unilateral attempts to improve relations with the Soviet Union, China, and Eastern Europe all accompanied this hard line in the EEC. At the same time, German national interests and Community progress continued to converge on the goal of European political unity. Unity became attractive because of growing German political influence drawn in large measure from economic strength. Erhard's refusal to concede to the French on the issue of political integration indicated a growing, new German confidence. The French boycott brought community institutions to a standstill and halted Kennedy Round negotiations. It was not until late January 1966 when the Council of Ministers hammered out an agreement, the so-called "Luxembourg Compromise," that the boycott was ended. The crisis brought into sharp relief the extent of the deterioration in Franco-German relations.

In important respects, these deepening European divisions can be traced to the unfolding of economic interdependence in the 1960s and these countries' attempts to adapt to its consequences. As the first part of this chapter has shown, each of these European states was affected differently by competing internal and external claims, and national circumstances determined that some would meet the challenges better than others. Their respective successes and failures were important factors in defining their interests in the European movement, interests that often proved incompatible on fundamental commercial and financial issues. The inability to reach common ground and tendencies for some to find more compatiblity with the United States (West Germany on the GATT negotiations and agricultural trade, and Britain on monetary issues and the defense of reserve currencies) made it easier for Washington to manage the politics of piecemeal change.

Multilateral Trade Negotiations

Multilateral discussions to reduce barriers to trade that were begun in the last years of the Eisenhower administration were resumed in 1961 under the new American leadership.[38] The first stage of negotiations, designed to secure adjustment assistance for non-Common Market members, received primary attention from the United States, recognizing that European concessions would be unilateral and not subject to the 20 percent limitations imposed by American legislation on the reciprocal negotiations. Understandably, the Europeans hoped to focus attention on the second stage of reciprocal reductions. Completed in May 1961, the first round of talks resulted in the Europeans making concessions on about 300 items, although, at French insistence, all agricultural goods were excluded. Generally satisfied with non-farm concessions, the Americans, determined to extract agricultural concessions, permitted the talks to proceed to reciprocal negotiations.[39]

During the second phase, the Europeans offered to reduce industrial tariffs across the board rather than negotiating item by item but, at de Gaulle's insistence, proposed minimal concessions on farm products. Moreover, at the end of 1961 de Gaulle tied Dillon Round progress and continued tariff cuts within the EEC to a European commitment to establish a Common Agricultural Policy. In mid-December, the GATT membership reached an interim agreement specifying a formula for reducing industrial tariffs, which was tied to the resolution of internal EEC agricultural problems and a GATT agreement on farm products. On industrial goods, the EEC would reduce its Common External Tariff by 20 percent and the U.S. would make 20 percent reductions in a somewhat smaller group of industrial products.

The European commitment to a Common Agricultural Policy in mid-January 1962 cleared the way for agricultural discussions in the Dillon Round, which were concluded by the end of the month. While that agreement excluded $400 million in farm exports that competed directly with European foodstuffs such as wheat, feed grains, tobacco, rice, livestock, and poultry, it did grant access to another $600 million worth of American agricultural trade.

The legacy of the Dillon Round was a mixed blessing for Washington. Designed as part of a broader strategy to rebuild American trade surpluses in the 1960s at a time when European integration threatened to deny important markets to American exporters, it can be viewed a moderate success. Before Congress, Kennedy claimed to have secured $4.3 billion in tariff concessions while giving up only $2.9 billion in return. While Washington sustained the momentum for trade liberalization and advanced its general objective of Atlantic commercial interdependence, the specific benefits from the Dillon Round were more uneven. Access to markets for industrial goods was enlarged both by European unilateral concessions and the across-the-board tariff reductions, but de Gaulle's determination to preserve European agricultural markets for French farmers produced less-satisfying results. De Gaulle's success in threatening progress toward European unity if French agricultural interests were not accommodated was effective both with the Germans and the Americans. One might question the wisdom of the French strategy in retrospect, given the current state of European agricultural production and pricing, just as we question the long-term viability of the broader American economic strategy throughout this analysis, but it made good sense in the short term to exercise influence to protect French farmers.

As the Dillon Round drew to a close, the momentum for further trade liberalization was sustained by the passage of the Trade Expansion Act in 1962. Exploratory talks for the new "Kennedy Round" of trade negotiations began in January 1963.[40] In the most-ambitious multilateral effort ever to reduce tariffs, it took until March 1965 just to decide what items would be included and what procedures to follow. From March 1965 to May 1966, the crisis surrounding the French boycott of the EEC brought GATT negotiations to a halt. The actual bargaining over tariff reductions took place in the twelve months prior to May 1967 under the pressure of the expiration of the American trade act.

Preliminary discussions in Geneva between 1963 and 1965 focused on procedures for reducing tariffs or the so-called disparities problem, the sensitive issue of agricultural trade and the growing discrimination caused by non-tariff barriers to trade.[41] Because of very different tariff structures in the United States and the European Community, each side argued for a different method in determining tariff reductions. The United States maintained a large number of both high and low tariffs with few in the middle range; following the tariff-averaging required for the CET, the Europeans set most rates in the middle range between 10 and 25 percent. Consistent with the authorization of the Trade Expansion Act, the United States sought across-the-board reductions of tariffs by 50 percent, negotiating individually only those items specifically excluded by GATT members. The Europeans argued that an across-the-board reduction favored the United States, since a 50 percent reduction of high U.S. tariffs would still leave in place a very high levy and an equal reduction of very low tariffs would affect trade very little, while a similar reduction of the moderate European levels would transform prohibitive moderate tariffs into minimal trade barriers. They sought instead to average tariffs on both sides of the Atlantic by proposing large cuts in high tariffs and smaller cuts in lower tariffs. After more than a year, an agreement was reached in May 1965 that accepted the American preference for across-the-board reductions but permitted participants to construct exemptions lists for items to be negotiated individually. After intensive bargaining, the EEC submitted a list that included 20 percent of all negotiable items.[42] The U.S. list was only slightly shorter.[43]

After the unsatisfactory results in the Dillon Round, Washington was determined to make agriculture a high priority in the Kennedy Round. Nevertheless, the EEC's slow progress in establishing the CAP prevented much movement in GATT negotiations. Without a common European price structure for grains, for example, an issue long debated by the French and the Germans, there could be little movement on an issue of great importance to American farmers. For Washington to hold other issues hostage to agriculture, there was unlikely to be any movement at all. Once the Europeans established a Community grain price in December 1964, an agreement on procedures for handling agricultural issues followed in March 1965. It specified that negotiations on farm products would be treated item by item rather than adopting reductions across the board.

The final problem area was the ill-defined realm of non-tariff barriers and how such discrimination should be treated. Such barriers had been largely ignored by the GATT forum, and their expanding use as many countries sought ways to adjust and adapt to the changing international division of labor convinced all that they needed attention. But the procedural problems in negotiating their elimination were far more numerous than with tariffs, and a full-scale assault on these new barriers would have to await the Tokyo Round in the 1970s.

After procedural issues were finally resolved, the EEC crisis of 1965 further delayed substantive negotiations. Following the Luxembourg Compromise, the wheels of the GATT slowly began to turn again and talks began in earnest in April 1966. The issues to be resolved before the expiration of the Trade Expansion Act on 30 June 1967 were many, and it often appeared that an agreement would not be possible. The negotiation of items on exemption lists, separate industrial sector negotiations on aluminum, pulp and paper, iron and steel, chemicals and cotton textiles, as well as the continuing problem of agriculture consumed the energies of the negotiators.[44] Growing, too, were protectionist sentiments in the United States as American trade fortunes began to decline and feelings that U.S. interests were not well served by such multilateral negotiations.

In the final months, three sets or problems stood in the way of an agreement: (a) the treatment of chemicals and particularly removal of the so-called American Selling Price (ASP), which imposed tariffs on imports of a small group of chemical products based not on the price set by the exporter but on the price charged by the American producers; (b) agricultural tariffs and especially European grain levies; and (c) steel tariffs that emerged as an issue in the last months of the talks as the clamor for protection against steel imports grew in the United States. Negotiators talked of a "package deal" that would find common ground on all three issues.[45]

By mid-May, this common ground was found. The grains agreement included both pricing arrangements and commitments among leading producers to provide food aid to developing countries. The pricing scheme provided little hope for American farmers seeking a larger share of the European market, but European aid commitments better distributed such burdens among Atlantic partners. Negotiations on meat and dairy products proved inconclusive. Once again, agricultural negotiations were disappointing for American interests. On the chemicals issue, the Community received no assurance that the ASP would be repealed, but they did agree to a 40 percent automatic cut in their own chemical tariffs, with the remaining 60 percent made conditional upon congressional repeal of the American Selling Price. On steel, William Roth, the American chief negotiator, revealed that the United States had withdrawn 80 percent of its tariff concessions on steel and another two-thirds of its offers on synthetic textiles in the final days of negotiations, claiming that trade conditions had changed markedly since offers were made in the early days of the Kennedy Round.

Analysts calculated that the Kennedy Round produced industrial tariff reductions that averaged 35 to 40 percent,[46] less than the 50 percent goal set by the Trade Expansion Act but far more than the achievements of other multilateral negotiations. The reductions brought most industrial tariffs to very low levels, leading most to conclude that future multilateral negotiations would give more attention to non-tariff trade barriers. President Johnson approved the Kennedy Round results in June, initiating reductions of some 6000 tariffs over five years between 1968 and 1972.

Several conclusions emerge from this treatment of Atlantic trade negotiations through the middle 1960s. First, the United States initiated both rounds of multilateral negotiations with the intent of increasing commercial interdependence among Atlantic states and building American trade surpluses in an effort to bolster confidence in the dollar and strengthen the balance of payments. Undoubtedly, Washington's efforts contributed significantly to the rapid growth of Atlantic trade during these years and to an era of unsurpassed trade liberalism. Nonetheless, the assumption that larger trade surpluses would follow free trade, which seemed to hold until 1965, was increasingly called into question after that time. As commercial interdependence deepened, free trade increasingly benefited those whose domestic economic policies were designed to assure that national industries remained competitive. While not all European states were able to find the right policy mix, all were attentive to these external constraints. American economic policies continued to be made with little regard for the world outside, and unbridled expansion, inflation, and increased government spending began to take its toll after 1965. As one industry after another began to be challenged, cotton textiles in the early 1960s and steel by the end of the Kennedy Round, Washington felt the pressure from home to engage in selective protectionism. Free trade remained a worthy goal, but threatened industries were entitled to "temporary" relief. As this more-qualified endorsement of free trade emerged, the belief that the United States could solve its monetary problems with trade expansion was also called into question, leading one to anticipate future changes in monetary policy.

While the protectionist impulse emerges in American trade policy toward the end of the Kennedy Round, one must not overstate its significance. For despite the tensions and troubles that one can always find within multilateral negotiations, the trade rounds were, as Ernest Preeg argued, an example of alliance strengthening and cooperation during a period when the Western nations were struggling with troublesome security dilemmas and tense political relations.[47] The broader political motives that were at the root of American support for the Common Market in the 1950s continued to underpin the commitment to liberal trade and interdependence in the 1960s. Without such objectives, the retreat into protectionism would surely have been more rapid.

A second conclusion from these commercial relations is that while it seems clear that American leadership was responsible for initiating and organizing the multilateral move to free trade, it is much less apparent that they controlled the outcomes of the actual negotiations.[48] Ernest Preeg argued that, in contrast to security negotiations within NATO where the possession of overwhelming nuclear capabilities gave the United States a trump card, the GATT negotiations were the first where the United States and Western Europe competed as equal partners.[49] In some respects, Washington became a prisoner of the principle of reciprocity that it had long championed in international trade. Reciprocity specified equal concessions on both sides as a basis for agreement. At other points, American influence was undermined by its earlier commitments to the EEC. De Gaulle proved to be a master at manipulating GATT negotiations to secure agricultural objectives within the Community that were consistently opposed to American interests. One could argue that without the Kennedy Round and the benefits that it offered to German exporters, de Gaulle might never have won a German commitment to the CAP.

But probably the most important reason for American negotiating disappointments was the size and complexity of the Kennedy Round negotiations themselves, preventing any state from dominating their outcome. With so many issues and with countries ranking the importance of such issues very differently, it is not surprising to discover that outcomes were dominated by no single state. It might also be expected that for countries with a rapidly growing dependence on foreign trade, such as West Germany, Japan, and a number of smaller European countries, negotiation strategies in the GATT would take on added importance. Close cooperation between government officials and private-sector actors, never a feature of American negotiating tactics, might be expected to ensure a more-faithful defense of commercial interests.

In short, the United States orchestrated the launching of a trade liberalizing scheme over which it had less and less control. A 35 to 40 percent average reduction in commercial tariffs certainly was consistent with the larger American objective of promoting free trade and interdependence, but trading partners proved to be able bargainers and defenders of their own interests in particular problem areas in the negotiations. Moreover, free trade pays dividends to those who give close attention to their international competitiveness, something that the bonds of interdependence imposed on trading partners but not on the United States. As the American protectionist impulses after the Kennedy Round reveal, the benefits of free trade were more regularly accruing to others.

The Monetary Relations

Money problems that were largely ignored at American insistence in the late 1950s demanded attention in the 1960s, and numerous proposals for altering the Bretton Woods system were actively debated. The United States advocated piecemeal changes that would address current difficulties but yet preserve the flexibility that the postwar regime provided for American external accounts. France opposed the privileges that were accorded reserve currencies and argued for a new system based on gold. West Germany took a middle postion, sharing French disenchantment with the postwar order, but unpersuaded by de Gaulle's remedy of radical reform.

National positions on monetary reform were considerably affected by the status of each country's currency and the balance of payments. The strength of French external accounts in the mid-1960s permitted de Gaulle an activist policy unavailable to leaders before or after him. German economic strength, but continuing political weakness, would dictate a less-vigorous defense of monetary interests and a reluctant willingness to shoulder the monetary problems of others. Growing sterling problems and mounting domestic impatience with austerity limited Britain's leverage in multilateral negotiations, prompting increasing dependence on

Washington for representation of its interests. Domestic pressure for policies of growth and expansion after the sluggish Eisenhower years shaped American strategies for reform. The remedies that emerged from the collision of these national positions closely followed American preferences for incremental change as opposed to radical reform. While they served American interests in the short term, they failed to address deeper problems that would return to plague the monetary system in the late 1960s and early 1970s.

Speculation against the dollar in the fall of 1960 convinced European finance ministers and central bankers of the need to consider monetary reform. Continuing speculation against the dollar and the pound in 1961 softened even the American opposition to reform.[50] In mid-1961 an Anglo-American plan was submitted for expanding IMF resources to help members meet attacks on weak currencies. Specifically, the proposal permitted the IMF to augment its resources by borrowing currency reserves from its members and making them available to countries whose currencies were the object of speculation. Not surprisingly, the initial beneficiaries of these new borrowings would likely be the dollar and the pound. The plan also specified in advance the actual amounts available and that funds could be drawn automatically, without the approval of the lending nation.

While the French recognized the need to exercise some international control over short-term capital movements, they opposed the Anglo-American plan for several reasons. Most important, they were uneasy with a scheme that could be used to finance balance-of-payments weaknesses and thereby diminish the pressure on weak currencies to take the appropriate domestic corrective measures. Making more monetary reserves available could also be inflationary. Moreover, Paris was uneasy with placing control of the arrangements in the hands of the IMF where American influence was strong. Finally, France objected to the "advanced commitment" and "automatic activation" provisions of the scheme, which effectively denied lending nations any control over its use.

After six months of negotiations the industrialized countries gave their support to the General Arrangement to Borrow (GAB), which made $6 billion in foreign currency reserves available to countries whose currencies were weakened by speculative attack. As a concession to the French, the new scheme was created independently of the IMF and administered by the so-called "Group of Ten."[51] Britain and the United States were assured a sizable pool of emergency funds; France was given some control over the fund's use. The London gold pool, discussed above, was created about the same time and provided added protection against speculation.

With reserves dwindling and the pound weakening, only the British raised the issue of monetary reform at the September annual meeting of the IMF in Washington.[52] To counter sterling weakness, Chancellor of the Exchequer Reginald Maudling proposed the establishment of a "mutual currency account" into which surplus countries would make guaranteed deposits from their surplus reserve accumulations of the world's major currencies.[53] Surplus countries would, in effect, take on some of the burden of adjustments, and the pool of currencies would be available to assist deficit nations. Under Secretary of the Treasury Robert Roosa denounced the British plan, arguing that existing IMF resources of $15 billion, which could be supplemented by $6 billion available under the GAB, were more than adequate for the task of currency stabilization.[54]

Anticipated improvements in the American balance of payments and fears of subsequent liquidity shortfalls brought a new interest in monetary reform to Washington in 1963. By mid-year several influential economic studies urged changes in the Bretton Woods system.[55] After considerable domestic debate, a new American position, supportive of reform, was outlined at the 1963 IMF annual meeting. Robert Roosa, who had criticized British plans for reform only twelve months earlier, discussed the new American plan in a *Foreign Affairs* article prior to the IMF meetings.[56] Roosa indicated American willingness to support studies of monetary reform, specifically those focusing on the expansion of world liquidity.

The principal reaction to the American proposal came from the French, who did not dispute the need for reform but objected to liquidity expansion as the principal remedy.[57] They suggested instead that the system's failing was its inability to require that chronic deficit countries, such as the United States and Britain, adopt appropriate internal measures to restore order to their external accounts. Reform, in the French view, should focus on ways to assure balance-of-payments accountability in the reserve currency countries.

Over French objections, the IMF membership voted to commission a study of world liquidity needs. As a concession to the French, two such studies were commissioned, one within the IMF, which Paris feared would be dominated by the Americans, and one by the Group of Ten, where the Europeans could exercise greater influence.[58] The Group of Ten study group met for the first time in December 1963 in Paris. Discussion focused on a proposal, first developed by Edward M. Bernstein, to create a new international currency unit that would reduce dependence on the dollar as the provider of international liquidity. Robert Roosa, the U.S. spokesman, argued that as American payments deficits were eliminated and dollar outflows curtailed by the mid-1960s, new sources of liquidity would be needed to supplement the inadequate supplies of newly mined gold. The French and the Dutch opposed Roosa's formulation, arguing that any new international asset should be designed to replace the dollar as a reserve currency, not merely supplement its role. By permitting the new reserve asset to supplement the dollar's role, the United States would merely be granted another source of financing for continuing payments deficits.

The Group of Ten concluded its study in June 1964 and published recommendations that reflected the French and the American differences.[59] The report concluded that existing liquidity levels were adequate to finance world trade for the present and "immediate future" but that continued expansion of world trade might require a new reserve asset in years ahead.[60] At American insistence, the study recommended that IMF quotas be moderately expanded and that quotas be adjusted upward in countries such as West Germany where initial allocations were clearly out of line. To meet French demands, the report called for greater discipline in deficit countries that would be imposed through a process of "multilateral surveillance."[61] The IMF report of its liquidity study was published at the same time and contained no major conflicts with the conclusions of the Group of Ten.

French and American differences surfaced once again at the IMF meeting held in Tokyo in September 1964 when the question of expanded quotas was raised. French Finance Minister Giscard d'Estaing rejected all schemes to create new reserves as thinly disguised efforts to finance American balance-of-payments deficits. He argued instead for a program of multilateral surveillance to impose discipline on U.S. monetary management.[62] Treasury Secretary Douglas Dillon warned of liquidity shortages once U.S. payments deficits were ended and stressed his support for incremental reform. Both the British and the Americans called for the creation of additional credit facilities within the IMF. The Germans shared the French view that there was no current liquidity shortage and that problems grew primarily from the lack of adequate monetary discipline in Britain and the United States, but Bonn was reluctant to challenge Washington in the French manner.[63]

In February 1965, the Anglo-American position prevailed and the IMF Executive Board voted to increase quotas by 20 percent. Implementation presented another problem. With one quarter of the quota increases to be paid in gold, Washington stood to lose sizable quantities of gold if other members decided to raise their gold contributions by exchanging accumulated dollars for American gold. To avoid these conversions, Washington invoked an obscure provision of the Bretton Woods agreement, the so-called "Pauper's Oath," which stipulated that if a nation's gold reserves and foreign exchange totaled less than its newly enlarged quotas to the Fund, the Fund may modify the requirement that one quarter of the quota increase be paid in gold. Under this provision, half of the Fund members qualified for reduced gold payments or no payments at all, thus protecting U.S. gold supplies. Such evasive maneuvering angered the French, who also opposed the plan to redistribute Fund quotas to reflect more accurately the economic strength of various states. The plan increased German quotas 52 percent, simultaneously giving Bonn greater voting power in the Fund than the French.

Several developments rekindled interest in monetary reform in 1965. First, the Ossola Commission, which had been appointed by the Group of Ten in 1964 to survey the wide variety of monetary reform proposals, completed its study and published a thorough summary of reform alternatives, which aided states in defining their own positions.[64] Second, the American balance of payments moved steadily toward surplus in 1965, increasing Washington's leverage in multilateral reform discussions. A strong dollar and payments surpluses would discredit those who argued that the U.S. was proposing changes merely to finance chronic deficits. Monetary reform also received support from new Secretary of the Treasury Henry Fowler, who became an advocate of more-ambitious reform. Fowler surprised the Europeans in July 1965 by calling for a global conference on monetary issues.[65]

The preliminary American position on this enlarged agenda of monetary reform was outlined in a book by former Under Secretary of the Treasury Robert Roosa in September 1965.[66] The Roosa Plan called for introduction of a new primary reserve asset or "Fund unit" to be administered through the IMF.[67] It would bear no connection with gold, but would be "as good as gold" and would be backed by currency contributions from the IMF membership. Roosa also advocated the creation of a secondary reserve asset for use in special circumstances.[68] Not unexpectedly, Roosa's recommendations stressed the U.S. interest in augmenting the existing gold-exchange standard rather than replacing it with an asset that would take over the reserve role of the dollar and gold.

President Johnson called for monetary reform at the IMF annual meeting in September. He stated that it was

> no longer appropriate or possible for one country alone—through its deficits—to be largely responsible for the creation of world reserves. . . . thus the United States has taken firm action to arrest its dollar drain . . . The long period of large U.S. deficits has come to an end. If growth is to continue and trade is to expand, we must provide an effective and adequate substitute.[69]

The meeting produced agreement to negotiate monetary reform, including giving consideration to the creation of a new reserve asset. In accordance with French wishes, it was agreed that the deputy finance ministers of the Group of Ten would study the problem and seek consensus by spring 1966. The debate at the IMF meeting indicated that agreement would not come easily. Both the Germans and the French stressed the need for domestic adjustment in deficit countries and the problems caused by an excessive dependence on international financing schemes and too much, rather than too little, liquidity.[70]

The U.S. case for insufficient reserve growth was bolstered in January 1966 when IMF data revealed no increases in international liquidity during the preceding year.[71] Yet progress in reform negotiations came slowly. Under their new Finance Minister Michel Debré, the French position hardened. In Debré's view, the only aspect of international finance meriting French consideration was the U.S. balance of payments; no reform measures would be considered.[72] In an effort to move negotiations forward, the West Germans offered a compromise proposal calling for the creation of a composite reserve unit. German efforts at mediation served to bring Washington and Bonn together, however, and to isolate the French.

After a series of unsuccessful meetings designed to accommodate the French, the Group of Ten met in The Hague in July and agreed to publish their report on monetary reform and to proceed to a second stage of deliberations that would include the remaining members of the IMF.[73] In accordance with Washington's wishes, the so-called Emminger Report acknowledged the need for a new international reserve asset to supplement gold and the dollar, but also indicated that many national differences remained about how that asset should be created and distributed.[74] The report also specified that new assets should be created by action of the full IMF membership and distributed to all its members. The amount distributed to each participant would be determined by member states' quotas, as the United States preferred, rather than a nation's gold reserves, as the French advocated.

De Gaulle refused to endorse The Hague agreement but maintained his presence in the negotiating process, fearing that a French departure would permit the adoption of wholly unacceptable procedures. In this respect, French participation in monetary negotiations lacked the leverage available in trade talks, where "empty chair" tactics brought EEC and Kennedy Round discussions to a halt.[75] By late 1966, the French government was actively seeking a workable compromise with the United States on reform.[76] At the end of January 1967, the French agreed to drop a demand for a change in the price of gold and participated in IMF talks held in London. This change in tactics coincided with the French decision to discontinue conversions of dollars for gold, a hint that the franc was weakening and that an independent French position was becoming less viable. De Gaulle's failure to win support for his policies in Europe also

increased unacceptably his isolation from EEC monetary policies. The
new strategy was designed to rebuild French influence within the EEC in
hopes of constructing a common European stance on monetary reform.

At the EEC Finance Ministers' meeting in January 1967 at The Hague,
Michel Debré dropped the French demand for a return to the gold
standard in an effort to gain support for two more moderate objectives
about monetary reform. First, he sought to increase the EEC's voting
power in the IMF such that the EEC could exercise a veto over Fund action, an option thus far enjoyed only by the United States. Second, although the July 1966 Group of Ten Report indicated a strong preference
for the creation of a new reserve asset, Debré argued that reform should
be limited to increased credit facilities within the Fund through the use of
new special drawing rights available to member countries on the condition of repayment. Debre's plan was not without implications for the
United States. His new focus on increased credit facilities came at a time
when the United States was approaching the limits of its automatic borrowing rights within the IMF, following their use to discourage gold conversions. By arguing for conditional drawing rights rather than asset
creation, Debré hoped to limit the American ability to continue this
strategy.

With the consensus emerging in Europe and growing balance-of-
payments problems that undermined arguments for new liquidity,
Washington was eager to reach agreement prior to the annual meeting in
September. In a March speech at a conference of American and European
banking and government officials at Pebble Beach, California, Treasury
Secretary Fowler hinted that without European cooperation in concluding reform discussions, Washington might consider unilateral action.

Tougher American rhetoric preceded by only a few weeks a conference
of European Finance Ministers in Munich during which the six hammered out a common position. In Stephen Cohen's words, the Munich
accord was essentially a Franco-German compromise:

> "In return for the French promise to support further contingency planning
> and the concept of unconditional drawing rights, the Germans agreed to
> shift their support from the creation of reserve units to a new drawing facil-
> ity within the Fund."[77]

In meetings of the deputies of the Group of Ten and the executive di-
rectors of the IMF through the spring and summer, the unresolved issues
between Washington and Brussels continued to be the EEC's voting
strength within the Fund and the repayment requirements associated
with the new drawing rights. On the latter issue, if repayment were required, as the French insisted, the new drawing rights would merely re-

semble other credit expansions that had been approved by the Fund. If repayment were not mandatory, as the United States preferred, the new drawing rights would take on the quality of a new reserve unit, supplementing the role of the dollar and gold.

Final agreement came after two meetings of the Group of Ten ministers in London in July and August. During the August meeting, the United States gave in to the EEC demand for a veto in the IMF, a concession won in large part because of the Europeans' determination to maintain a common position. The repayment question, which never enjoyed European unanimity, was finally settled on terms closer to American wishes. A nation would be obligated to repay the Fund only if its use of the new drawing rights exceeded an average of 70 percent of its allocations over a five year period. In effect, the United States succeeded in creating a new reserve asset, while the French managed to assure only limited control over its use. At the annual meeting of the IMF in Rio in September, the membership approved the reform proposal.[78]

CONCLUSION

While trade initiatives remained important in the early and middle 1960s, monetary adjustments became the central focus of American strategy to support economic interdependence and preserve domestic autonomy. Not only did the United States shape the agenda for regime adjustments as it had for trade, but it also exercised considerable influence over the outcomes of those negotiations, something it frequently failed to do on commercial issues.[79] Through bilateral and multilateral measures to finance ongoing deficits, prevent speculation against the dollar, and discourage conversions of foreign-held dollars for gold, Washington prevented monetary problems from standing in the way of expansion and renewed prosperity at home. By insisting on changes that would only slightly modify the rules of Bretton Woods, American officials assured the continuing integration of international financial markets.

The Americans may have gotten their way on most issues of monetary reform, but their insistence won few friends in Europe. Throughout the period, there was growing opposition to American monetary policies, not only in France where de Gaulle called for a fundamental restructuring of the monetary system, but also in West Germany and in other West European countries who shared the diagnosis of monetary ills, if not the prescription for remedy. Yet unity among European states remained elusive. Contrasting economic fortunes country-by-country defined and redefined national interests on reform issues that seldom permitted agreement. Sterling weakness during these years almost silenced British officials in reform negotiations who were generally content to follow the

Americans whose interests paralleled their own. French assertiveness was tied to the temporary strength of external balances, and Paris proved to be more flexible once weaknesses reappeared. Most important, economic well-being in all European states was increasingly tied to the workings of the dollar-based system and the financial interdependence it promoted. To sever these bonds too hastily through fundamental changes in the monetary rules could have had far more damaging consequences than the irritating American abuses. In effect, the dollar enjoyed the advantages of incumbency; the privileges that were provided by its central rule were bothersome but were preferred to the uncertainties of the alternatives. American success was also assured by a new toughness in Washington on monetary matters, not unlike the protectionist backlash that was growing in the final year of the Kennedy Round. As American economic fortunes declined in the late 1960s, U.S. negotiators were inclined to take unilateral action in defense of American economic interests rather than engage in the long and frustrating process of negotiation and compromise typical of the early and middle parts of the decade.

4

Monetary Crisis and the New Protectionism: 1968–1973

The conclusion of the Kennedy Round of trade negotiations in the spring of 1967 and the agreement among monetary officials to create Special Drawing Rights several months later ended the era of patchwork reform in Atlantic economic relations. The Kennedy Round facilitated the growth and expansion of international trade in the 1960s, but in so doing it accelerated shifts in the international division of labor and drew protectionist responses from those countries unable to adjust to commercial change and new competition. The ad hoc monetary procedures designed to cope with chronic deficits and currency speculation worked well as long as speculation remained moderate and deficits modest. Neither of these conditions obtained in the late 1960s, and monetary flows overwhelmed these temporary arrangements and required more fundamental change. In the words of Robert Keohane and Joseph Nye, the era of "complex interdependence" was at hand, and changed conditions required new strategies of management.[1]

The management of economic interdependence was complicated in all advanced industrialized states by the rising domestic expectations that accompanied prosperity in the 1960s. In almost all Western countries, the last years of the decade recorded economic expansion, steadily rising income levels, low levels of unemployment, and expanded social welfare services. The principal objectives of the postwar welfare state had been achieved, or at least the political battles were under way to assure their realization.[2]

In the United States, in particular, the late 1960s and early 1970s were consumed with domestic political battles aimed at ensuring that all shared in the new prosperity. The protection of civil rights, the elimination of economic inequities, and the pursuit of social justice were the issues around which politicians rallied. To the extent that leaders focused on international matters, Vietnam received most of the attention. Washington's response to growing trade and monetary problems was, not unreasonably, to ignore these problems through a strategy that came to be called "benign neglect" and, when that failed, to adopt tough and unabashedly self-interested tactics in seeking regime changes that would improve American external fortunes.

The new American approach also reflected a reordering of U.S. foreign policy priorities that gave less attention to Western Europe. American administrations through the mid-1960s gave management of the Western Alliance their utmost attention, but the accelerating involvement in Vietnam and the emerging strategic accommodation with the Soviet Union made European affairs of less pressing concern. Such neglect certainly did not increase European tolerance for continuing payments deficits and growing American protectionism.[3] But while resentment of American self-interest and economic actions reached a postwar high and British admission to the EEC and a commitment to monetary integration offered new hope for unity, the Europeans once again fell prey to national divisions that diluted their combined power.

This chapter will show that even though confidence in the dollar reached a postwar low and the U.S. trade account recorded its first deficit of the 20th century, negotiators in Washington continued to control the pace and shape the direction of Atlantic regime change between 1968 and 1973. They orchestrated fundamental changes in the rules of the monetary system and simultaneously sold "temporary" protectionist arrangements to reluctant trading partners. Autonomy was again preserved without disturbing the fundamental tenets of interdependence. Nevertheless, the costs of autonomy were high and the weaknesses in the domestic economy increasingly evident. Washington was less and less able to compete in the interdependent world of its own design. Political power continued to undermine economic strength.

THE DETERMINANTS OF FOREIGN ECONOMIC POLICY

The United States

American monetary and trade policy in the Nixon years took a very different course from that of the two preceding administrations, which reflected, among other things, important changes in the international economy that were the result of the successful promotion of economic interdependence. In the early part of the decade, monetary policy had aimed for short-term support for a sagging dollar and for protection of the American gold supply until lingering payments deficits could be eliminated by expanded trade surpluses. Those surpluses would follow from a regime of freer trade, the heart of Washington's trade policy. By the end of the decade it was clear that existing correctives were no longer adequate to manage short-term capital flows responding to interest rate realignments and expectations about exchange-rate changes. New strategies were required to cope with the internationalization of capital markets. Moreover, freer trade, which was supposed to result in larger trade surpluses, not only seemed to contribute to their decline, but offered opportunities to new competitors who were challenging U.S. producers abroad and at home. These shifts in the international division of labor gave new political clout to American protectionists, who clamored for relief.

The label attached to American monetary policy in the late 1960s was "benign neglect."[4] After almost a decade of efforts to correct the deficiencies of Bretton Woods and to make American payments deficits more palatable to economic partners, the new approach was to do less, and often to do nothing at all, to manage money flows or to defend the dollar. The shift to "benign neglect" was facilitated in late 1967 and early 1968 by the collapse of the London gold pool, the establishment of a two-tier system of gold pricing that fixed government-held supplies of gold at $35 an ounce while letting privately held supplies fluctuate with market demand and quiet understandings between Washington and Bonn that discouraged the exchange of German-held dollars for gold. The combined effect of these developments and understandings was to sever internally the link between the dollar and gold and to move the system to a *de facto* dollar standard. As the United States became, in effect, the world's banker, the value of the dollar was now determined by the sum of other nations' decisions about their currencies' worth vis-à-vis the dollar. Should others' confidence in the dollar change, it was up to them to adjust the value of their currencies accordingly. The United States had no obligation to engage in exchange-rate realignment; indeed, such meddling was likely to do more harm than good. The obligation that Washington did have was to manage its domestic economy prudently by assuring moderate levels of growth, price stability, and government spending levels that did not exceed fiscal revenues, objectives that were far from realized in the late 1960s and early 1970s.

In some respects, the strategy recalled Eisenhower's concentration on non-inflationary growth and balanced budgets and his belated recognition that a failure to hold to these objectives could result in growing economic troubles abroad. Yet, the domestic economic circumstances were vastly different in the 1960s, and there is serious question whether American leaders ever expected to be able to meet their obligations of prudent economic management or whether "benign neglect" was really a rationalization for doing what they pleased. Nevertheless, in its new approach Washington laid claim to a flexibility in domestic economic management that was denied to other Atlantic states.

If the internal purpose of "benign neglect" was to protect the freedom of action for domestic economic policy-makers, the external effect was to move Washington to support more exchange-rate flexibility rather than to rely on balance-of-payments financing measures popular in the 1960s. Between 1969 and 1972 the Nixon leadership encouraged revaluations of other major currencies, the adoption of wider trading bands, and finally the movement to flexible exchange rates.[5] "Benign neglect" could sustain domestic autonomy without interfering with free currency convertibility and the commitment to interdependence.

There was little evidence of "benign neglect" in 1968, but President Johnson's more-prudent domestic economic policies made it more believable in 1969. Following the deterioration of the American balance of payments in 1967 and the speculative attack against the dollar early in the following year, Johnson relied on the old tools to improve payments prospects and fight speculation. He also introduced mandatory controls on bank lending and corporate investment abroad.[6] External measures were complemented by a growing acceptance of the view at home that policies of domestic restraint were needed if serious inflation was to be avoided. While hardly popular in an election year, Johnson sought congressional approval of a 10 percent surcharge on corporate and personal income taxes, and Congress reluctantly passed the legislation in May. The tax hike, coupled with restraints imposed by the Federal Reserve, slowed the inflationary surge by late in the year and, unexpectedly, produced the first balance-of-payment surplus since 1957. The latter was more the product of luck than good management, since payments improvements were founded on capital flows responding to temporary controls and interest rate realignments that overshadowed a continuing deterioration in the trade account.

The Nixon administration made few changes in domestic policy in 1969. Tight money provided the basic ammunition for the battle against inflation and coincidentally aided the balance of payments. High interest rates at home drove American banks into the unregulated Euro-dollar market for funds to sustain their levels of domestic lending.[7] This borrowing abroad totaled almost $9 billion in 1969, contributing to a $2.7 billion surplus on the official reserve transactions calculation of the balance of payments, compared with a $7 billion deficit on the liquidity balance that does not include these flows.[8] With these temporary payments improvements and the attention of speculators directed at other currencies in 1969, "benign neglect" was an easy posture to assume.

The fear of turning the economic slowdown into a severe recession and continuing worry about an inflation level in excess of 5 percent resulted in some relaxation of fiscal and monetary restraints in 1970. By lowering the discount rate, the Federal Reserve did give new life to the domestic economy, but it also reordered the structure of international interest rates and redirected short-term capital flows out of the United States. Cheaper money at home made it too costly for American banks to continue to pay the premiums on earlier Euro-dollar loans, and their liquidation turned an $8.7 billion capital inflow in 1969 into a $6.2 billion outflow in 1970.

While "benign neglect" appeared to work well in the late 1960s when the domestic brakes were applied, it became a less-viable strategy in 1970 and 1971 when, facing economic slowdown and unemployment of 6 percent, the administration moved to revive economic activity at home. Capital outflows in 1970 were succeeded in the following year by a steady deterioration in the trade account. On the official reserve transactions basis, the balance-of-payments deficit approached $30 billion in 1971, and the trade account moved toward its first deficit in memory.

With the 1972 election in view, Nixon clung resolutely to the strategy of "benign neglect" through the first half of 1971, unwilling to sacrifice domestic recovery for the well-being of external accounts and confidence in the dollar. If the American balance of payments continued in deficit, surplus countries could either continue to accept deficit dollars or revalue their currencies. And when speculation hit the dollar full force in May, leading the West German Bundesbank to opt for a temporary float of the mark to slow the dollar inflows, Vice President Spiro Agnew underlined the priority of domestic policy: "We will not put the U.S. economy through the wringer to deal with a temporary situation."[9] Or, as Joanne Gowa argued:

> The Nixon Administration's officials . . . took the primacy of the domestic economy as given. They consigned to the realm of non-decisions the option of deflation as a partial remedy for the ills besetting the Bretton Woods regime. Autonomy in domestic economic policy-making was far more important than the survival of the postwar monetary regime in the calculus of the Nixon Administration.[10]

Yet the hemmorrhage of dollars continued, as did worrisome signs from the trade account, and by the end of May some leaders in Washington were suggesting that "benign neglect" was inadequate and that a more-assertive policy was required.[11] Renewed speculative attacks on the dollar in mid-August, coupled with the disappointing reports on the recovery of the domestic economy, convinced the President and his economic advisors of the need for a bold and aggressive new approach. The New Economic Policy (NEP), outlined at a weekend meeting at Camp David and announced on August 15, imposed a 90-day freeze on wages and prices to be followed by a program of wage-price restraint and a 10 percent investment tax credit.[12] These measures to fight inflation and assist domestic recovery simultaneously were coupled with measures to shift to others the burdens of deteriorating external accounts. Convertibility between the dollar and gold was formally severed (conversions had been slowed by informal understandings since 1967), and a 10 percent surcharge was imposed on American imports. By eliminating the option of converting foreign-held dollars for gold and making clear that the surcharge would be removed only following appropriate exchange-rate changes, the policy was designed to put maximum pressure on Western Europe and Japan to revalue their currencies. Those realignments, including a modest devaluation of the dollar, were successfully negotiated by the end of the year.

The experiments with temporary floats and the realignment of exchange rates in 1971 convinced some in the administration that monetary interests would be better served by flexible exchange rates, or at least greater exchange-rate flexibility. Flexible rates, it was argued, would permit continued domestic policy autonomy in a monetary system with the dollar as the primary reserve asset, and at the same time market forces, rather than difficult government negotiations, would determine the appropriate exchange rates.

The administration's determination to assure continuing economic recovery through the fall 1972 election resulted once again in deterioration in commercial accounts and renewed pressure against the dollar. The appointment of George Shultz as Secretary of the Treasury in May 1972, replacing John Connolly, brought to office a strong supporter of exchange-rate reform.[13] Nixon's decision to terminate the second phase of wage and price controls and institute a voluntary third phase set off renewed pressure against the dollar in early 1973. It took a 10 percent devaluation of the dollar in February to quiet markets temporarily and, when pressures resumed again in March, Washington led the move to flexible exchange rates.[14] By May, the utility of the floating rate regime was evident. In that month pressures against the dollar mounted once again, drawing demands from Europe and particularly the French, that the United States intervene in money markets in support of its currency. Washington slipped back into its posture of "benign neglect" and ignored French demands for intervention.

The liberal momentum in American trade policy was lost at the conclusion of the Kennedy Round, and the years that followed have frequently been called the era of the new protectionism.[15] No new liberal trade initiative was placed before Congress in the late 1960s, as there had been in 1958 and 1962, and instead most proposed legislation sought to impose quantitative restrictions on imports. In November 1967, bills before Congress were asking for quotas that would affect 40 percent of all American imports.

The growing number of requests for meeting the challenge of imports did not alter at a general level the American commitment to the principle of free trade, but it did heighten the government's sensitivity to the real difficulty faced by a discrete group of important industries. Textiles and steel were the most vocal and the most politically influential. In many cases, the charge was made that importers captured growing shares of the American market by receiving government subsidies, paying absurdly low wages, or engaging in predatory trading practices. The theme was that gains were won by violating the rules of free trade and that the American government should work to assure fair trade in the international marketplace. Fair trade replaced free trade as the slogan of American trade policy in the late 1960s and early 1970s.

Claims of unfair trading practices were taken more seriously in these years in part because of a steady and worrisome deterioration of the trade surplus. This deterioration had other causes as well. The rapidly expanding domestic economy increased steadily the demand for imports. Persistent inflation that continued into the early 1970s and an overvalued dollar diminished the competitiveness of exports. Consistent with other American foreign economic policy, the recourse to selective protectionism shifted the burden of declining trade surpluses to others in the short term, but it also delayed the adaptation necessary to renew American competitiveness.

The most-acceptable routes to protectionism were to negotiate voluntary export restraints (VERs) or orderly marketing arrangements (OMAs). The VER was an agreement between exporter and importer specifying how much product the exporter could sell annually in the importer's market. The expectation was that the quantity specified would be less than the exporter would have been able to sell without the restraint agreement but more than might be allowed if the importer had invoked formal quantitative restrictions. The OMA was a negotiated agreement among exporters about how the market was to be shared. Both the OMA and the VER avoided quotas or high tariffs and given their voluntary nature could be said to conform with the formal rules, if not the spirit, of free trade.

The VER, used first by Kennedy in the early 1960s to slow the inflow of Japanese textiles, was the route preferred by Nixon as protectionist forces gathered in Congress and threatened to pass more restrictive legislation. It is also worth noting that these and subsequent VER negotiations were not directed at European trading partners, but at Japan and newly industrializing countries, particularly those in east Asia. By the late 1960s, shifts in the international division of labor had spread well beyond the Atlantic region.

Nixon's efforts to secure a restraint agreement with Japan to fulfill a campaign promise to southern textile interests produced a complicated set of negotiations stretching over two years.[16] While one can legitimately question the value of such efforts to protect American firms and enhance U.S. trading fortunes, they became the preferred method for addressing the challenges of other textile-producing countries and subsequent competition in other industries such as footwear, color television sets, steel, and automobiles.[17] They were a politically acceptable way of maintaining the posture of free trade while meeting the growing pressure for relief at home.

The prospect of a trade deficit in 1971 led the Nixon administration to take more-direct action. A principal reason for the NEP in August was to achieve a turnaround in the trade account. While the 10 percent import surcharge was designed to bring some immediate relief, Treasury Secretary John Connolly pressed hard between August and December for exchange-rate changes and greater access to European and Japanese markets that would result in a $13 billion improvement in the U.S. trade account. The temporary imposition of the import surcharge and the realignment of currency parities in December 1971 did not bring the hoped-for improvement in the trade balance. Indeed, the deficit more than doubled to $6.3 billion in 1972. Congressional response to continuing deficits was to call for stronger protectionist action. The Foreign Trade Act of 1972, the so-called Burke-Hartke bill, would have imposed wide quotas on a large number of imports and would have limited U.S. foreign direct investment to protect American jobs. In opposing the bill as an open invitation to retaliation, the administration argued that exchange-rate changes were likely to be the most useful way to adjust commercial balances. Treasury Secretary Shultz's support for flexible exchange rates can be viewed as part of this strategy to provide needed adjustments in trade.

In 1973, Nixon attempted to seize the legislative initiative at home and return to multilateral negotiations abroad in order to advance American trading interests. The Trade Reform Act, submitted to Congress in April, was an interesting mix of liberalism and protectionism and is a striking contrast to the 1962 Trade Expansion Act. The legislation asked first for unlimited presidential authority to raise, lower, or eliminate tariffs. On the important subject of non-tariff barriers, the administration asked for wide-ranging powers to negotiate their elimination, but it did subject executive action to congressional veto. The bill also provided new and more-rapid safeguard procedures to assist industries and workers injured by imports and sought authority to impose restrictions on states engaging in unfair trading practices. Finally, the legislation called for sweeping presidential powers to impose short-term import taxes or quotas to bring external accounts back into equilibrium. These requests for sweeping new presidential powers came at a time when Congress was intent on finding ways to limit executive authority, not expand it, and the prospects for passage of the trade bill were limited from the start. The AFL–CIO denounced the bill and reaffirmed their support of the Burke-Hartke alternative. Delaying tactics in the House and Senate killed the chance of approval in 1973.

The urgency surrounding such legislation diminished significantly in the second half of 1973 when, bolstered by two dollar devaluations, large agricultural sales to the Soviet Union, and the new boom in European economies, the American trade account moved back into surplus. The revival of U.S. trading fortunes and Nixon's resignation improved the prospects for passing comprehensive trade legislation in the following year. The Trade Reform Act of 1974 became the enabling legislation necessary for launching the next multilateral trade negotiations in the GATT, the so-called Tokyo Round. Fair trade in American markets and free trade abroad would be the objectives of American negotiators.

Western Europe

At no time since World War II was the United States more vulnerable to an economic challenge from Western Europe than it was in the years 1968–1973. The steadily eroding trade balance and the speculative attacks on the dollar offered a united Western Europe the chance to participate in regime change as equal partners. The Europeans, however, failed to capitalize on American weaknesses because shifting fortunes in the domestic economies of leading states repeatedly prevented common action.

The most-striking change occurred in France where the frequently abrasive independence of de Gaulle was quieted by domestic claims in 1968 and a deterioration of French external accounts that put the franc under attack. Through the 1960s de Gaulle's design to restore French independence had been premised on two assumptions that were called into question in 1968. Politically and strategically, de Gaulle depended on a steady reduction in East-West tensions that would mask French dependence on the United States and allow France greater diplomatic flexibility in Europe and abroad. The Soviet invasion of Czechoslovakia in August 1968 made clear the limits of the Cold War thaw and the continuing importance of the Western alliance for French security. Foreign economic independence depended on the willingness of French citizens to support the austerity measures necessary to ensure trade surpluses and the strength of the franc. That support slipped away in 1968 and, in mid-May, French workers demanded a better distribution of the expanding national wealth. The price of restored order was a larger package of wages and benefits that set off moderate inflation and diminished international confidence in the franc.

By late spring, pressure against the franc required de Gaulle to make use of currency "swaps" and IMF drawing rights so useful to Britain and the United States earlier in the decade.[18] By mid-summer, France was caught in the "stop-go" dynamics reminiscent of the British experience. In July, inflation and continued pressure on the franc required an interest rate hike from 3.5 to 5 percent, tax increases totaling $500 million, and another $1.3 billion in international assistance. It was ironic that France was also required to sell gold worth $100 million to augment its depleted supply of dollars. But when pressure against the franc subsided in September, French groups were quick to demand an easing of internal constraints to reduce unemployment and permit economic expansion. Predictably, relaxed conditions set the stage for yet another attack on the franc.

France's losing battle against inflation contrasted with German successes and resulted in a confrontation between the franc and the mark in November.[19] At a late November meeting of the Group of Ten in Bonn to resolve the monetary crisis, the French argued for a revaluation of the mark while the Germans held firm for a franc devaluation.[20] And while the impression was left that the French would make the exchange-rate change, de Gaulle, seemingly unable to make this concession to the Germans, refused to devalue and instead chose the route of harsh domestic austerity.[21]

The new plan, which included a wage-price freeze, government budget cuts, strict currency controls, and tighter enforcement of French tax laws, was not received enthusiastically at home. Moreover, improvement in French external accounts was undermined by tight money policies in the United States, which encouraged American banks to borrow from their subsidiaries abroad, including those in France. French monetary authorities who had sought to unload the American currency only a short time earlier now found dollars in short supply. The slow recovery of external balances led de Gaulle to delay action on the domestic reform promised earlier, which in turn touched off a new round of strikes and domestic unrest in March. Unhappiness with the president's handling of the domestic crisis was registered in an April national referendum, the defeat of which was followed by his resignation.

Georges Pompidou brought to French economic policy changes of emphasis and style. Less consumed with independence and political rank, the new French president and his finance minister, Valery Giscard d'Estaing, were more attentive to the need to make foreign and domestic economic policy compatible. The problems they faced, however, were no less troublesome. Titling their new program the "disinflation of expansion," Giscard increased interest rates and limited government spending to slow the outflow of capital and limit price increases. When these modest restraints proved insufficient, Pompidou opted for an 11.1 percent devaluation of the franc in August and introduced an austerity program to prevent the erosion of the exchange-rate advantage by domestic infla-tion.[22] Internal measures included a wage and price freeze, new and tighter limits on government spending, restrictions on consumer credit, an acceleration tax collections, and greater incentives for individual sav-ing and for manufacturers to produce for export. In a gesture to the un-ions and low-income groups, minimum wage rates in industry were raised and increased payments were made to pensioners. To defend the franc, a $985 million loan from the IMF was arranged, and $1.6 billion in additional assistance was secured from various sources.[23] The success of this program, aided by a revaluation of the German mark in October, en-hanced French economic prospects in the early 1970s. Improvements in external balances permitted the relaxation of domestic restraints, re-sulting in productivity increases and annual GNP growth of 5 percent through 1973.

The French strategy to rebuild external accounts between 1969 and 1973 was to control imports by limiting the growth of domestic consumption and to keep the franc undervalued, thereby assisting French exports. Maintaining an undervalued franc became increasingly difficult in 1971 and thereafter when speculative pressure shifted to the American dollar and others, like the Germans, sought relief from dollar inflows through currency floats. Unwilling to let the franc float, not only because of ex-pected damage to export competitiveness but because of the relatively painless solution it offered to dollar problems, the government adopted a two-tiered pricing system for the franc (an official price and a private market price) to discourage dollar inflows.[24] Between 1969 and 1973, the franc appreciated only 17 percent vis-à-vis the dollar, while the German mark appreciated by 43 percent. This reluctance to give up the fixed-rate regime and the German's growing preference for flexible rates divided the two countries on issues of monetary reform in the early 1970s. Not un-til the French were required to absorb large dollar inflows during specula-tion against the dollar in February 1973 did Pompidou alter his commitment to fixed rates and agree to let the franc float. French confi-dence was also shaken by worrisome signs of inflation in the domestic economy, which required the reimposition of austerity measures late in the year.

By and large, Pompidou's efforts to balance internal and external con-straints were successful in the late 1960s and early 1970s. They reflected a more-modest view of the French role in the international economy and in international politics generally, one better suited to addressing the chal-lenges of Atlantic interdependence. Nevertheless, more sensitivity to French domestic interests often resulted in sharp differences with Euro-pean neighbors regarding trade and monetary management.

British economic policy in this period must be set against the backdrop of the 1967 sterling devaluation. Devaluation concluded two decades of efforts to sustain a leadership role for Britain in the world economy.[25] Economic policy in 1968 was designed to ensure the effectiveness of the devaluation. The bank rate was raised from 6.5 to 8 percent, defense spending was cut, taxes were increased $2.2 billion, and ceilings were imposed on wages and dividends.[26] Moreover, additional international assistance was required to protect dwindling reserves. European central bankers extended existing loans for another year in February and provided another $2 billion in July.[27] In June, the IMF made available another $1.4 billion in stand-by credits. In July central bankers extended another $2 billion in long-term loans. Additional foreign assistance and tougher austerity measures were required in 1969, and it was not until the end of the year that external accounts showed steady improvement. By early 1970 most analysts concluded that British external recovery was well under way. The stability of sterling and growing strength in the trade account permitted some optimism in 1970 and 1971. The British recorded a trade surplus of $12 million in 1970, the first since 1958, and that surplus grew to $738 million in 1971. The outflow of capital from the United States in these two years also aided the British balance of payments and contributed to growing confidence in the pound. Yet improvement abroad and some loosening of austerity measures at home did not prevent a defeat of Harold Wilson at the polls in June 1970 and a return to power of the Conservatives under Edward Heath.

Fearful of renewed inflation, the new Tory government delayed moves to expand the internal economy in 1970 and 1971. With unemployment standing at 3.9 percent in early 1972, the Heath government introduced a $3 billion tax cut to accelerate economic growth. Economic activity did pick up in the second half of 1972 and unemployment began to decline, but expansion was also accompanied by new signs of inflation and union demands for overdue wage increases. Two large settlements with miners and railway workers early in the year led the government to initiate a series of "tripartite" talks (labor, government, and management) to head off inflationary settlements in the fall. When those discussions failed in November, Heath imposed a compulsory 90-day wage-price freeze in an attempt to subdue inflationary pressures.

Predictably, the realignment of currency parities at the end of 1971 and increased domestic activity in 1972 prompted a deterioration in external accounts. Increased demand for imports moved the British trade account into deficit by year-end. Lower interest rates in the United Kingdom and a revaluation of the pound against the dollar slowed the inflows of short-term capital that had assisted the British balance of payments. In June 1972, speculation against sterling rapidly drew down reserves of foreign exchange so carefully rebuilt over four years. Determined not to repeat the sterling crisis of 1967, London discontinued its defense of the $2.60 Smithsonian rate on 23 June, permitting the pound to float down to a level of $2.40 in October.

The failure of the wage-price freeze to slow inflation, and the anticipated upward pressure on food prices accompanying EEC membership, brought further action in June 1973. Phase II of Heath's economic program limited annual pay increases to 7 percent, froze prices, rents, and dividends, and established a pay board and price commission with supervisory powers. The new measures brought strikes and work disruptions and failed to keep inflation below 10 percent. An equally unsuccessful Phase III combined with the expected consequences of the October oil price increases drove Heath to declare a state of national emergency on 13 November. Nevertheless, his plans to shore up the balance of payments, restore order to the domestic economy, and settle bitter labor disputes with the coal miners and the electric power workers were unsuccessful through the end of the year. Domestic economic activity was limited to a three-day work week, and the trade deficit for the year stood at a record $3.3 billion. Elections in late February returned Labor to power, but not until mid-March was the miners' strike settled and the four-month-old state of emergency lifted. Even so, the continuing impact of the oil crisis made 1974 Britain's most-difficult year, economically, of the entire postwar period.

Britain had come full circle by late 1973. The sterling devaluation of late 1967 had been coupled with a harsh domestic austerity program designed to right the trade balance and restore confidence in British currency. By 1970, these measures succeeded in slowing domestic production and restraining levels of consumption at home while pushing the trade account into the black and rebuilding the stock of monetary reserves. Renewed stability in external accounts once again permitted the government to address domestic repercussions of the recovery operation, which included stagnating industrial activity and record-high unemployment levels. The concessions to domestic needs in mid-1972 once again triggered a new round of trade and monetary problems that became worrisome in 1973. The impact of the oil crisis on external accounts and domestic inflation by late in the year compounded the economic crisis. The declaration of a national emergency and the move to a three-day work week marked a new low in postwar British economic fortunes.

The care with which Britain had to balance internal and external constraints permitted little flexibility in trade and monetary positions assumed in international negotiations. Flexibility was sufficient in the early 1970s to permit acceptable terms of entry into the EEC, but it seldom allowed London to play a leading role in negotiations on monetary reform.

In part, British silence reflected a continuing convergence of monetary interests with Washington. To the decision-makers in London, who were tired of repeated attacks on sterling, for example, the move to flexible rates made good sense.

In contrast to the other countries, whose leaders were all struggling with weak currencies and devising policies to reverse the deterioration in external accounts, West German officials had to cope with the consequences of currency strength and persistent trade surpluses. As the most-attractive convertible currency, the mark repeatedly drew in inflationary capital and came under pressures for revaluation that threatened to undermine the competitiveness of German exports. Such "rewards" for prudent economic management made the Germans more assertive of their economic interests, as the French discovered during the monetary crisis in the fall of 1968. Bonn was increasingly willing to translate economic strength into political power. Still, there were international constraints on German influence, particularly in their relations with the United States.

Growing influence in the late 1960s and early 1970s was founded on the strong performance of the German economy at home as well as abroad. The mild recession in 1966–1967 brought about a rapid decline in imports and moderate growth in exports, yielding a trade surplus of $3 billion in 1966 and $5 billion in 1967. In late 1967 domestic leaders sought to rekindle domestic expansion without sacrificing improvement in trade. Economics Minister Karl Schiller promoted easier credit policies, devised industrial investment incentives and, most important, convinced labor and management to forego price increases and inflationary wage settlements. Economic growth accelerated rapidly in 1968, unemployment dropped sharply, inflation was contained, and German exporters still managed a $5 billion surplus.

Economic successes in 1968 made Bonn the target of other Western states looking for economic assistance. Both Britain and the United States argued for larger military "offset" payments and, while Bonn resisted more vigorously than in the past, an accommodation was eventually reached. The firmest German resistance to pressure for aid came during monetary negotiations with Paris after the French domestic crisis in May. As noted above, Bonn repeatedly stood firm against French pressures for a mark revaluation through renewed currency speculation in the fall. Such German determination did not bode well for Franco-German relations already under some strain.

The German refusal to revalue was also based on domestic political calculations. With general elections less than a year away, the Christian Democrats (CDU) were mindful of the political impact of a stronger mark. The Ruhr industrial area, long a CDU stronghold in the north, was a region highly dependent on exports. German farmers, the southern strength of the CDU, stood to suffer even more through lower agricultural prices.[28] Revaluation remained an issue in 1969. Continued pressure against the franc resulted in speculative flows into the Federal Republic, which, coupled with an already expanding German economy, posed a growing inflationary threat. In May, the CDU-SPD coalition split over the appropriate response. Economics Minister Schiller, backed by Bundesbank President Karl Blessing, argued for a 7 percent unilateral revaluation. Chancellor Kurt Kiesinger and Finance Minister Franz-Joseph Strauss, more mindful of political consequences, would consider revaluation only if it were achieved within a larger scheme of currency realignments. When the May currency crisis drew in another $5 billion and Kiesinger again refused to devalue, Schiller resigned his chairmanship of the government's economic cabinet.[29]

The revaluation issue was not put to rest by the franc devaluation in August, although Kiesinger claimed that it was a vindication of his policy to defend the mark. Anticipating a postelection revaluation, speculators put heavy upward pressure on the mark in the days before the October voting, forcing a closing of German currency markets. The two major candidates, Willy Brandt and Kurt Kiesinger, then agreed to let the mark float before setting a new exchange rate after the election. The mark floated for four weeks before it was re-pegged at a healthy 9.3 percent above its old parity. Under the crush of speculation, Bonn was persuaded early of the need for greater exchange-rate flexibility and later became an ally of Washington's evolution to flexible rates.[30]

Some argued that the revaluation was too large since it was followed by a large outflow of speculative capital, which actually produced a shortage of foreign exchange.[31] High interest rates in the United States also contributed to the outflow that reached $2.7 billion by early November. By late in the year, Germany was required to withdraw $1 billion from the IMF and sell $500 million in gold to shore up its liquidity position. The bank rate was raised from 6 to 7.5 percent in March 1970 to protect against further withdrawals. The restructuring of American interest rates in mid-1970 eliminated the problem, and by the end of the year the Bundesbank was once again concerned about inflationary dollar inflows.

Indeed, the major challenge to the health of the German economy in 1970 and 1971 came from the outside. By June 1970, the Bundesbank had become the primary depository for foreign funds seeking to avoid the dollar's deteriorating position, requiring considerable bank action to hold down the mark. To compensate for this imported inflation, Economics Minister Karl Schiller announced fiscal measures in July to reduce German consumer spending.[32] By late in the year German officials were in a dilemma about where to set interest rates. Higher rates were an effective way to contain domestic expansion but, with rates declining in the United States, Bonn could not allow German rates to climb much above American levels without attracting inflationary capital flows from abroad. Determined to keep rates high enough to slow the domestic economy and unwilling to resort to foreign exchange controls that revived memories of the 1930s, Economics Minister Schiller pushed European action on a joint currency float that had been discussed in the EEC since 1969.[33] The proposed float would loosely link European currencies together to float against the dollar. Drawing on the experience of the mark's transitional float in late 1969, Schiller argued that joint European action would slow the inflow of unwanted dollars. The principal opponents of the float were the French, who had only recently given up a campaign to return to the gold standard and were more comfortable with the use of exchange controls.

Unable to win French support for a common European response to the dollar crisis of May 1971, the Germans decided on a unilateral float to regain some control over their domestic money supply.[34] The mark was joined in its float by several other European currencies following the announcement of Nixon's New Economic Policy in August, but the French decision to establish a two-tiered pricing system for the franc made impossible a common European response to the more-aggressive tactics of the Nixon administration.

Economic managers in Bonn faced the same challenge of dollar inflows in 1972 once the Smithsonian agreement restored fixed exchange rates. The German bank rate was again determined largely by external circumstances and was kept low so as not to attract foreign funds. Early in the year domestic debate was revived on the use of foreign exchange controls to limit the inflow of dollars. Schiller remained opposed to their use, but Bundesbank President Karl Blessing argued that they were necessary to assure some control over the domestic economy in an era of currency convertibility. When Blessing's logic prevailed in the German economic cabinet in late June and modest exchange controls were imposed, Schiller resigned as economics minister.

Speculation against the dollar brought additional capital into the German economy in 1973. In February, the Brandt government announced a program of internal measures—tax increases, budgetary cuts, and savings incentives—to address inflationary pressures. When the 10 percent devaluation of the dollar in the same month failed to curb the inflows, the Germans, with the Americans, were ready to make the transition to flexible rates.

As the country with the strongest Western currency in these years of monetary crisis, West Germany showed clearly that surplus countries were as vulnerable to the vagaries of the world economy as were small and medium-sized deficit countries. Domestic economic management was regularly circumscribed by the changing costs of international capital and by the success or failure of weak currency countries in addressing monetary ills. Regular exchange-rate changes had important consequences for the competitiveness of German exports, so crucial to overall economic performance. National autonomy conceded much to the dynamics of economic interdependence. Yet, the West Germans had grown accustomed to making domestic policies conform with international constraints and, not surprisingly, they prospered both at home and abroad in these years. Moreover, their economic success was frequently translated into greater political influence in European and Atlantic affairs. West Germany had grown up with international constraints and had learned to adapt domestic policy to external limits.

THE POLITICS OF FUNDAMENTAL CHANGE, 1968–1973

The central focus of Atlantic economic relations between 1968 and 1973 shifted from trade to money, and changing American interests were an important factor explaining that shift. After experimenting with temporary correctives in the early 1960s, the experience of the late 1960s and early 1970s convinced Washington that major changes were needed in the Bretton Woods regime. The internationalization of capital markets, the growth of a community of currency speculators, and the problems of managing persistent inflation put serious pressures on the dollar and the fixed exchange system, exposing the inadequacies of the regime's adjustment process. Moreover, as discussed above, American support for large multilateral trade liberalization initiatives vanished after the Kennedy Round, amid calls for ad hoc protectionism. Shifting national comparative advantages brought new interest in measures for adjustment that would have to accompany any progress toward liberalization.

The greater importance attached to monetary developments led Washington to argue that continuing American economic problems abroad were due mostly to European strategies to undervalue their currencies, which were facilitated by the fixed rate system and the dollar's reserve status. Undervalued currencies explained the deterioration in the American trade account and speculative pressures against the dollar. Greater exchange-rate flexibility became increasingly attractive as the Europeans failed to make the appropriate revaluations. Further, it was argued that American problems were aggravated to a lesser extent by unfair trading practices that justified temporary protectionist relief, although these practices were to be found primarily among non-European trading partners. Consistent with the behavior of American leaders since the 1950s, the roots of economic difficulties and declining competitiveness were seldom sought at home. Such was the "advantage" of being the leading economic power with the ability to shape and reshape international rules in ways that would shift the burdens of adjustment to others.

The sections that follow examine three sets of relations: intra-European economic relations, Atlantic trade relations, and Atlantic monetary relations. The first section looks at both European trade and monetary relations. As was the case in Atlantic economic relations generally, Europe shifted its concerns from trade to money in these years and, in particular, to the forging of a monetary union, made attractive in part by continuing disenchantment with the dollar. Nevertheless, intra-European differences remained as intractable in monetary affairs as they had been in trade, and such disagreements were again exploited by American leadership. The second section looks at Atlantic commercial relations and the appeal of protectionism, which reached its peak with Nixon's import surcharge in August 1971 before declining somewhat and permitting a limited commitment to multilateral negotiations in the 1973 Tokyo declaration. The third section traces Atlantic responses to recurrent monetary crises in these years and the evolution to flexible exchange rates. Only a shaky commitment to free convertibility remained of the principles established at Bretton Woods.

West European Economic Relations

The late 1960s and early 1970s provided mixed signals for those following progress toward unity in Europe, particularly for the purpose of playing a more equal role with the United States in trade and money matters. On the brighter side, it was in these years that French opposition to British EEC membership was overcome and the commercial division that began in 1958 was ended. Moreover, the original six EEC members completed the second transitional phase in their march toward unity by achieving a common market and making the financial commitments required to launch the Common Agricultural Policy. To show their determination to sustain momentum into the third phase, the six also gave their support during a 1969 meeting at The Hague to the development of plans for a European monetary union. This union took on increasing attractiveness in the early 1970s when the dollar was under attack and EEC members viewed a common currency as an alternative to the dollar. The design of plans to achieve monetary union by 1980 and efforts to narrow currency fluctuations through a joint float (the so-called "snake") were further evidence of interest in seeking European solutions to monetary problems, rather than following the American lead.

Yet, economic relations in Western Europe were still shaped principally by the shifting fortunes and interests of individual states. And progress toward unity at the general level often masked continuing national differences on particular issues of money and trade as well as ongoing uneasiness about who would lead a fully integrated community. Franco-German differences on monetary reform, growing from different historical circumstances and diverging economic fortunes in the late 1960s, raised questions about the viability of designs for monetary union. Anglo-French splits on commercial issues and the role of agricultural policy suggested that disagreements formerly aired outside the Community would now be part of regular EEC business. Growing German confidence and assertiveness in EEC affairs led the French to question their own commitment to unity if it entailed a Europe under German leadership.

The politics surrounding British entry demonstrated the continuing vitality of divisive national calculations on an issue ostensibly supportive of supra-national loyalties.[35] The successful pound devaluation and the recovery strategy challenged the French contention that British membership would be a financial burden. With both the United Kingdom and France struggling with austerity measures and seeking to restore order to external accounts in the late 1960s, their monetary interests increasingly converged. The convergence was first evident in November 1968 when the British backed the French in pressing for a revaluation of the mark in the Group of Ten meetings in Bonn. London knew that a simple franc devaluation might shift speculative pressure back to the pound although, for political reasons, discussions of British membership had to await de Gaulle's resignation. When Pompidou assumed the presidency in the spring of 1969, the British, with the active support of the West Germans, renewed their application. Pompidou was amenable to talk on British entry but indicated to Bonn that his approval would be contingent upon finding an acceptable permanent formula for financing the CAP.

The deterioration in Franco-German relations, which reached a low point during the November 1968 monetary crisis, was, in part, responsible for changing French attitudes toward British membership. Bonn's successful resistance of the French pressure for revaluation represented a kind of political coming of age for West Germany, a development Paris viewed with some alarm. While the Germans continued to couch national interests in terms of Community objectives and European unity, France was undoubtedly uneasy with a Community that granted growing influence to Bonn. Britain, always more comfortable with a less closely knit and confederal view of Europe, became more attractive to Paris in these times of declining confidence. London would not only insist on the preservation of national sovereignty, as the French were determined to do, but could also serve as an effective counterweight to the Germans.

The December 1969 Hague Conference was remarkable for the range of political commitments it extracted from European leaders. Bonn gave assurances to Paris on financing the CAP, which in turn cleared the way for negotiations on British membership in 1970. The six showed renewed support for the European movement by undertaking the task of monetary union.[36] In many respects, the "spirit of the Hague" reflected a political desire on the part of the new leaders in France and West Germany to rebuild relations between the two countries. Pompidou recognized that French independence and isolation from Community affairs only increased German influence among the other members. Brandt understood the importance of strong Franco-German relations in bridge-building efforts with Eastern Europe and the Soviet Union. Skeptics at the Hague meeting argued that economic implications and difficulties were overlooked or ignored in the quest for political harmony.[37] The most-important difficulty was the significant surrender of national sovereignty that would be required to create a common currency and achieve a monetary union. And as the 1970s would show, there was much truth in this assessment.

Nevertheless, the Hague meeting did set in motion negotiations that would culminate in British membership. Those talks began in 1970 and centered on the length of the adjustment period before Britain would be fully bound by all EEC policies, the size of London's contribution to the EEC budget, the role of sterling, and treatment of Commonwealth countries. Agreement was reached in June 1971, followed by House of Commons approval in October.

The dollar crises of the early 1970s and Washington's unilateral actions in 1971 increased the attractiveness of the commitments made at The Hague. The nine members of the soon-to-be expanded Community met in Paris in October 1972 to act on these objectives. Common industrial, monetary, social, and foreign policies were discussed, and all members accepted the three-step Werner Plan for monetary union by 1980.[38] The Nine also agreed to work toward political unity, although they left the pathway deliberately ambiguous at French and British insistence.

Nineteen seventy-three proved a most-difficult year to sustain the momentum of the Paris summit. Britain managed the transition to EEC membership in January, but growing domestic economic difficulties made the costs of participation less acceptable by mid-year. By the end of the year, the deepening economic crisis led the Labour Party and the Trade Union Congress (TUC) to call for a national referendum to reconsider Britain's membership. Changing national circumstances rapidly reduced the flexibility of British policy-makers and diminished the prospects for common action in Europe. Such national constraints and divisive actions were not uncommon in the unsettled decade of the 1970s. The separate national responses to the challenges of the 1973–1974 oil crisis were probably the most notable examples.

Progress toward monetary union was also difficult to sustain during the speculative crises of the early 1970s, particularly when West Germany and France adopted divergent strategies to cope with them. The German preference for currency floats to regain some control over the domestic money supply made more difficult the commitment to stabilize European exchange rates on the way to a common currency. Bonn's proposal for linking currencies together in a common float against the dollar accommodated the stabilization requirement in most respects, but worried others that the mark would pull their weaker currencies to levels that would undermine the competitiveness of their exports. Moreover, the common float required member states to expend precious national reserves to maintain their currency parities within the prescribed European range, a cost that frequently became unacceptable when a national currency experienced heavy exchange-rate pressure. The early refusal of the French to float at all and their adoption of a two-tiered pricing scheme for the franc further deepened divisions surrounding the appropriate strategy for moving toward monetary union. In short, exchange-rate stability and predictability were necessary prerequisites for the first steps toward monetary union, and the events of the early 1970s provided considerable instability and the promise of unpredictability as the flexible exchange-rate regime gained support.

The continued weakness of the pound and the Italian lira through the remainder of 1972 and 1973, as well as growing speculative pressure against the French franc in late 1973, repeatedly tested the resources that European cooperation offered. When the EEC Finance Ministers met in December 1973 to secure support for moving into the second stage of their planned monetary union, it was reluctantly agreed that the tough decisions, such as the pooling of monetary reserves, would have to be temporarily put aside. The new era of flexible exchange rates and exorbitant oil costs after 1973 made national economic managers faced with double-digit inflation, currency speculation, and unfavorable trade balances even less willing to relinquish national instruments of economic control. A united Europe that could negotiate with Washington as an equal partner became a steadily more-distant objective.

Atlantic Trade Relations

The absence of any American trade legislation providing the framework for multilateral negotiations between 1968 and 1973 changed the character of Atlantic trade relations from the preceding decade. Negotiations were more often undertaken bilaterally rather than involving all Atlantic states, and they were as often designed to limit trade as to expand it. The changes can be explained first by the successes of the EEC to eliminate internal tariff barriers and by the achievements of the Kennedy Round to reduce tariffs among all GATT members by 35 to 40 percent. The already low levels of industrial tariffs hardly warranted another multilateral effort to reduce them further. There was a growing recognition that the most-troublesome barriers to trade were of the non-tariff sort, but adequate procedures had not yet been designed to define such barriers satisfactorily or to negotiate their elimination. Moreover, discussions of non-tariff issues often questioned the legitimacy of domestic economic and social policy instruments employed by governments to foster industrialization and to strengthen economic competitiveness. Such policies assumed greater political importance to elected governments as they struggled to adjust to rapid shifts in international comparative advantage.

The second reason for the changing character of Atlantic trade relations, which is closely related to the first and was discussed more fully in the section on American policy above, was that many domestic groups in all Western states, and particularly in the United States, no longer viewed trade liberalization as an unqualified good, as most had up until this time. The oldest and most politically influential industries, the so-called "smokestack industries" such as textiles, steel, and even automobiles, looked for protectionist relief as the challenge of imports grew. Labor unions, a bulwark of American trade liberalism after the 1940s, argued that multinationals and foreign producers were eliminating domestic jobs.[39] The politics of trade policy in the late 1960s reflected the breakup of the postwar liberal coalition and made it difficult for Western leaders to mount any new liberal initiatives.[40] The negotiations for VERs and OMAs that became attractive options for American (and European) political leaders were often undertaken by a leadership seeking to avoid more blatantly protectionist legislative action at home. These temporary schemes were designed both to sustain a larger commitment to free trade and to accommodate powerful interests. While declining commercial fortunes in the United States reinforced the protectionist arguments to make the United States the most-influential spokesman for this new strategy, the schemes of organized free trade gained favor in some European countries as well.[41] And, as noted above, American efforts were more frequently directed at non-European states such as Japan and other rapidly growing countries in East Asia. As the benefits of liberal trade extended beyond the Atlantic region, both the United States and Western Europe found it necessary to make commercial adjustments.

Washington did make one major effort to apply pressure on its European allies to assist in the reversal of American trading fortunes in these years. Convinced that much of the deterioration of the trade account could be explained by an overvalued dollar, the Nixon administration sought to link monetary and trade policy in the service of the latter. "Benign neglect," which was aimed at forcing revaluations of European currencies, sought indirectly to provide assistance to the trade account. When that strategy failed to secure the desired exchange-rate changes, Nixon took direct action in August 1971, imposing the 10 percent import surcharge and insisting that its removal would require exchange-rate changes and trade concessions sufficient to yield a $13 billion improvement in the U.S. trade balance. Among the commercial changes demanded were immediate improved access to European markets for a number of agricultural products—wheat, tobacco, citrus fruits—and a long-term restructruing of the CAP.[42]

Acceptable parity changes were negotiated prior to the Smithsonian Agreement in December 1971, when the surcharge was lifted, but discussions surrounding additional trade concessions extended well into 1972. When the discussions were completed, the United States had secured additional unilateral trade assistance from Europe and Japan in the form of increased access to foreign markets for American goods and some "voluntary" reductions of exports to the United States. The agreement, announced in February 1972, also outlined an accelerated timetable for negotiations under the GATT to assess the damage done to non-members by the expansion of the EEC from six to nine states and a commitment to seek a new round of multilateral negotiations some time in 1973. Having achieved what it believed to be the necessary conditions for the restoration of a healthy trade surplus, and indeed the United States did record such a surplus in 1973, the Nixon administration moved away from the tough-minded unilateral action undertaken in 1971.

Western Europe's willingness to be bullied by American officials in the early 1970s can be explained in part by the uncertainty about what Washington was prepared to do to protect its commercial interests. Trade surpluses had long been taken for granted in Washington as an indicator of American global strength; no one was quite sure what response their disappearance might evoke.[43] Talk of a trade war was taken more seriously under such circumstances, since the dismantling of commercial interdependence threatened to do much more damage to Europe and Japan than to the United States. Some modest concessions to Washington in these years were a small price to assure the preservation of the postwar trading system.

Following the 1972 agreement, the European reaction to a more-moderate American tone and new interest in multilateral negotiations was one of caution. Determined to meet Washington's new initiatives from a position of strength, the EEC hammered out a common stance near the end of 1972. They insisted that the talks be based on the principle of reciprocity, that the structure of the CAP was non-negotiable, and that defects in the monetary system could not be remedied by commercial changes alone. Trade liberalization must be accompanied by simultaneous progress toward reform of the international monetary system. When these demands were introduced into the discussions convened in Tokyo, all anticipated resistance from Washington and protracted negotiations.

In sum, the expanded use of non-tariff barriers to trade and the growing importance of national adaptation and adjustments to a rapidly changing international division of labor was redefining the character of trade issues in the late 1960s and early 1970s and negotiations in the years that followed were bound to be different. Unfortunately, Washington again resorted to the exercise of power and extracted concessions from others, both through bilateral VERs and multilateral negotiations, in the early 1970s to rebuild short-term trade balances. Such influence discouraged the kinds of adaptation that would be required to compete in the late 1970s and 1980s.

Atlantic Monetary Relations

By the late 1960s, there was abundant evidence of the success of the Bretton Woods system in promoting monetary interdependence. Currency convertibility made it easy to move capital from one market to another, permitting investors to cross national borders to seek the highest returns for their money and allowing borrowers to scour international financial markets for the cheapest source of funds. The rapid growth of the Euro-dollar market from almost $3 billion in 1962 to over $100 billion in 1973 provided a large and unregulated pool of funds to augment what national economies were unable to provide.[44] This array of capital options encouraged economic actors, such as multinational firms, to think boldly about investment opportunities and, with time, their strategies came to depend in large measure on these international financial arrangements. The rapid economic expansion of the 1960s owed much to the opportunities provided by the Bretton Woods system and the monetary interdependence it fostered.

At the same time, some costs were associated with currency convertibility and the easy movement of capital. Most important, those flows diminished the effectiveness of national policy instruments in managing economic growth, limiting inflation, and maintaining order in external accounts. The responsiveness of international capital movements to changes in national interest rates led to consequences contrary to the intentions of domestic monetary policy. The easing of rates to make funds available for domestic expansion often resulted in capital outflows when returns were more favorable abroad. The tightening of monetary instruments to moderate expansion and upward pressures on prices frequently attracted foreign funds and encouraged borrowing in foreign markets, sustaining the pressures of inflation. Moreover, the ease with which capital could be moved made currency markets extremely sensitive to national exchange rates, leading money managers to move out of those currencies where confidence in national economic performance began to slide. In a system of fixed rates with cumbersome and politically sensitive procedures for rate adjustments, speculative conversions could rapidly deteriorate into a serious monetary crisis.

The ease of capital movement also complicated the accommodation of continuing American balance-of-payments deficits. The punishing effect of such movements on deficit countries, as the British and the French learned all too well, and to a lesser extent on surplus countries, made American deficits problematic in the early 1970s when Washington engaged in a strategy of "benign neglect." In the face of such deficits and American unwillingness to do anything about them, surplus countries like West Germany resorted to currency floats as the best of a number of unattractive alternatives.

The consequences of mixing free convertibility, fixed rates, and American deficits had been manageable in the early 1960s when deficits were small, currency movements were modest, and Washington was able to sell interim measures to limit the pressure on exchange rates. Neither of the first two conditions obtained by the early 1970s, and it was clear that more-fundamental regime changes were required. These changes, the severing of convertibility between the dollar and gold in 1971 and the move to flexible exchange rates in 1973, achieved a somewhat uneasy accommodation between the consequences of financial interdependence and the international monetary regime, an accommodation that also preserved the American ability to set domestic policy autonomously. While some have talked of the death of Bretton Woods it is worth noting that the most-important features of that regime—its discouragement of foreign exchange controls and implied support for currency convertibility—were retained by the system that succeeded it.[45] These are the features, rather than fixed exchange rates or the convertibility of the dollar with gold, that are crucial to the continued vitality of monetary interdependence.

The British battle to defend the pound in the 1960s was really the beginning of this era of monetary crisis, although the patchwork procedures to manage rapid capital flows were up to the task prior to 1967. Sterling devaluation in 1967 and London's subsequent management of British financial recovery altered Atlantic monetary relations in two ways. First, the experience served to counter a prevailing assumption that the pound, which had long served as a reserve asset, must not have its value changed. The successful devaluation expanded the range of acceptable policy options open to government officials, including those in the United States, in coping with currency troubles, but it also signaled to those in the private sector that any currency was subject to parity change and, therefore, a possible source of speculative profit. Second, the British move set off delayed movement against currencies that had been protected from speculation as long as the pound was under attack.[46]

Speculators first focused on gold and the dollar in early 1968. The volume of London gold pool operations grew alarmingly in early March, prompting the closing of the London market on 15 March and the convening of a meeting in Washington to negotiate new arrangements to manage trading in gold.[47] France, having withdrawn from the gold pool in November 1967, was not invited to the Washington conference, which undoubtedly irritated de Gaulle. As a consequence, American negotiators met only moderate resistance in restructuring regime rules regarding the treatment of gold. They had two general objectives: to maintain the official price of gold at $35 per ounce without constantly fighting speculators to keep it there, and to discourage others from making conversions for American gold, as had been French policy until only shortly before that time.

To address the first objective the Washington conference agreed to create a two-tiered pricing structure for gold. The official price would be maintained at $35 per ounce, and government holdings of gold would be used only as reserves to settle imbalances in external accounts. The participating governments also agreed to minimize the leakage between official holdings and private markets. The price of gold in private markets would be permitted to fluctuate with changes in supply and demand, which would thus limit speculation to trading in private markets. To minimize conversions of foreign-held dollars for gold, the United States secured informal understandings with foreign central bankers that they would discourage exchanges. Such assurances were tied to upcoming negotiations to implement the 1967 SDR agreement; the creation and allocation of SDRs would supplement members' reserve holdings and diminish their need for gold. This second American objective was aimed to reduce the role played by gold in the monetary regime, a goal that the French, who had been calling for a return to the gold standard, continued to oppose.

One issue that was not settled by the Washington conference and that lingered until late 1969 was where gold producers, such as South Africa, would be permitted to sell gold.[48] In keeping with their objective of diminishing gold as a reserve asset, American authorities argued that all sales should be made to private markets, in effect freezing official sources at their current levels. The Europeans, with a larger historical association with gold and a recognition that holding less gold would likely mean holding more dollars, favored a scheme that would permit South Africa to sell to official sources under specified circumstances. The South Africans opposed the prohibition on official sales, arguing that selling large quantities of gold on private markets would depress the price and reduce their revenues. Subsequently, they employed several strategies to disrupt the two-tiered scheme, such as refusing to sell gold in private markets in an effort to drive up the price and convincing some official holders to purchase specified amounts. In September 1968, the Europeans attempted to mediate between the Americans and the South Africans with the so-called Emminger Plan, which reflected European interest in maintaining some limited official access to newly produced gold. The proposal, with German and British backing, specified that South Africa would be permitted to offer gold to both the IMF and other official sources if the South African balance of payments was in deficit and the private market price was near $35 an ounce. While the Americans showed some interest in the European plan prior to the IMF annual meeting, the South Africans rejected it as too restrictive.

Under Secretary of the Treasury Paul Volcker took on the South African gold problem for the new administration. Considerable differences remained in the early months of 1969, but a falling price of gold on private markets in the summer and fall and a steadily deteriorating balance of payments in South Africa pushed the Pretoria government toward a settlement near the end of the year. At the same time, the American position was strengthened by a small balance-of-payments surplus in 1968 and a temporary dollar shortage in 1969, which reduced demand for gold. By late November, the free market price threatened to drop below $35. In mid-December Volcker met with South African officials in Rome and secured a temporary agreement, the conditions of which were not markedly different from the Emminger Plan of a year earlier.[49]

With all but the question of new gold settled following the Washington conference, the London gold market reopened and drew little attention from private traders. The private price of gold rose slightly above the official price in 1968 but settled back near the $35 price for all of 1969.

Two weeks after the Washington meeting on gold, the Group of Ten ministers and governors met in Stockholm to act on the 1967 Rio agreement to create Special Drawing Rights. The gold agreement was negotiated on the assumption that SDRs would soon be available to fill any unanticipated liquidity shortages. Unhappy with their exclusion from the Washington meeting and the agreement it produced, the French came to Stockholm opposed to any new reserve creation, arguing that attention should be directed to British and American payments deficits.[50] Attempts by the other Europeans to find some common ground with France proved unsuccessful.[51] The Stockholm negotiators eventually did produce a set of procedures for creating SDRs to be discussed at the fall IMF annual meeting, but they came without French approval. But with the rapid loss of reserves that accompanied domestic crisis in Paris in May, the French position softened.

When the IMF took up the question of SDR creation in October, prospects for agreement were enhanced by fears of a liquidity shortage following the official gold losses during the last months of the London gold pool and an anticipated American balance of payments surplus. Paul Volcker, the U.S. spokesman, argued for prompt action on SDRs to meet the liquidity shortfall. The Volcker Plan was a "front loading" approach, calling for a large first-year allocation of SDRs, with lesser amounts to be distributed over four subsequent years. Heavy Euro-dollar borrowing by American banks in early 1969 created a temporary dollar shortage in European central banks, increasing the attractiveness of the Volcker Plan. It is ironic that the Germans, not the French, were now cautious about the size of SDR allocations. The recipients of large capital inflows during the months of speculation against the franc, Bonn's reserves were more than adequate. Washington pushed for a $5 billion initial distribution, while Bonn argued for a figure closer to $2 billion. The Germans offered a compromise in the Group of Ten meeting in July that was accepted: $9.5 billion would be allocated beginning 1 January 1970, with $3.5 billion created in the first year and $3 billion in each of the two following years. The agreement also specified a 35 percent expansion of IMF quotas over the same three-year period.[52]

Other than gold and SDR negotiations aimed at liquidity concerns, Washington generally assumed the posture of "benign neglect" on monetary issues between 1968 and 1970. Exchange-rate adjustment problems, the new disease afflicting the Bretton Woods regime in these years, was regarded as Europe's concern, and with speculation focused on the mark and the franc, this view was easily sustained. And indeed the Franco-German confrontation on the exchange-rate issue left some lasting scars that did not bode well for future European monetary cooperation. The French experience with devaluation and tough austerity measures reaffirmed their support for fixed parities and monetary discipline for others as they encountered similar problems. The Germans, while stressing frugal internal management in their own economy, found that they were increasingly the unlucky recipients of funds escaping other, less-frugal economies. As a practical response, Bonn became increasingly disenchanted with the fixed rate regime and its clumsy adjustment process and became more supportive of exchange-rate flexibility.

The shortcomings of the fixed exchange rate regime and the merits of flexibility had been actively discussed by academics and policy-makers for some time.[53] In the late 1960s such analysts often used the Franco-German currency crises to test their hypotheses about various ways to introduce greater flexibility into the monetary system—wider trading bands, the "crawling peg," or transitional floating. While the United States encouraged the study of greater flexibility, it did not endorse any new arrangements.[54]

The evolution to a more-flexible regime was pushed along by the force of events in 1971. The renewal of monetary crisis, triggered by Nixon's decision to heat up the economy after a two-year fight against inflation and Bonn's determination to slow their domestic boom, reversed the flow of short-term capital. The money flows from Europe to the United States, which had provided protective cover for otherwise unsatisfactory American balance-of-payments positions in 1968 and 1969, now began piling up in European central banks. Ironically, the first allocation of $3.5 billion in SDRs came in 1970 in addition to $10.8 billion in foreign exchange absorbed by Western Europe, Japan, and Canada. The renewed dollar glut put pressure on Washington to reduce dollar holdings abroad by permitting conversions for American gold, something the administration was determined to avoid. When continuing dollar outflows resulted in a speculative attack on the dollar in May 1971, the administration's refusal to take action left other countries to their own devices. Unable to find common ground, the Germans and the Dutch adopted the transitional float, and the French stood firm in their insistence on a dollar devaluation vis-à-vis gold.

The even larger speculative rush in August and Nixon's decision to act unilaterally to close the gold window and to insist on revaluations abroad renewed Atlantic negotiations on monetary reform, focusing squarely on the problem of exchange-rate adjustment.[55] The immediate response abroad was predictably divided. The Germans and the Dutch, who had been floating since May, encouraged a common EEC float. Again France refused, this time opting for the two-tiered pricing scheme for the franc. The Japanese and the rest of the Europeans experimented a short time with the defense of old parities but, finding it too costly, eventually succumbed to various floating arrangements.

Negotiations began in earnest in September at a meeting of the Group of Ten deputies in Paris. Initially, Washington focused little on monetary reform, instead demanding temporary concessions that would improve the American trade position—currency revaluations, greater market access for American exports, and increased military "offset" payments—in exchange for removal of the 10 percent import surcharge. The Europeans countered with a call for a small devaluation of the dollar vis-à-vis gold and a return to convertibility.

Little progress was made toward an agreement in subsequent talks in London at the IMF meeting at the end of September where Treasury Secretary John Connolly continued to take a hard line.[56] The turning point did not come until mid-November, when Arthur Burns and Henry Kissinger convinced Nixon that further delay would have negative consequences for both domestic economic policies and for larger American foreign policy interests.[57] Meanwhile, the EEC finance ministers meeting in

France carved out a common position, insisting that any settlement must include a devaluation of the dollar against gold.

Talks were resumed in late November in Group of Ten meetings in Rome. The American spokesman, Paul Volcker, took a somewhat softer line, calling for an 11 percent average revaluation of other currencies vis-à-vis the dollar, widened trading bands from 1 to 3 percent either side of parity, and some trade and defense assistance. Most important, for the first time, he initiated discussion of a hypothetical devaluation of the dollar. That agreement eluded the Rome negotiators was due more to internal European differences than to American reluctance. Specifically, the French and the Germans disagreed about the structure of the currency realignment. Exchange-rate pressures in the fall had resulted in a 9.5 percent appreciation of the mark, while the French government intervention had kept the commercial and financial rates for the franc near the old fixed parity. Paris resisted losing this advantage in any currency realignment, and Bonn wanted to improve its competitive position in Europe. Brandt and Pompidou met in early December to arrange a compromise.

The breakthrough in the larger negotiations came when Pompidou and Nixon met in the Azores on 13 and 14 December and agreed to raise the dollar price of gold from $35 to $38 per ounce, to continue negotiations on the realignment of other currency partities, to widen the existing trading bands, and to seek agreement on trade concessions. Robert Solomon has argued that the limited French victory on devaluation was in part due to the French ability to sustain their position in negotiations when others, including the United States, were growing increasingly anxious for a settlement.[58] But he also devalued the importance of the American concession by acknowledging that "We [U.S. policy-makers] comforted ourselves with the knowledge that the continued inconvertibility of the dollar would give the United States considerable leverage in future negotiations over reform of the system."[59] That Pompidou agreed not to press for the return to dollar convertibility as part of the bargain made the American concession of even lesser consequence.

The Group of Ten convened again in Washington at the Smithsonian Institution only days after the Azores meeting. Two days of bargaining yielded a dollar devaluation of 8.57 percent in relation to gold. The mark and the yen were revalued 13.58 percent and 16.88 percent, respectively, against the dollar, while the pound and the franc were set 8.57 percent higher vis-à-vis the American currency or unchanged in relation to gold. In exchange for the realignment, the United States agreed to lift the 10 percent import surcharge. With negotiations on European trade concessions not complete, the United States also reserved the right to delay the required congressional approval of the increased gold price until the commercial package was finalized. The ministers agreed as well to widen trading bands from 1 to 2.25 percent as a modest contribution to greater exchange rate flexibility. The Smithsonian agreement also duly noted unresolved monetary difficulties and expressed a commitment to work for more fundamental reform "over the longer term."[60]

All in all, the tough tactics of the administration produced an agreement that came very close to the objectives set out by Nixon in August. Significant exchange-rate changes were achieved, modest unilateral trade concessions were forthcoming, and a small move toward greater exchange-rate flexibility was made, with the door left open to future changes. Only a modest devaluation of the dollar was conceded, the importance of which was diminished by the decision to sever convertibility between the dollar and gold. All these changes were accomplished without any concessions to the management of the domestic economy.

Although President Nixon declared the Smithsonian Agreement to be "the most significant monetary agreement in the history of the world," the agreement did not eliminate the causes of crisis from Atlantic monetary relations.[61] Because it attempted to return to a fixed rate system to manage the problems brought on by monetary interdependence while permitting the most-important national actors to resume a posture of "benign neglect," the Smithsonian regime had little prospect of a long life. Washington's unwillingness to intervene on behalf of the dollar or to discuss the European request for "miniconvertibility," which would have permitted the Europeans to purchase enough U.S. gold to pay off IMF debts, led to considerable resentment abroad and undermined further the basis for cooperative monetary management.[62]

It was in 1972 that the blueprints for monetary union were most attractive in Europe. In early March, an agreement was announced to narrow currency fluctuations, specifying that EEC members would maintain their own exchange rates within a narrower 2.25 percent trading band, even though the Smithsonian Agreement now permitted fluctuations of 4.5 percent. Anticipating membership in the following year, the British joined the so-called "snake-in-the-tunnel" in early May.

British domestic economic problems in June provided the first severe test of both the European "snake" and the Smithsonian Agreement. Defending the pound in the "snake" rapidly became too costly for Britain and, in late June, London was forced to withdraw and to let sterling float. British action shifted speculative pressures to the dollar in late June and early July, during which European central bankers attempted to defend the Smithsonian rates and to maintain the European "snake," even though they were required to take in almost $6 billion in the first two weeks of July alone. By mid-July, most European states, including the Germans, resorted to foreign exchange controls to slow the inflows. The volume of dollar outflows and the proliferation of exchange controls also brought a more-active contribution from the United States. The Federal Reserve Bank of New York reactivated its "swap" agreements with central bankers abroad that had been discontinued in August 1971 and also intervened in foreign exchange markets to prop up the dollar.

Uncertainty and nervousness returned to currency markets in early 1973 when Nixon replaced mandatory wage and price controls with less-restrictive and voluntary guidelines that money traders viewed as increasing the likelihood of inflation. Speculation peaked in the first ten days of February, and the Germans and the Japanese accumulated the most dollars. Treasury Secretary Shultz surprised financial observers on 12 February by announcing a 10 percent unilateral devaluation of the dollar.[63]

Viewed as a courageous move by some and only the latest of American mercantilist tactics by others, the devaluation provided only a temporary lull in speculative activity.[64] By the end of February, the dollar was again under severe attack. The frenzied pace of speculation pushed the Atlantic states to the reform option increasingly preferred by American leaders, a flexible exchange-rate regime.[65] The question soon became not whether such a flexible regime should replace the system of fixed exchange rates, although the United States did present the option of another Smithsonian variety of realignment, but rather how the new regime should be managed. At a March 4 meeting of the EEC Finance Ministers in Brussels, the Germans, who wanted to salvage what they could of the plans for European monetary union, proposed a joint float of all European currencies against the American dollar. The Italians and the British, already struggling with their own currencies, were unwilling to enter any scheme that might further deplete their reserves. The French, who had stubbornly refused to consider flexible rates all along, proved surprisingly receptive to the floating option in exchange for a preliminary 3 percent revaluation of the German mark.

The Europeans' principal concern was American behavior in any generalized floating regime. At a meeting of the Nine plus the United States, Japan, Sweden, Switzerland, and Canada in Paris on 9 March, the EEC presented a "catalogue of suggestions" to govern U.S. actions.[66] These suggestions included an American willingness to intervene in currency markets on behalf of the dollar; an agreement to mop up dollars abroad by selling long-term Treasury bonds; a determination to tighten domestic credit policies to attract dollars from abroad; and a new policy that would require multinationals to report the composition of their currency holdings and to limit redistribution of those holdings. Shultz expressed U.S. readiness to cooperate in new arrangements, but he avoided any specific commitments regarding the European requests. A second March meeting produced agreement on the mechanics of moving to floating rates. Six of the nine EEC states (Germany, France, the Netherlands, Belgium, Luxembourg, and Denmark) would float together, agreeing to limit internal fluctuations to 2.25 percent. Britain, Ireland, and Italy decided to float outside the "snake" for the time being, and Japan decided to float alone. By the end of March, Washington had successfully orchestrated its second major change in the "rules-of-the-game." Together, the inconvertibility of the dollar with gold and the acceptance of floating exchange rates gave Washington the option of resuming the posture of "benign neglect" in the management of external accounts. And should the dollar remain under attack, the Europeans were faced with accumulating unwanted American dollars through periodic market interventions, or watching their currencies float upward and suffering the consequences in their trade accounts.

It is significant that these two important changes in the international monetary system were made outside the established channels of monetary reform. The failure of international institutions to bring about such reform was not for lack of trying. The IMF gave considerable attention to the negotiation of significant changes in the monetary rules, and its failure to make much headway is worth examining briefly.[67] The impetus for discussions of monetary reform came both from the problems left unresolved by Nixon's initiative of August 1971 and the Smithsonian Agreement concluded in December. In the Smithsonian communiqué, the assembled financial leaders identified a series of problems that would warrant further treatment.[68]

In June 1972, the IMF membership agreed to create a new Committee on the Reform of the International Monetary System and Related Issues (the so-called Committee of Twenty), which included the old Group of Ten countries plus representatives from ten developing countries. When the Committee of Twenty began its work late in the year, the U.S. and West European financial leaders had settled upon two quite different strategies of monetary reform that reflected their contrasting positions in the existing system.[69] For a deficit country like the United States, the most-telling defect of the existing order was the asymmetry of the adjustment process that encouraged surplus states to go on accumulating surpluses and required deficit states to shoulder the burdens of adjustment. The American strategy was to design measures to shift some of the adjustment costs to surplus states.

As the regular recipients of American deficits, the telling asymmetry for the Europeans was that the United States, unlike all other states, was able to avoid the obligations of an international debtor by refusing to convert foreign-held dollars for other reserve assets. Convertibility was the key first step to monetary reform. If dollars were convertible, Washington would be required to conduct a more-responsible balance-of-payments policy.

The American desire to secure greater adjustment assistance from surplus countries was outlined in Washington in a proposal submitted to the first formal meeting of the Committee of Twenty in November. The so-called Volcker Plan called for the establishment of an "objective test" that would begin by determining "normal" reserve levels for all states and then require adjustment measures if reserves exceeded defined points either above or below that normal level.[70] When states failed to make the appropriate adjustments, inducements or sanctions would be applied by the IMF. The EEC Finance Ministers and central bankers opposed the Volcker Plan's reliance on "objective" reserve indicators to trigger payments adjustments. At the second meeting of the Committee of Twenty in late January, several European proposals were advanced by different deputies, each calling for a return to full convertibility as a prerequisite to a comprehensive reform, but differing in their treatment of the existing overhang of dollars that had accumulated in their central banks. Washington's unwillingness to consider convertibility on such terms allowed negotiators little room for maneuver. Stalemate was the result, a not-unsatisfactory outcome to Washington but one that in early 1973, when speculation resumed, meant that Europe would have to go on accepting dollars, impose unwanted exchange constraints, or let their currencies float up against the dollar.

The reform dialogue took a different turn after March 1973 when it inherited a monetary regime altered by the course of events. The Committe of Twenty assembled again in Washington at the end of the month to reconsider the prospects for reform. The participants treated the float as a temporary necessity, agreeing that more permanent arrangements should promote stable but adjustable currency values.[71] The United States reiterated its position that exchange adjustment should be linked automatically to specified reserve accumulations, and the Europeans repeated their opposition to the use of "objective" indicators, although they did permit the establishment of a technical group that would study the potential of such indicators more generally.

The objective of the next Washington meetings in May was to outline a broad strategy for reform. Once again, the old differences surfaced, the United States pushing for objective indicators and adjustment requirements for surplus countries, the Europeans looking for an early return to convertibility. Positions were clarified and some margin for compromise was identified in July, and there was hope that a compromise scheme addressing both convertibility and adjustment could resolve remaining differences in September. It is regrettable that neither side was willing to approve the compromise developed by the technicians and the initiative collapsed. The Committee did resolve to seek comprehensive reform again in 1974.

These efforts were dealt a further blow by the oil embargo in mid-October and the quadrupling of petroleum prices in December 1973. The monetary uncertainties generated by the oil shock reinforced the need for a flexible adjustment process and postponed indefinitely any consideration of a return to a par value system. This de facto acceptance of floating rates shifted attention from comprehensive designs for reform to the immediate problems generated by the petroleum crisis itself. The new and fluid context required reformers to feel their way forward, uncertain about what the future would hold for more-grandiose schemes and plans. The meeting of the Committee of Twenty in Rome in mid-January 1974 confirmed this shift to an incremental and piecemeal approach to reform, and dashed the hopes of those who had believed that meaningful change was possible by mid-year. This new piecemeal strategy, which focused on such issues as appropriate guidelines for managing floating currencies, was compatible with American interests. As U.S. leaders became accustomed to the workings of the free-floating regime and came to understand the advantages it offered to the dollar, enthusiasm for more comprehensive reform continued to decline.[72]

This largely unproductive exercise with multilateral reform in the early 1970s underlined the difficulty of negotiating major regime changes. Even modest changes had proven extremely difficult, as the creation of Special Drawing Rights demonstrated in the 1960s. But in these earlier negotiations, movement was facilitated by a strong American commitment to reform and the willingness of Washington to use its influence to bring the talks to a successful conclusion. The Nixon administration's strategy to bring about major changes in the 1970s was to act unilaterally and to depend much less on multilateral channels. Unilateral action combined with events in international financial markets brought the desired changes quickly and without the normal compromises required to secure multilateral agreement. The United States, willing to use the Committee of Twenty deliberations if they would further American interests but content to let them fail if others made unacceptable demands, therefore invested little in the deliberations.

In some respects, this is evidence confirming the view that hegemonic power is required to make needed structural changes in the monetary system; negotiated reform is both too slow and yields generally unsatisfactory results.[73] While the changes brought about by American assertiveness in these years may have achieved some needed exchange-rate flexibility in the monetary system, they also permitted Washington to go on making domestic economic policy with little concern for its external consequences. Hegemonic power could also encourage a state to take action contrary to its long-term economic interests.

CONCLUSION

The major conclusion of this chapter is that although these were years of apparent American weakness, marked by falling confidence in the dollar and a deteriorating trade account, Washington nevertheless controlled the pace and direction of regime change in both commercial and financial affairs. On the trade side, U.S. officials responded to the growing chorus of domestic voices calling for relief from rising imports in key economic sectors. With the proliferation of non-tariff barriers, fair trade, not free trade, was the cry of those at home facing major shifts in the international division of labor. In financial matters, American leaders responded to an emerging monetary interdependence that made the old rules of Bretton Woods unsustainable and required new arrangements to safeguard the role of the dollar, preserve balance-of-payments flexibility, and maintain domestic economic priorities. Those who proclaimed the end of hegemony greatly overstated the erosion of American power.

A second conclusion is that while American strategies continued to achieve their objectives, new tactics were necessary to adapt the old regimes to new times. Where the Americans had engaged their European partners in cooperative arrangements in the early 1960s, they alternatively ignored common problems, adopting a spirit of "benign neglect," or took tough unilateral action to secure desired objectives. Where economic strength permitted compromise and concessions in the 1950s and 1960s, new feelings of economic weakness justified self-interested actions and the bold exercise of economic power.

The irony of American successes in these years was that in overcoming the inherent contradiction between autonomy and interdependence once again by restructuring the rules, the United States postponed any serious effort to adapt to life in the international economy, either to the new division of labor in commerce or to the many manifestations of interdependence in finance. It was becoming more evident in the early 1970s that American performance abroad was increasingly important to domestic prosperity and also that by many critical measures—trade, technology, innovation, productivity, currency strength—that performance was declining steadily when compared with the records of its chief foreign rivals. The extent of this decline received considerable attention in those years, perhaps best summarized by Peter G. Peterson, in a report prepared for President Nixon prior to the decisions of August 1971.[74] Still, the predominant impulse was to blame others and to pass on to them the costs of adjustment rather than to seek causes at home.

5

Living with Interdependence: The Oil Crisis and Beyond, 1974–1984

The preceding chapters have argued that the United States pursued successfully the contradictory goals of international economic interdependence and autonomy in the management of the domestic economy for almost three decades after the war. Interdependence or the emergence of what Albert Bressand has called the "worldeconomy" was achieved by putting liberal money and trade regimes in place, which gave rise to a steadily growing volume of Atlantic commerce and the internationalization of financial markets.[1] The recourse to selective protectionism and the reappearance of modest exchange controls in the late 1960s and early 1970s did not disrupt significantly these patterns of interdependence, nor did they indicate a fundamental shift away from support for liberal norms. At the same time, American power to set the rules in both money and trade permitted Washington to shield the U.S. economy from the consequences of interdependence and to define domestic economic policies unhindered by external constraints.

The costs of "success" were high in the 1970s not only for American economic performance, but for prosperity in the Altantic region as a whole. Absent the pressing concerns about foreign competition and the constraints imposed by the balance of payments, American domestic policies encouraged the expansion of social programs and the growth in government spending; they imposed regulations and controls on the private sector rather than offering incentives and rewards; and they resulted in chronic inflation throughout the decade.[2] While these chapters certainly do not pretend to suggest that the absence of such international economic pressures fully explains either the adoption of these policies or their consequences, they do lend support to the idea that political leaders and affected groups might have viewed such initiatives with less enthusiasm, or at least designed them differently in the face of a very serious economic challenge from abroad.[3] Indeed, some of the logic supporting cutbacks in government programs and deregulation that became politically attractive in the mid- and late 1970s followed from a growing belief that domestic policies seriously disadvantaged American firms in the international marketplace. Nevertheless, the legacies of autonomy for the United States in the 1970s were regular trade deficits, foreign challenges to key postwar industries, declining labor productivity relative to other countries, threats to technological leadership, and an unstable dollar.

More important, the American habit of autonomy made it more difficult to manage the consequences of interdependence among industrialized states. In other words, Washington still held the outdated belief that national actions and remedies were adequate to cope with the problems of a commercially and financially integrated international economy. Rather than become a leader in the coordination of economic policies among key industrialized states, Washington continued to believe that it could realize its objectives by acting alone. This inclination to follow national routes to prosperity is not unique to the United States; indeed, it explains many European failures to achieve greater economic unity, and it grows from national leaders' unwillingness to relinquish the already blunt instruments for responding successfully to domestic demands. Nevertheless, an appreciation by Washington that common problems require common solutions would have improved the prospects for all. "Benign neglect" as a servant of American intents might have made sense when the level of American involvement in the international economy remained low; it became counterproductive when that involvement grew rapidly in the late 1960s and early 1970s. The principal consequence of economic interdependence is that it ties the fortunes of participating states together. It forces a convergence of economic interests, it makes the problems of one the problems of all, and it demands coordinated solutions. But, as Bressand observed about the last decade, "seldom have so many common interests run into so many common problems to produce so little common action."[4] The American unwillingness to think in terms of joint problems to be solved collectively contributed to this dearth of common action.

The oil embargo and the quadrupling of petroleum prices in 1973 set out in sharp relief these consequences of the contradiction between autonomy and interdependence. First, the OPEC action demonstrated what Washington had attempted to deny all along: the United States too had become caught in the web of interdependence it had for so long fostered and was crucially dependent on participation in the international economy for its own prosperity. Oil provides just one example of such dependence and its ramifications. Not only was foreign oil necessary to run American industry, but its higher costs contributed to domestic inflation and further weakened the trade account. Deteriorating external balances put downward pressure on the exchange rate of the dollar, which in turn encouraged petroleum producers to raise prices to recover exchange-rate losses. The oil crisis made clear that American economic prosperity at home depended upon making domestic performance compatible with the vagaries of the global economy. Or, as William Diebold put it, "more than ever before, we cannot put our own house in order except by relating the American economy to the rest of the world."[5] Autonomous management of the domestic economy made sense only as long as the level of American dependence remained low. When that dependence reached a point where autonomous actions became self-defeating, that is, when they undermined economic well-being by triggering harmful consequences from abroad, as came to be the case in the early 1970s, they ceased to be attractive even at home. It is regrettable that the patterns of postwar economic policy-making at home gave little guidance about how to tailor domestic choices to conform with shifting international circumstances. In other words, even if this dependence had been recognized, American political leaders were not prepared to address it.

The second consequence of the oil crisis was that it plunged all Western countries into a severe recession, the escape from which, these interdependent economies soon learned, was dependent upon a coordinated effort among them. As Robert Putnam and Nicholas Bayne argued, "no one country, even the largest, could successfully sustain policies against the trend of what the others were doing."[6] The need for coordination was exacerbated by the move to flexible exchange rates, which the United States had viewed only a short time earlier as a scheme that would expand the freedom of domestic economic management. Flexible rates, as the Americans learned in 1977 and the French learned in the early 1980s, quickly translated the balance-of-payments deterioration that generally followed domestic expansion into heavy pressure against the national currency, which in turn demanded corrective action and aborted recovery at home. And even though the futility of unilateral action had become clear to all by the late 1970s, the means for coordination were not easily found. The evolution of economic interdepenence, which predictably would undermine the utility of national policy instruments, had not been accompanied by the introduction of methods of coordination and common action. "Benign neglect" argued that adaptation and coordination should be undertaken by others. Struggles to create a European monetary union underlined the reluctance of national leaders to give up what remained of national control and to act together, even in the face of a strong American challenge. Bressand wrote:

> We are still striving to overcome an international economic crisis through national economic policies. Models of closed national economies still gov-

ern much of our thinking and we wonder with incredulity at their failure—be it on the Keynesian or on the Monetarist side. Modest coordination proposals aimed at prompting a much needed world recovery still arouse controversy and scepticism—when in fact national policy-makers have obviously lost control over their much cherished spheres of national economic autonomy.[7]

This chapter examines the efforts of the United States, in particular, and, more generally, the industrialized countries (Canada and Japan have become more-active participants in this process) to cope with the problems of adaptation and international coordination made explicit by the oil crisis. It is a chapter about learning to live with interdependence instead of avoiding its consequences through the manipulation of regime rules. Because of the unavoidable evidence of domestic economic decline, Washington began to understand the bankruptcy of its earlier strategy in these years and reached out with considerable uncertainty for a new approach to restore economic strength. Much less attention was directed to using American power to redefine the rules-of-the-game; those rules that were in place in 1973 are adjusted only marginally over the course of the decade. The theme of the chapter is that new American efforts take two forms, each of which tackles one of the two problems posed by interdependence. Unwilling to take on the difficult task of domestic adjustment, the Ford and Carter administrations focused on international coordination as the viable route to recovery. Their failures combined with his own commitment to fundamental economic reform led Reagan to address the challenges of domestic adjustment and revitalization but, aided by enormous budget deficits and a renewed abundance of oil, in a manner that ignored the requirements of international coordination.

This post-oil crisis era is treated in a format different from the chapters that preceded it. The first section briefly examines monetary and trade negotiations after 1973, supporting the view that Washington regarded regime change as a less-appropriate way to serve its economic interests. The second section discusses new American efforts to bring about coordinated recovery after the oil crisis and explains the failures of these attempts by drawing upon the varying patterns of national economic management that have been treated more fully in earlier chapters. The final section explores the shift in approach introduced by Reagan and the prospects it offers for American revitalization and Atlantic cooperation.

MONETARY AND TRADE RELATIONS

The oil crisis of 1973–1974 had the effect of cementing the monetary and trade arrangements that had been newly adopted in the late 1960s and early 1970s. While some marginal changes were negotiated in both regimes, the main contours have remained unaltered for more than a decade. The massive transfers of funds precipitated by the hike in petroleum prices and the serious payments imbalances that followed required the flexibility of the exchange-rate system adopted in 1973. There was little hope for a return to fixed parities in an environment of divergent inflation patterns, rapidly shifting trade fortunes, and frequent speculative movements against weak currencies. Similarly, oil price increases had far-reaching consequences for national trade fortunes, as they disrupted patterns of comparative advantage and increased pressures for selective protectionism. Yet, the oil embargo also reaffirmed the commitment to free trade. Imports depended upon access to petroleum to fuel their industrial economies. And they counted on foreign markets for their exports to pay new and higher oil bills.

As discussed in Chapter 4, efforts by the Committee of Twenty to devise a comprehensive blueprint for reform were disrupted time and again by the unsettled monetary circumstances of the early 1970s. The oil crisis convinced the group of the futility of this ambitious exercise, and in a report published in June 1974 the committee recommended an evolutionary approach to reform and suggested the appointment of an interim committee to carry on this work.[8] At the 1974 Annual Meeting of the IMF, the Interim Committee was appointed and focused its attention principally on the monetary ramifications of the oil crisis.[9] Three sets of issues received attention: (a) how to accommodate payments imbalances; (b) what guidelines, if any, should be devised to assist the adjustment of exchange rates; and (c) how to treat gold in official holdings and private markets.

The most-immediate problem brought about by the quadrupling of oil prices was serious payments deficits in almost all oil-consuming states. Pressure was subsequently applied to the IMF for new financing facilities to assist countries with chronic deficits. Concern for payments imbalances brought the more-active participation of key OPEC states who, as creditors, were expected to provide some of the needed funding. Early financing was achieved by the so-called IMF oil facility created in 1974 from contributions made by Saudi Arabia and other industrialized states. While other proposals were considered, none gained sufficient backing to generate consensus in the Interim Committee. A proposal that bore on the immediate financing problem, but emerged separately from it, called for the general increase in IMF quotas and proportionately larger increases for OPEC members to reflect their growing financial power in the monetary system. Proposals circulated called for doubling OPEC quotas from 5 to 10 percent of the total. But with larger quotas came greater voting strength within the Fund, and the United States was insistent that its quota share not drop below the 20 percent that gave it an effective veto over Fund decisions. Only in December 1975, when the required vote for passage on major decisions was raised from 80 to 85 percent and the effective veto dropped from 20 to 15 percent, did the United States agree to a quota increase and redistribution in favor of the OPEC states. Nevertheless, these marginal increases in financing contributed little to the problems faced by deficit countries. In the end, the key contributions to the management of payments imbalances came not from multilateral negotiations, but from the lending activities of private multinational banks and from the deepening world recession that sharply reduced imports and reversed trading fortunes in 1975 and 1976.[10]

Oil price increases also had an important impact on the debate surrounding exchange-rate management. The United States continued to be the most supportive of flexible rates, arguing that more stable parities were unsustainable in an era of large capital transfers and frequent speculative flows.[11] The French continued to be the major opponents of a long-term commitment to exchange-rate flexibility, arguing that floating itself contributed to continuing monetary instability in addition to granting considerable policy flexibility to Washington. In negotiations through 1975, French and American differences were narrowed. The French came to accept the idea that a return to pegged rates was impractical and that some guidelines for managing the float were the next-best alternative. The Americans were willing to accept such guidelines as long as they were not defined too rigidly. Agreement between the two states came during the first major power economic summit held in November 1975 at the Chateau de Rambouillet in France. The French conceded the continuing operation of the floating regime, while the Americans agreed to language calling upon national monetary authorities to combat "erratic fluctuations" in exchange rates and to consult regularly with one another to seek ways to diffuse speculation against vulnerable currencies. The French did manage to convince others of the need for "managed floating," but the "surveillance" guidelines remained sufficiently vague to permit national leaders to choose when they wished to apply them. The negotiated compromise was offered as an amendment to the IMF's Articles of Agreement and was presented at the Interim Committee meeting in Jamaica in January 1976. It was subsequently ratified by the Fund's membership.

The idea of more regular government intervention in currency markets or managed floating became attractive to all countries as they gained more experience with the flexible exchange-rate regime. While flexible rates offered more regular adjustments in currency values to reflect shifting national economic fortunes, there was a tendency, because of the rewards of speculating in changing currency values, for markets to overcorrect or "overshoot."[12] Such overcorrections resulted in wide swings in exchange rates and disruption of domestic economic policies and foreign trade. A number of proposals were made, including the defining of so-called "target zones" for currency values, designed to narrow the range of fluctuations through joint intervention.[13] While such plans were appealing in theory, they were much more difficult to put into practice because of conflicting national views about what constituted an appropriate national exchange rate. Therefore, little progress was made toward implementing the guidelines for a managed float in the late 1970s. And the Reagan administration's commitment to market solutions for exchange-rate problems raised the more-basic issue once again of whether government intervention was appropriate at all.

The third concern of the Interim Committee was what future role gold should play in the international monetary system. Again, the French and the American positions were at odds.[14] Continuing its long-term strategy to reduce the importance of gold in the regime, Washington pressed for the IMF to sell its gold. Such sales would reduce further the role of gold as an official reserve asset, drive down gold prices in private markets, and provide needed Fund revenues that could be channeled into aid for LDCs. The French, alternatively, did not retreat to de Gaulle's insistence on the return to the international gold standard, but rather called for the resale of gold by the IMF to the states who had contributed it as part of their assessed quotas. This restitution would then permit states to use gold along with other currencies as part of their international reserves. The outline of an agreement began to take shape by mid-1975. All parties to the negotiations agreed that no additional payments in gold to the IMF should be required. Moreover, the United States softened its opposition to national authorities selling gold at other than official prices, which prompted movement toward eliminating the official price of gold altogether. Washington also showed some willingness to move on the question of restitution if the French would reciprocate by permitting IMF gold sales to aid poor countries. At the end of August 1975, the so-called Washington Agreement on gold was finalized. It was decided that one-sixth of the Fund's gold would be restituted to the membership, and one-sixth would be sold on the open market to benefit LDCs. The agreement was to run for two years, during which time, the national authorities agreed, they would not add to their existing stock of gold. After that time, they could engage in gold sales in open markets if the agreement were not renewed. Washington's willingness to accept a two-year limit on the agreement was strongly criticized at home by some who predicted a renewed appeal for gold when governments and central banks were free to buy and sell gold on the open market. It was argued that such flexibility would undermine American efforts to demonetize gold in the international economy.

The work of the Interim Committee was concluded at a January 1976 meeting in Jamaica.[15] The meeting formally endorsed the negotiated agreements on quota increases and payments imbalances, guidelines for floating exchange rates, and sales and restitution of IMF gold. Most important, the Jamaica meeting gave a stamp of approval to the flexible exchange-rate regime negotiated in 1973 and represented a commitment of the leading participants to manage the new environment created by the oil price increases. It also left much unresolved, aspects of the regime that still remain unsettled in the 1980s. While quotas were raised significantly in the early 1980s, a new allocation of SDRs was approved, and talks continued on issues such as managed floating and a "substitution" account that would permit foreign central bankers to reduce the size of their dollar holdings, the basic outlines of the monetary system have remained unchanged. American conservatives, including Reagan himself, have raised the idea of a return to the gold standard, and others have talked of a "new Bretton Woods" but, to date, major structural reform has generated neither sustained interest nor the prospect of agreement.[16] Barring an international financial collapse, continuing American support for the current regime and the problems of negotiating any significant change would appear to keep the current rules in place for the foreseeable future.

The pattern established in the late 1960s of selective protectionism in an otherwise liberal trading system that emerged as a response to rapid changes in the international division of labor was repeated through the 1970s. Continuing challenges to a wide array of key American and West European industries, particularly from Japan and the newly industrializing countries, reinforced the habit of recourse to voluntary export restraints, market-sharing schemes, and negotiations on non-tariff barriers to trade. The list of affected industries grew longer – textiles, footwear, color television sets, steel, automobiles – but strategies for addressing their problems were all variations on a similar theme.[17]

Just as the Jamaica Agreement legitimized the new flexible exchange rate regime in monetary affairs, the Tokyo Round or Multilateral Trade Negotiations (MTN) and their focus on non-tariff barriers and "fair trade" performed a similar function in commerce.[18] In many respects, the Tokyo Round was a "revolution in trade politics," developing new procedures and codes of conduct for addressing trade issues that could not be accommodated by the old GATT rules.[19] At the same time, it was not a full-scale retreat into protectionism and isolationism in commercial relations. As Robert Keohane suggests, it may have actually represented an increase in commercial cooperation among leading trading countries, although frequently this cooperation slowed the overall growth of trade volume.[20]

The appeal of protectionism was also strengthened by the severe recession of 1974–1975 and the long, slow process of global recovery. Deep recession resulted in surplus capacity, even in the most-vital of industries, and intensified competition among firms seeking to maintain sales in smaller markets.[21] The clamor for public subsidies and other forms of government assistance was particularly strong in an era when domestic firms legitimately claimed that without such assistance they would be forced to close their doors. Trade problems were also aggravated by the uncoordinated expansion of national economies. The U.S. unilateral expansion in 1976 and 1977 resulted in a growing demand for imports unmatched by foreign purchases of American exports and a rapidly widening trade gap. The American trade account recorded a $5.6 billion deficit in 1976, followed by record deficits of $26 billion in 1977 and $28 billion in 1978. Even larger deficits have followed the American expansion in 1983 and 1984. Trade difficulties have also followed from wide swings in currency values. Improvements in the trade account followed the weakening of the dollar in 1978 and 1979, but the continued strength of the American currency in 1983 and 1984 has brought on deficits of record size.

Washington responded to trade difficulties in 1976 and 1977 by seeking market-sharing agreements to address the demands of domestic producers of steel, color televisions, shoes, sugar, and textiles. In early 1977 the new Carter administration pursued bilateral market-sharing agreements much in the way that "voluntary" export limits on textiles were pursued with Japan in the late 1960s. By May, Washington had secured a three-year pact with Tokyo to cut imports of color television. In June, both Taiwan and South Korea agreed to four-year plans to limit the export of shoes.

Textiles and steel received attention in 1977. The multi-fibre agreement for textiles expired in December 1977, and Britain, France, and the United States all sought a new agreement that would afford better protection of national industries. Intense negotiations with Japan yielded a new four-year agreement at the end of the year. Of even greater concern was the surge of imported steel into American and European markets. As early as 1976, the U.S. steel industry sought relief in the form of quotas and higher tariffs and received some assistance for specialty steel. The issue was taken up again in mid-1977 and, in a move to avoid more-restrictive direct measures, Under Secretary of the Treasury Anthony Solomon proposed a "trigger pricing" scheme that would set minimum prices for imported steel and require protectionist measures against foreign steel brought in below those levels. Initial prices were announced in January 1978 and raised by 5 percent four months later. While the arrangements slowed imports of foreign steel, they did little to remedy domestic competitiveness.

Pressure for protectionist relief has continued for textiles, footwear, and steel into the 1980s as American industry has struggled to find the right mix for a new competitiveness. Moreover, the pattern has been repeated in the automobile sector where a struggling industry has pressed for temporary relief from the successful penetration of Japanese imports.[22] Voluntary restraints were again negotiated with Tokyo in the hope that a slowing of imports would give the major American companies the opportunity to restructure and revive.

This selective protectionism has not been a strategy followed by the United States alone. The French claim to have been the originators of the concept "organized free trade" as a response to particular problems facing important French industries, such as textiles, steel, aircraft, and shipbuilding. Former Prime Minister Raymond Barre summed up the reasons for French action:

> France cannot allow international competition to develop under conditions that would throw its economic stuctures into confusion, bring about the sudden collapse of whole sectors of its industry or agriculture, put thousands of workers out of work and jeopardize its independence by eliminating essential activities.[23]

The need for organized free trade grows out of new features in the international economy—persistent sectoral overcapacity in times of slow growth, advantages enjoyed by low-wage countries in particular industries, monopolistic tendencies in sectors such as Japanese shipbuilding and American aircraft, and the rapid price increases for needed raw materials and commodities, most notably oil. Domestic strategies of adaptation and adjustment must be permitted to operate simultaneously with structural changes in international trade.

In Europe, the West Germans have not shared French enthusiasm for organized free trade, arguing that this sectoral protectionism is highly contagious and ultimately discourages national competitiveness. In the words of one official, structural change in international trade poses no threat to free trade:

> Free trade is synonymous with structural change. It is obviously difficult to accept the required process of adjustment in a period of high unemployment, but the record of the 1930s . . . should have taught us once and for all that protectionism cannot resolve the problems of unemployment.[24]

Despite German opposition, several protectionist arrangements have been discussed and negotiated by the European Community since the mid-1970s. Textiles, steel, and chemicals have been on the Community's agenda of sectors seriously damaged by imports. European cartels and market-sharing schemes have regularly drawn support from the French and the Italians.[25]

Problems of structural change and global commerce were also addressed in the Tokyo Round of trade negotiations under the auspices of the GATT. The American Congress passed the long-delayed Trade Reform Act in late 1974, empowering the President once again to engage in multilateral trade talks over five years. The problems of recession in 1975 and American electoral politics in 1976 prevented any serious negotiations before 1977, when the problems of structural change in the world economy were addressed by the major trading partners at the London economic summit in May. Barre and the French argued for "organized free trade" as a guiding principle for the MTN and, during November meetings, Washington submitted a list of demands to get negotiations started. By early 1978 Europe, Japan and the United States had made offers to cut industrial tariffs, the latter specifying reductions of 40 percent. Later in the year they focused their attention on non-tariff barriers to trade. Negotiators devised codes of conduct specifying acceptable commercial behavior on a variety of issues: public subsidies and countervailing duties, government standards and technical regulations, customs valuations, government procurement policies, procedures for import licensing and temporary "safeguard" measures to assist domestic industries seriously injured by imports. The participants also took up the issues of new rules for agricultural trade and sectoral arrangements in aircraft, steel, and meat and dairy products.

Substantial progress was made in all areas prior to the Bonn economic summit in July, with the exception of agriculture and the code of conduct on subsidies and countervailing duties. In agriculture, the United States held out for greater access to European and Japanese markets for fruit, vegetables, and poultry, while the Europeans argued for marketing arrangements in wheat, coarse grains, and meat and dairy products. Agreement on a subsidies code was delayed by differences over the criteria for imposing countervailing duties. The Europeans argued for clear evidence of harm to domestic producers, while Washington preferred a less-rigorous test.

Continuing negotiations through the rest of the year resolved most of the remaining issues. In April 1979, the industrialized countries reached agreement on the MTN package, which included tariff reductions averaging about 33 percent to be phased in over eight to ten years; codes of conduct for subsidies and countervailing duties, government procurement, product standards, and import licensing and customs valuation; and sector agreements in aircraft, steel, and agriculture, specifically meat and dairy products. A general agreement on agriculture also opened up new markets for American farm products and established an international council to facilitate the resolution of commercial differences on agricultural matters.[26] Favorable action by both houses of Congress in July completed the American approval of the MTN.

In many respects, the MTN agreement was an accurate reflection of the state of international commercial affairs in the late 1970s. It reaffirmed the basic commitment of the industrialized countries to international trade but at the same time recognized the serious commercial challenges that these countries faced from new competitors and the need and the right to take corrective and frequently protectionist action to shore up the competitive position of key industries. Given the fact that many common commercial challenges came from newly industrializing countries in the Third World, Atlantic states frequently found their interests converging, which facilitated multilateral agreement. Most Third World countries, however, expressed opposition to these new international rules and refused to endorse the outcome of the MTN.

THE POLITICS OF RECOVERY

While monetary and trade relations after the 1973-1974 oil crisis served primarily to fix in place and to modify marginally the regime changes that evolved in the early part of the decade, the new American dependence on foreign oil and the severity of the 1974-1975 recession led U.S. leaders to realize that successful economic recovery could not be managed by the United States acting alone, that other help would be needed to pull Atlantic economies out of the deep slump. This shift away from "benign neglect," which had presumed that Washington could make policy with little regard for the world outside, was not coupled with any diminished commitment to achieve domestic economic objectives, but simply with the recognition that interdependence required policy coordination with others. Adopting policies to promote expansion and growth without the assurance that other states were moving in the same direction would result in a rapid deterioration in the trade account and downward pressure on the dollar, developments that had been ignored earlier but were now more and more unacceptable in an age of growing petroleum dependence. Domestic expansion would result in sharply higher oil imports, renewed inflationary pressures at home, and an unusually large deterioration in the trade account. If other countries engaged in similar expansion, American exports would grow, moderating the deterioration in the trade account. Moreover, a rapidly deteriorating trade position would probably put the American dollar under attack in foreign exchange markets, and a weakening dollar would encourage OPEC to consider new oil price increases to offset declining revenues denominated in dollars.

The effort to involve others in the process of recovery made use of the annual economic summits among the major industrialized powers that were initiated at Rambouillet in France in November 1975.[27] Summitry had become an effective vehicle of the Nixon-Kissinger détente process undertaken with the Soviet Union in the late 1960s and early 1970s, and Henry Kissinger raised the idea of an Atlantic summit in the early 1970s to deal with sharpening disagreements in the Western Alliance.[28] Support for an economic summit was advanced by new leadership in France and West Germany. French President Valery Giscard d'Estaing and German Chancellor Helmut Schmidt, both former high-ranking economic officials, appreciated the importance of taking on tough international economic problems and were supportive of collective approaches to address commercial and financial difficulties. Giscard raised the idea of an economic summit among the leaders of the industrialized countries in the summer of 1975 and secured American, German, and British approval by the end of July. Broad support for the economic summits grew also from the era of frictions and bad feeling that had characterized alliance economic relations in the early 1970s and a desire to return to a more-cooperative mode. Moreover, the oil crisis and its ramifications, while certainly not producing a unified response, was common to all and did contribute to a convergence of interests among oil consumers. The crisis also had the effect of putting all Atlantic economies in phase—that is, deep in recession—for the first time in memory, giving some hope for arriving at compatible domestic responses.[29]

The U.S. strategy of global recovery took on the nickname the "locomotive"—implying that the engines of growth in the strongest states (West Germany, Japan, and the United States) would steadily pull the states with less-vibrant economies out of recession by becoming active markets for those states' exports. Complicating what seemed a reasonable approach was a stubborn inflation that persisted throughout the worst of the recession. Any rekindling of domestic economies was bound to aggravate further these inflationary impulses and, while the United States was prepared to endure some inevitable pressure on prices for the expected payoffs in business activity and employment, both the Germans and the Japanese were not. With their historic sensitivity to inflation, their higher dependence on oil, and the importance of trade to overall economic performance, the Germans were understandably uneasy with what they viewed as imprudent American policy. The Japanese were even more dependent upon foreign oil, more of which they would require during a period of rapid economic growth. While much of the Rambouillet summit was consumed with debate surrounding proposed rules for managing the flexible exchange-rate regime, the assembled leaders from France, Britain, West Germany, Japan, Italy, and the United States did produce a declaration encouraging "coordination for growth."

Coordination in 1976 was further complicated by Britain's troubles with the pound. Sterling fell sharply in international monetary markets through the year, prompting Labor Prime Minister Harold Wilson's resignation in March. By September, the government was at the limits of its borrowing privileges, and it took a $3.9 billion rescue package in January 1977 before the speculators retreated. The pressure on the pound and the determination of international lenders to extract deflationary measures from the British government made London a poor candidate to assist in the process of economic recovery, although they were supportive of expansion abroad. Pressure on the pound also affected the French franc, prompting Paris to withdraw from the European "snake" in March. An EEC summit in Luxembourg in April revealed divergent domestic economic priorities among the leading states and little opportunity for the construction of common policies.

Western leaders met in June 1976 in Puerto Rico to discuss what had gone wrong since Rambouillet. A commitment to coordinated recovery had produced very meager results. The heavy pressure on the pound in foreign exchange markets and the persistence of high levels of inflation in Britain led some to argue that the floating regime was itself a cause of inflation, especially in weaker states.[30] Fears were also voiced that coordinated recovery would bring additional inflaton, creating more uncertainty in exchange markets. The consensus at Puerto Rico was therefore to proceed more cautiously with the strategy of growth until inflationary pressures could be brought under better control. The prospect of American elections in November and the uncertainty generated by the possibility of new leadership led most economic managers to adopt a "wait and see" posture for the remainder of the year. Inactivity resulted in a gradual slowdown that set the stage for a more-activist strategy of coordinated growth in the new year.

Cooperation and coordination received a big boost with the election of Jimmy Carter and the appointment of many of the architects of "trilateralism" to high positions in the new administration. Arguing for a more-prominent place for Western Europe and Japan in the elaboration of American foreign policy, the "trilateralists" focused particularly on the management of economic issues. Richard Cooper, Carter's Under Secretary of State for Economic Affairs, labeled this new strategy "coordinated stimulation," claiming that it was designed to "strengthen the domestic economic performance and create jobs without triggering inflation." It would also encourage strong states to "expand as rapidly as they can consistent with sustained growth and the control of inflation, thereby absorbing a greater portion of the aggregate deficit of the oil-importing countries and stimulating growth in the weaker economies."[31]

The politics of coordination proved particularly vexing throughout the first half of 1977. Repeated efforts were made to gain commitments from Bonn and Tokyo to follow the American lead in stimulating its economy, the most notable of which came during the third economic summit convened in London in May. Primary attention was directed at ways to stimulate the domestic economies of Western states and to reduce high levels of unemployment. The American tactic was to urge governments to set and to meet growth targets that would assure some balance among all states, but Bonn and Tokyo refused to adopt growth targets in the succeeding months.[32] Failure to produce consensus on a recovery strategy and the determination of Washington to proceed with its accelerated rate of expansion unilaterally guaranteed troublesome adjustment problems that would appear a year later.

Disappointment with German and Japanese policies of reflation and a steady deterioration in the American trade account led Treasury Secretary Michael Blumenthal to make known his belief that the dollar was overvalued in the summer of 1977. His statements produced downward pressure on the dollar in foreign exchange markets. Unable to convince Bonn and Tokyo to reduce their growing trade surpluses by stimulating their economies, Washington hoped to achieve some corrections in trade balances through realigned currency values. Once under way, however, speculation against the dollar proved very difficult to control. By October, the dollar was under heavy selling pressure, even though Washington secured minimal concessions to growth and stimulation from the West Germans. By late in the year, word that the American trade deficit would approach $30 billion, expectations that inflation would soon rise in the expanding American economy, and the continued growth of oil imports all combined to diminish further the attactiveness of the dollar.

By early 1978, the results of uncoordinated stimulation had resulted in a serious economic crisis. Huge American trade deficits coexisted with enormous German and Japanese trade surpluses; a steadily weakening dollar was accompanied by a rapidly appreciating mark and yen. Continuing American expansion and the failure to devise an energy program that would cut oil imports combined to keep the dollar weak in foreign exchange markets and drew pressure from abroad for Washington to intervene to support the American currency. In early January, the Treasury and the Federal Reserve announced that they would defend the dollar by drawing on a $20 billion "swap" network. This new willingness to support the dollar responded not only to European pressures, but also to the unhappiness expressed by King Khalid of Saudi Arabia about the impact of a devalued dollar on his oil revenues. Washington and Bonn announced a new bilateral scheme to counter speculation in March. The expiration of the 1975 Washington Gold Agreement in January 1978 also gave the option of selling official supplies of gold to depress the market price and support the dollar. In May, the Treasury launched six months of gold sales, offering 300,000 ounces per month. Washington continued to formulate domestic policy in accordance with priorities set at home, but it was clear that the fate of the dollar was having important consequences on the achievement of domestic objectives, particularly in the management of inflation.

Through all these months of crisis for the dollar, the West Germans repeatedly lectured Washington about the virtues of discipline in the management of the domestic economy. European unhappiness with the dollar also gave new life to the proposals for European monetary union that had been put aside after the move to floating rates and the disruptions of the oil crisis. In June 1978, Schmidt and Giscard met to discuss a European monetary stabilization plan. In early July, the EEC leaders assembled at Bremen and endorsed the creation of a European Monetary System (EMS) through which members would pool a portion of their monetary reserves, to be made available for stabilizing national exchange rates.[33] The plan, which was successfully launched in early 1979, was viewed less favorably by Britain and Italy. London decided not to join, but indicated a willingness to reassess their participation upon the improvement of their own monetary fortunes. The Italians agreed to join on the condition that the lira would be allowed to fluctuate 6 percent either side of the European floating rate, rather than the 2.25 percent required of other currencies.

In addition to specific measures to support the dollar in early 1978, the Carter administration attempted to redefine its approach to macroeconomic coordination to make it more acceptable to the Europeans. The West Germans had never accepted the "locomotive" strategy, as Helmut Schmidt argued before the Bundestag as late as January 1978:

> Even though we want to contribute to an expansion of the world economy, we do not want to have any part in a new round of inflation . . . to want the Federal Republic to be the locomotive which, as some people abroad suggest, should . . . pull others out of recession would mean overestimating the Federal Republic's strength. Together with others this can be done, but not on our own.[34]

Rather than place the burden of recovery on the economies of two or three countries, the new approach attempted to distribute the tasks more widely. Articulated at the OECD meetings in February 1978, the "Coordinated Reflation Action Program" was now to include Britain, France, Italy and the Benelux states. The analogy of a "convoy" replaced that of "locomotive."

In many respects "coordination" for recovery was less likely to succeed in 1978 than in either of the two previous years, since Western economies were already out of phase.[35] The American economy showed all the signs of dangerous overheating while the Europeans were still struggling with recession. Coordination would now have to involve a mix of inducements to and restraints on growth in the various economies.

The difficulties of coordination were evident in the preparations for and the conduct of the Bonn economic summit in July 1978. Prior to the meeting Deputy Secretary of State Warren Christopher outlined the American strategy:

> Next month in Bonn, West Germany, President Carter will reaffirm our commitment to a deeper level of genuine economic cooperation among the industrial nations. There he will meet . . . to discuss how coordinated action can contribute to each nation's efforts to achieve its economic objectives. . . . To achieve this goal, each nation must do its share. Some can give additional stimulus to their economies thereby increasing exports for others; some can make special efforts to resist protectionist pressures. For our part the United States will pledge to restrain our oil imports and to intensify our fight against inflation.

Christopher goes on to compare this approach with that early in the decade:

> It stands in notable contrast to the unilateral actions of the United States in 1971, when a prior Administration suspended the operation of the international monetary system. This action, together with a 10 percent surcharge on all imports, was taken without consulting our major economic partners. We have learned that in the long run, such unilateral action is self-defeating. The way we have chosen at the Bonn summit is the better course.[36]

The summit itself resulted primarily in U.S. concessions on energy and commitments by others to growth. Carter agreed to cuts in oil imports of 2.5 million barrels per day by 1985 and to measures to reduce inflation. Schmidt committed the Germans to a stimulus package totaling 1 percent of GNP, and the rest of the "convoy"—France, Italy, Japan, and Britain—agreed to modest policies of expansion.[37] Putnam and Bayne argued that the Bonn meeting was the most successful of the summits that preceded it and those since then, in part because domestic and international interests of the leading states were generally compatible.[38] The Europeans and the Japanese were willing to commit to modest reflationary programs after long enduring recession; Washington saw the wisdom of invoking anti-inflationary policies that would be helped by a strong energy program. And the leaders generally delivered on the commitments made in Bonn, although the consequences were not all that the participants had hoped for.

The most-troublesome problem after the Bonn summit was the renewed pressure against the dollar that continued in the fall. On 1 November President Carter acted decisively to curb inflation and to support the dollar in foreign exchange markets. The discount rate was increased from 8.5 to 9.5 percent, and a $30 billion pool of foreign currencies was readied to fight speculation against the dollar. The latter drew upon expanded currency "swaps," the sale of bonds denominated in foreign currencies, and borrowing from the International Monetary Fund.[39] The belief that any anti-inflation program had to be accompanied by measures to support the dollar followed from data published by the Council of Economic Advisors demonstrating that a 20 percent trade-weighted depreciation of the dollar was responsible for as much as one-third of domestic inflation.[40] Domestic economic well-being was tied closely to performance on external accounts.

The new American resolve to intervene in foreign exchange markets brought a halt to the decline of the dollar late in the year, and in January 1979 the dollar began a tenuous recovery. At a four-power summit (Britain, France, West Germany, and the United States) in Guadeloupe in the same month, Washington was cautiously optimistic about recovery. In April, gold sales were halved, a further sign of monetary confidence.

The threat to monetary stability in 1979 came from OPEC's decision in June to raise oil prices 60 percent. The erosion of the dollar's value in foreign exchange markets and the continuing strong demand for petroleum convinced the oil producers that the time was right for a move to higher prices. One week after the OPEC announcement, Western economic leaders convened their annual economic summit in Tokyo, which then focused on the anticipated problems of higher energy costs. Western leaders pledged to cut oil imports two million barrels per day by 1985 and to seek alternative energy sources. They also tackled the problem of coordinating domestic economic policies, but after four years of seeking joint strategies for expansion, the Tokyo summit and those that followed took on the challenges of curbing expansion and reducing inflation.[41] The new oil prices threatened to push inflation to even higher levels. The Germans continued to insist on tighter monetary policies and reduced oil imports in the United States to slow inflation and support the dollar. But even West European states, following a year of moderate expansion, were concerned about new inflationary pressures in their own economies. All states agreed to greater recourse to domestic austerity measures, although the obligations were less clearly outlined.

Anxieties raised both by oil price increases and the problems of overheating triggered pressures against the dollar following the Tokyo summit and reversed the progress toward stability. Currency traders, particularly Arab money managers, sold dollars and bought gold as a hedge against inflation and currency instability. The price of gold climbed to $300 an ounce in July and then moved above $400 in September and

October. Continuing dollar difficulties and inflationary pressures brought additional action from Washington. On 6 October, the Federal Reserve Board raised the discount rate from 11 to 12 percent, acting in part on the belief that a satisfactory American slowdown required interest rates that equalled or exceeded the inflation rate.

The 1979 oil price hike, the generally unsatisfactory results with economic coordination, and the continuing problems of inflation pushed the United States to rely more on its own resources to manage economic difficulties in the new decade. The steady rise in interest rates in early 1980 moderated inflation, but it also brought domestic recession. Nevertheless, Federal Reserve Board Chairman Paul Volcker was determined to maintain monetary discipline in the face of presidential politics in order to win the battle against inflation and to rebuild confidence in the dollar. The political acceptance of this strategy, despite its short-term costs in employment and sustained levels of economic activity, was part of a growing recognition that economic well-being was dependent on competitiveness in international markets and a stable and strong currency. Both required the elimination of inflation through domestic economic adjustments. Shifting the costs of adjustment to others was no longer a viable strategy. Unable to coordinate economic adjustment among the leading industrialized states, Washington retreated to independent action and greater self-reliance, positions that were compatible with the economic philosophy of the new president elected in November.

INTERDEPENDENCE IN THE 1980s: THE REAGAN YEARS

The first round of oil price increases in 1973–1974, coming as it did after years of particularly acrimonious relations in the Western Alliance, generated serious problems of recession and inflation in all industrialized states, but also resulted in efforts to resolve these difficulties through coordinated action, particularly macroeconomic demand management. Most important, after the years of "benign neglect," was a growing recognition in Washington that economic well-being at home was contingent on making domestic policy compatible with international economic developments. The resolve was as strong as ever to respond first and foremost to domestic economic priorities, but there was a growing realization that success could not be achieved in splendid isolation, that global economic changes could upset the best-laid plans at home. The consequences of interdependence had now taken hold in the American economy, and economic coordination among the leading states was viewed as the appropriate response to gaining some control over its consequences. The annual economic summit was the vehicle adopted to assert this control and to foster coordination among the industrialized economies. To find common ground among countries who faced different domestic economic problems, held different views about the proper trade-off between inflation and unemployment, and had to be accountable to their own electorates was much more difficult than simply to ignore these countries altogether, which had been the luxury of "benign neglect." The failure to achieve much coordination in the task of recovery and the disruptive consequences of unilateral expansion encouraged American leaders to entertain new options in the late 1970s and 1980s.

The view that gained acceptance in the United States after the second round of oil price increases in 1979, amid expectations of renewed inflation and recession, was that significant changes were required in the management of the American domestic economy, regardless of what was achieved in the way of coordination abroad. At the root of this new approach was a basic critique of government and the view that the growth of state intervention in the American economy in the 1960s and 1970s had had a seriously detrimental effect on economic performance. Government's unbridled expansion into all aspects of American life, so the argument ran, had slowly choked off the vitality of the marketplace, slowed the pace of economic growth, undermined the potential for an innovative revival, and allowed foreign producers to penetrate and prosper in American markets. This critique of government intervention began as early as the mid-1970s. One particular thread focused on the impact of government regulation of business activity and called for strategies of deregulation that won adherents among Democrats as well as Republicans.[42] Market incentives were promoted to achieve regulatory objectives rather than relying on the costly and clumsy hand of government.[43]

The years of recession and inflation in the 1970s reinforced the view that the economic policies of the 1950s and 1960s were no longer appropriate for the challenges of the 1980s. Moreover, the belief that other industrial countries, most notably West Germany and Japan, were adapting more successfully to the post-oil crisis era led some to look for lessons in the experiences of others.[44] Those who looked abroad generally argued not that government intervention itself was at fault, but that the intervention in the United States had been of the wrong kind – penalizing business enterprises with costly policies that inhibited productive activity rather than supporting such enterprises with assistance and incentives. Closer cooperation and collaboration between business, labor, and government, the pattern prevalent in Japan and West Germany, should replace the confrontational and adversarial relations so common in the United States.[45] Government could be a partner with business in rebuilding the industrial base; a carefully articulated industrial policy that focused on America's innovative potential, rather than protecting the industries of the past, was the key to economic revival.[46]

Regardless of the preference for industrial policy or the freer play of market forces, belief was widespread that major changes were required in the way the United States did business. Neither coordinating economic management with others nor passing the burden of external adjustment to economic partners was a viable strategy for a return to moderate growth, low inflation, and acceptable levels of unemployment. Ronald Reagan's victory at the polls in the fall of 1980 was, among other things, a reflection of the electorate's desire for major economic change and disenchantment with the policies that brought double-digit inflation, persistent recession, and the loss of jobs to more-competitive foreign producers. Reagan's unshakable faith in markets and his long-standing opposition to big government determined the form that this economic change would take. The new administration took office determined to squeeze inflation from the domestic economy through the use of monetary policy, to improve the climate for business through supply-side incentives and deregulation, and to make deep cuts in government expenditures.

In many respect, Reagan's approach to foreign economic policy closely resembled the "benign neglect" strategy of the late 1960s and early 1970s. His view was that attention should be directed to the domestic economy; if the United States succeeded in reducing inflation and restoring the vigor and competitiveness of American industries, the exchange rate for the dollar would stabilize and surpluses would return to the American trade account. As a consequence, administration officials refused to intervene in foreign exchange markets, arguing that the value of the dollar should be determined by market forces. International stability would be assured if others adopted at home the same prudent, market-oriented policies practiced in Washington. That Reagan's policies shared much in common with those of Margaret Thatcher in Britain, and that they were viewed somewhat more favorably by Helmut Kohl in Bonn than by his predecessor, Helmut Schmidt, provided growing support for this market orientation in economic negotiations at the annual economic summits and diminished the appeal of coordination. The important exception to this drift to the right and support for conservative management was in France, where François Mitterand and the Socialists assumed power in 1981.

The difference between the "benign neglect" of the early 1970s and the early 1980s was that during the latter period, the American government did follow through with actions that restored confidence in the dollar. Most important, high interest rates were sustained through 1980 and 1981 in an effort to drive down inflation. Tight monetary policy resulted in the severe recession of 1982, but it also brought inflation under control, improved trade fortunes, and renewed the attractiveness of the dollar. Benign neglect was more acceptable initially because American domestic policy was consistent with restoring order in external accounts.

Nevertheless, high interest rates soon became a major irritant for foreign economies. High American rates and the appreciating dollar forced economic officials abroad to keep their own rates high to discourage capital outflows and depreciations of their own currencies that would undermine the competitiveness of their exports. But high rates discouraged economic recovery following the second round of petroleum price increases. The summits of 1981 in Ottawa and 1982 in Versailles gave considerable attention to these problems caused by American monetary policy.[47]

While the Germans complained loudly about the effects of American rates but followed prudent policies of their own, Mitterand and the Socialists in France acted unilaterally to expand the French economy in 1981, only to suffer the inevitable consequences of a deteriorating trade account and punishing speculation against the franc. Economic conditions required stiff austerity measures in 1982 and 1983, and the franc has remained weak well into 1984. As Washington learned in the late 1970s, policies that run contrary to those practiced in other countries are likely to enjoy little success in the age of interdependence.

The Reagan administration's determination to follow a monetarist course and its unflinching belief that the free play of market forces would permit American firms to restore their international competitiveness gave a different flavor to the annual economic summits of the early 1980s. Rather than taking on the tasks of macroeconomic coordination, the summits became an opportunity for Reagan and Thatcher to extol the benefits of monetarism and the virtues of diminished government intervention in economic activity generally. As Robert Putnam and Nicholas Bayne put it:

> The prevailing sentiment was that governments in the past had tried to do too much. They would be wiser to do less themselves and to leave the markets to do more. The summits therefore moved away from precise commitments in this field back to more general statements of intention and consensus.[48]

This diminished role for government in economic policy-making permitted Western leaders to take on more political issues or economic issues of political consequence, such as East-West trade.

While Reagan's deflationary policies of 1981 and 1982 were compatible with a strategy of "benign neglect," just as high interest rates protected the dollar and permitted a similar approach in 1968 and 1969, the modest reduction of interest rates in late 1982 and 1983 did not expose the dollar to the pressure experienced by the dollar in 1971, which required more-active government intervention. The difference was that in the 1980s interest rates did not move sharply lower, but remained high as a result of record budget deficits that required the government to compete with private borrowers for scarce funds.

As the American economy enjoyed a strong recovery in 1983 and 1984, budget deficits and high interest rates again delayed overdue recoveries in the economies of other industrialized states. At the 1983 and 1984 summits in Williamsburg and London, all the participants, including ideological allies such as Margaret Thatcher and Helmut Kohl, pressed Reagan for action to reduce the deficits and permit a decline in interest rates, but the President was unmoved. Confident of the recovery underway at home, he was unwilling to raise taxes or cut military spending, the two quickest means to reduce the budget deficits. Reagan's position was bolstered by the continuing strength of the dollar. High rates drew in capital from abroad and strengthened the position of the dollar in foreign exchange markets. The developments in the trade account were less encouraging. American recovery generated strong demand for imports, but the overvalued dollar and weak demand from recession-plagued economies abroad undermined export performance. Record trade deficits were the result in 1983 and 1984.

Reagan's policies can be credited for bringing inflation under control and orchestrating a domestic recovery that offer the potential for restoring competitiveness in some of American industries.[49] Yet, the determination to ignore the international consequences of these policies, the legacy of "benign neglect," may soon undermine these achievements. Two likely scenarios suggest tough times ahead for the United States and for the management of interdependence. First, if American budget deficits persist, interest rates remain high, and the dollar remains strong well into the mid-1980s, American industries, no matter how much more efficient and productive, will have a difficult time holding their own against foreign competition. A continuing deterioration of the trade account of the sort experienced in 1983 and 1984 would more than offset the incentives and benefits offered to American business by Reaganomics. The most-likely early sign would be rapidly growing pressures for protectionism. Second, if action is taken to reduce the deficits, American interest rates fall, and capital moves abroad, severe downward pressure on the dollar is likely to result, which may have favorable consequences for the trade balance but may well result in monetary crisis, rapid short-term capital movements, pressure on oil prices, and a return to the inflation of the 1970s.

In sum, Reagan domestic economic policies of the early 1980s have provided one viable route (industrial policy might be another) to renewed vigor for the American economy. The control of domestic inflation and an improved climate for business activity appear to offer new opportunities and create incentives for American firms to restore their competitiveness in the international marketplace. But while the administration has recognized the need to compete with foreign competitors, it has designed domestic policies with little regard for their consequences in an interdependent global economy. In this latter respect, the Reagan years are a retreat to the insistence on autonomy in the management of the domestic economy that prevailed into the early 1970s. No doubt, the current global oil glut and the decline in petroleum prices contributes to the feelings of American independence that prevailed up to the 1973–1974 oil embargo. The peculiar circumstances of high interest rates, budget deficits, and a strong dollar also add to this feeling of well-being and conceal the lurking problems with the trade account or a renewed run on the dollar. The bonds of interdependence may be ignored for a while, but so doing invites more-painful adjustments in the future. The American leaders of the Carter years discovered the enormous difficulties of coordinating the economic policies of democratic states, and in many instances they failed badly. But they recognized that industrialized countries, even the largest, could not head off on their own without doing considerable damage to themselves and frequently to others and without creating management problems for the global economy as a whole.

CONCLUSION

Interdependence demands prudent economic management at home and a willingness to respond flexibly to the problems of coordination that inevitably arise among interwoven economies. The United States was generally responsive to the latter demand in the late 1970s, although it seldom provided effective leadership. Washington has been responsive to the former demand in the 1980s, but its neglect of the latter threatens to undermine the progress made at home.

Meeting both requirements is never easy for leaders in sovereign democratic states, since they have to be responsive to the demands of citizens and groups whose interests more regularly contradict, rather than conform with, the demands of the international economy. That such conflicts have made it extremely problematic to define interests in common is the experience of the European states. The problems of adapting to interdependence are particularly difficult for Washington. Here a large and historically isolated economy, coupled with the postwar power to manipulate international rules to its advantage, did not require the United States to act prudently at home or to respond flexibly to the problems of international coordination. While the results have been far from satisfactory, modest efforts have been made to meet these demands of interdependence over the past decade. Only time will tell how well the lessons have been learned.

6

Conclusion

In the absence of enforceable law, shared norms and agreed-upon procedures are highly valued in international relations.[1] Agreements, treaties, and alliances regularly identify common interests and acceptable behavior among friends and with adversaries. The usefulness of such patterns of rules or "regimes" has spread from traditional political-diplomatic and security affairs to the full range of issues encompassing modern international affairs.[2]

Among the most successsful "regimes" of the first two decades after the war were those that managed monetary and trading relations among Western states. The GATT–Bretton Woods regimes presided over reconstruction in war-torn Europe and Japan and managed an era of unprecedented growth in industrialized states through the 1960s. As the principal postwar economic power, the United States organized the economic order according to liberal rules and then managed it in ways that permitted a strict separation of American domestic and foreign economic policy. This ability to conduct domestic policy with little regard for external accounts offered significant political advantages and policy flexibility to leaders in Washington, features that did not go unnoticed among allies abroad. The inherent economic logic of this liberal order, however, was to weave together the fortunes of these advanced industrialized states through trade, foreign investment, and capital flows. By the early 1960s, the Germans, the French, and the British all appreciated the benefits that the liberal order provided for their recovered economies, but they also came to understand the limits that interdependence could place on domestic economic management. They learned early of the need to devise strategies to meet often-contradictory internal and external demands. And, as these chapters have shown, some adapted better than others. Continuing power to manipulate regime rules permitted American policy-makers at home to avoid external economic constraints, but it also removed the pressure to make needed changes to sustain the competitiveness of U.S. goods in the international marketplace.

As liberal rules yielded a global economy, the American insistence on domestic autonomy became more and more difficult to sustain. Growing problems in external accounts were regularly blamed on others. Declining trade surpluses in the late 1960s were said to result from "unfair" practices abroad, not poor industrial performance at home. Speculative attacks on the dollar were said to be caused by undervalued foreign currencies, not by domestic inflation brought on by waging war in southeast Asia or building the "Great Society." The turnaround in the trade account and recovery of the dollar were to be achieved in 1971 not by putting the "domestic economy through the wringer," but by cutting convertibility between the dollar and gold, by securing favorable currency realignments, and by extracting trade concessions from others. The move to flexible exchange rates in early 1973 was the final effort to preserve American flexibility in domestic economic management.

Not only did it become more difficult to assure domestic autonomy, but the United States became more and more dependent on global exchange for continued prosperity at home. International trade came to represent a growing percentage of GNP, foreign direct investment became an integral part of the strategies of large American firms, and international activities assumed an important share of the business of U.S. banks. Most important, growing quantities of foreign oil were required to fuel American industrial expansion. In the 1960s, European partners had been seduced by liberal rules in much the same way, and their reluctance to challenge the regime that granted special advantages to the United States is, in part, explained by the knowledge that such rules were of continuing importance for their own prosperity.

The 1973–1974 oil crisis made all too clear the extent of American dependence on the global economy for its economic well-being and Washington's inexperience in formulating needed domestic adjustments to address the external shock. The interminable battle for a domestic energy policy is just one example of the failure to formulate an effective response. American power had made such adjustments unnecessary in the 1950s and 1960s; it provided little help in coping with the complex interdependence of the 1970s and 1980s.

U.S. efforts over the past decade to adapt to life in the global economy and to restore U.S. economic strength have produced mixed results. With the consequences of the oil crisis dominant in policy-making, the Ford and Carter administrations understood the need for collective responses and coordinated management among the industrialized states, but they had little success in organizing common action.[3] Moreover, the decisions to proceed with unilateral expansion when cooperation could not be secured abroad resulted in inflation, trade deficits, pressure on the dollar, and another round of price increases that further undermined the competitiveness of the American economy. The Reagan years have demonstrated the will "to put the domestic economy through the wringer" to rid it of inflation and begin the process of restoring industrial competitiveness. But the faith in market solutions and the current glut of oil have resulted in little attention to the management of interdependence, despite evidence of a growing need to stabilize exchange-rate fluctuations, slow the spread of protectionism, and address the problems of Third World debt. International crisis in any of these areas could quickly unravel domestic accomplishments.

The experience of the past decade is evidence of what Daniel Bell has called the "double bind" of advanced industrialized states.[4] Modern elected governments are servants of two masters. They must meet the high expectations of domestic populations for steady non-inflationary growth, full employment, and a wide range of social welfare benefits. To fall too far short on any of these measures risks being turned out of power. At the same time, they must give attention to sustaining favorable commercial balances, managing capital flows, and maintaining confidence in their currency. Failure to meet these external demands may result not only in pressures from one's economic partners, but may also undermine the economic objectives set at home. It is regrettable that policy prescriptions to meet these internal and external demands are frequently incompatible, particularly when undertaken without coordination with other states. Domestic expansion results in the deterioration of external accounts; policies to restore order abroad result in slower growth and unemployment.

Such policy dilemmas plagued European states throughout the 1960s when the United States was able to isolate domestic management by exercising control over regime change. This ongoing need for each government to define national strategies that would respond both to domestic demands and external constraints made a common European strategy always elusive and is the principal reason why their challenge to the United States remained weak.

While the United States recognized in the early 1970s that the rewriting of regime rules was no longer an effective way to cope with the constraints of interdependence, there has been understandable resistance to the loss of domestic flexibility, as the attitudes and policies of the Reagan administration demonstrate. Such resistance is common to all democratic states, although in different degrees. The first priority of all elected governments is to meet domestic needs. Only when the threat from outside or the vulnerability to the international economy can be effectively demonstrated are domestic sacrifices likely to follow. German international political weakness after World War II was often useful to the government in Bonn to secure domestic economic sacrifice. The importance of exports to domestic growth in West Germany and Japan has been a useful lever against growing domestic demands in the 1960s and 1970s. American dependence on foreign oil yielded some moderation in claims at home in the 1970s, and the challenge of imports in the late 1970s and 1980s has also produced some willingness among unions to forego improved wage and benefit packages in the hopes of saving jobs and restoring industry strength. Nevertheless, improved competitiveness and industrial revival inevitably bring renewed domestic claims, as de Gaulle learned in 1968 and American automobile firms are learning in the 1980s.

In short, while the economic instincts of many government leaders are to try to achieve some balance between domestic and foreign economic objectives, political realities demand that primary attention be focused at home. This conclusion implies that intergovernmental efforts to manage interdependence are likely to produce a very uneven record for the foreseeable future.

The utility of any historical study of this sort can be judged by how well it analyzes a given set of events and by its potential for generating conclusions useful in understanding similar periods in the past or instructive in predicting the future. The preceding chapters took on the first task; these concluding pages tackle the second.

This study of Atlantic economic relations points to two general conclusions worth examining in other historical contexts. The first centers on the behavior of economically strong and powerful states in the international economy and the impact that such hegemonic behavior has on the structure of economic relations and the distribution of wealth among the participants. The second focuses on the foundations of foreign economic relations, how they change over time, and what such change implies about stability in the international political economy.

The first conclusion is that a state that adopts a market economy at home and enjoys vastly superior wealth and power abroad, what others have called an economic hegemon, is likely to use its power to structure economic relationships with other states in ways that will diminish its own wealth relative to those states over time.[5] The international economic regimes preferred by such hegemonic powers are likely to be those employing liberal commercial and financial rules to manage relations among states.[6] Free trade expands the opportunities of the leading state's competitive domestic producers; the clamor for trade barriers is likely to be less where foreign producers seldom challenge in domestic markets. Free flows of capital facilitate the growth of trade and open up new opportunities for foreign investment. In the short term, economic liberalism abroad is the logical handmaiden of a vital market economy at home.[7] As the analysis has shown, however, while economic liberalism may faithfully serve the interests of the hegemonic power for a brief time, it may soon come to serve the interests of its principal rivals even more.

This tentative conclusion follows for two reasons. First, while such regimes are the logical extension of the interests of strong market economies, they are also the principal vehicles of the internationalization of capital markets, investment decisions, production techniques, managerial skills, and technological knowledge leading to what we have been calling a condition of economic interdependence. Successfully functioning liberal regimes encourage large firms and enterprises to undertake strategic planning and economic decison-making that extends calculations about opportunities and costs beyond national borders.[8] New opportunities for trade and investment and the availability of capital diffuse some of the economic advantages of the leading state to its principal rivals and redefine the international division of labor. The longer such liberal rules prevail, the more widespread this diffusion and the more specialized production will become. Such a conclusion is consistent with predictions made by economic liberals, although they would not necessarily agree that such a new division of labor would necessarily diminish the economic strength of the leading power if it adjusted successfully to the changing marketplace.

The tendency toward economic decline is reinforced by the advantages of power that accrue to the hegemonic state. That power is required initially to put liberal rules in place and to enforce them when countries with weaker economies are less convinced of their benefits. But, with time, this power over others becomes an attractive instrument to avoid the inevitable, but politically difficult, adjustments that all states are regularly required to make at home once interdependence begins to take hold. Power permits the costs of adjustment to be shifted to economic partners abroad through regime changes or exceptions to regime rules. By shielding the domestic economy from the realities of this interdependence, power both preserves the liberal regime and contributes to the economic decline of the hegemonic state.

At some point, the loss of economic strength or wealth in the leading state may be followed by a loss of power, particularly if domestic politics frustrate the adaptation of economic policies at home to the changing environment abroad. Such, in the postwar years, has been the fate of Britain, unable to balance internal and external demands. The Conservative government's use of monetarist medicine in the 1980s to restore British economic competitiveness and to halt the stop-go swings in domestic policy is a belated and painful effort to reverse economic fortunes. American interest in structural economic change that was triggered by the oil crisis and the Reagan administration's efforts to redefine economic policy to help restore American competitiveness are part of the effort to rebuild economic strength before it results in a loss of economic power. While the tasks of rejuvenation are many, the size and resources of the American economy would seem to offer more potential for adaptation than exists in Britain.

Conversely, new economic strength should eventually translate into new sources of economic power. West Germany and Japan would appear to be the most-logical candidates, but both have been cautious about permitting their currencies to assume reserve currency status, a sure sign of growing monetary influence. When oil-producing countries have shown an interest in using the mark as a reserve currency, officials at the German Bundesbank have been wary of any changes permitting greater flexibility in German balance-of-payments management, for fear of encouraging less prudence in the management of domestic policy.

The second conclusion to be drawn from the Atlantic experience follows from roles played by power and interdependence in the organization of the international political economy and the relationship between the two. It argues that hegemonic power and economic interdependence can each act as the foundation for stable and prosperous monetary and trading regimes among industrialized states, that a regime based on political power will precede and provide the prerequisites for one based on economic interdependence, and that the transition from one regime to the other will result in considerable instability in both trade and monetary relations. It agrees with those who subscribe to the hegemonic stability thesis and argue that American power no longer serves as an adequate foundation for managing the international political economy; but rather than lamenting the loss of hegemonic leadership as an inevitable sign of economic instability and regime decline, it suggests that the disorder of the 1970s was an expected part of the transition to a regime based on interdependence.[9]

It has been suggested above that the establishment of monetary and trade regimes based on liberal rules requires the action of a state of superior economic strength and unchallenged political power. Liberal trade and monetary rules are attractive to a strong and competitive economy; hegemonic power increases the prospects for compliance. American hegemonic leadership was required to assure the successful implementation of the liberal regimes after World War II, just as British political and economic dominance fostered the era of free trade in the 19th century. Political power provided the glue for the liberal order in the early years of the *Pax Britannica* and the *Pax Americana*.

Political power also gives liberal rules a chance to work, expanding networks of international trade and facilitating the international movement of capital. As the benefits of this economic interdependence are diffused more widely, support for the liberal regimes grows in other states whose prosperity is increasingly dependent upon them. Shared support for the benefits of economic interdependence gradually replaces hegemonic power as the cement for the foundation of the international political economy.

Frictions and problems are most likely in the transition from a system based on the realities of politics and power to one bounded by the logic of economics and markets. For, as we have argued, there is a strong temptation on the part of the leading state to use its power to avoid the action required at home to correct its external accounts and instead to shift the burden of adjustment to others. This was the course taken by the United States through the 1960s and early 1970s. Such action not only jeopardized American economic performance over the long term, but it also seriously aggravated already-difficult problems of coping with the consequences of interdependence. Washington's actions hastened the partial retreat into protectionism on trade issues and complicated the management of short-term capital flows and currency speculation. Its belated commitment to economic policy coordination among advanced industrialized states also narrowed the range of possible common action.

The Atlantic experience indicates that while the transition from regimes based on power to those structured by interdependence is difficult, it is possible. Over the last decade Washington has recognized that the unilateral exercise of economic power to rewrite the rules further undermines the economy at home, and that accommodating the realities of the global economy is necessary to sustain economic prosperity. Procedures for managing interdependence are far from satisfactorily defined, and early experience has not been particularly encouraging, but all seem to recognize the need for some minimal accommodation to sustain the regimes that none can afford to allow to fail.

Notes

CHAPTER 1

1. Among those who have focused on the decline of the United States as a global economic power from varying perspectives are Robert Gilpin, *U. S. Power and the Multinational Corporation* (New York: Basic Books, 1975); Peter J. Katzenstein, ed., *Between Power and Plenty: Foreign Economic Policies of Advanced Industrialized States* (Madison: University of Wisconsin Press, 1977); Fred Block, *The Origins of International Economic Disorder* (Berkeley: University of California Press, 1977); Robert O. Keohane and Joseph S. Nye, *Power and Interdependence* (Boston: Little, Brown, 1977), Part II; David Calleo, *The Imperious Economy* (Cambridge: Harvard University Press, 1982); Robert Reich, *The Next American Frontier* (New York: Times Books, 1983); and Mancur Olson, *The Rise and Decline of Nations* (New Haven: Yale University Press, 1982).

2. Perhaps the strongest case for this view is made by Charles P. Kindleberger, *The World in Depression, 1929–1939* (Berkeley: University of California Press, 1973). See also Stephen D. Krasner, "State Power and the Structure of International Trade," *World Politics* 28 (April 1976): 317–46. For a thoughtful and thorough refinement of the theory, see Robert O. Keohane, *After Hegemony: Cooperation and Discord in the World of Political Economy* (Princeton: Princeton University Press, 1984). For other refinements and refutations, see Robert O. Keohane, "The Theory of Hegemonic Stability and Changes in International Economic Regimes," in Oli R. Holsti, Randolph M. Siverson, and Alexander L. George, eds., *Change in the International System* (Boulder, Colo.: Westview Press, 1980), pp. 131–62; John G. Ruggie, "International Regimes, Transactions, and Change: Embedded Liberalism in the Postwar Economic Order," *International Organization* 36 (Spring 1982): 379–415; Arthur A. Stein, "The Hegemon's Dilemma: Great Britain, the United States and the International Economic Order," *International Organization* 38 (Spring 1984): 355–86; and Timothy McKeown, "Hegemonic Stability Theory and Nineteenth Century Tariff Levels in Europe," *International Organization* 37 (Winter 1983): 73–91.

3. For a superb early argument to this effect, see Albert O. Hirschman, *National Power and the Structure of Foreign Trade* (Berkeley: University of California Press, 1945). See also Krasner, "State Power." Public choice arguments from economics also support this view. See, especially, Mancur Olson, *The Logic of Collective Action: Political Goods and the Theory of Groups* (Cambridge: Harvard University Press, 1965).

4. Among those subscribing to this view are Benjamin J. Cohen, "The Revolution in Atlantic Economic Relations: A Bargain Comes Unstuck," in Wolfram F. Hanrieder, *The United States and Western Europe* (New York: Winthrop Publishers, 1974), pp. 106–33; David Calleo and Benjamin Rowland, *America and the World Political Economy* (Bloomington: Indiana University Press, 1973); Marina von Whitman, "Leadership Without Hegemony," *Foreign Policy* 20 (Fall 1975): 138–64.

5. The term "regime," long employed by students of international law, has recently been defined by Stephen D. Krasner as "sets of implicit or explicit principles, norms, rules and decision-making procedures around which actors' expectations converge in a given area of international relations." See Krasner, "Structural Causes and Regime Consequences: Regimes as Intervening Variables," *International Organization* 36 (Spring 1982): 186. My use of the term *regime* will follow Krasner's definition in this analysis. For the most-thorough treatment of the dynamics of international regimes, see Krasner, ed., "Interna-

tional Regimes," *International Organization* (Special Issue) 36 (Spring 1982). For an article raising doubts about the utility of the concept, see the article by Susan Strange in the same volume. Richard Cooper provides a useful discussion of monetary regimes in "Prolegomena to the Choice of an International Monetary System," in C. Fred Bergsten and Lawrence Krause, eds., *World Politics and International Economics* (Washington D.C.: Brookings Institution, 1975).

6. David Calleo and Benjamin Rowland, *America and the World,* Chap. 10.

7. Charles P. Kindleberger, *The World in Depression,* and Marina von Whitman, "Leadership."

8. Perceived changes in the nature of international power and who has it have prompted scholars in recent years to rethink their ideas about power in international relations, in general, and in economic affairs, in particular. On power in international relations in general, see Seyom Brown, "The Changing Essence of Power," *Foreign Affairs* 51 (January 1973): 286–99; James G. Marsh, "The Power of Power," in David Easton, ed., *Varieties of Political Theory* (Englewood Cliffs, N.J.: Prentice-Hall, 1966); Stanley Hoffmann, "Notes on the Elusiveness of Modern Power," *International Journal* 30 (Spring 1975): 207–24; Klaus Knorr, *The Power of Nations* (New York: Basic Books, 1975); and the articles by William P. Bundy, Stanley Hoffmann, Robert Legvold, Ralf Dahrendorf, and John C. Campbell in *Foreign Affairs* 56 (October 1977). On the nature of economic power, see Benjamin J. Cohen, *American Foreign Economic Policy* (New York: Harper & Row, 1968), Chap. 1; Charles P. Kindleberger, *Power and Money* (New York: Basic Books, 1970); Klauss Knorr, *The Power of Nations* (New York: Basic Books, 1975); and C. Fred Bergsten, *The Dilemmas of the Dollar: The Economics and Politics of United States International Monetary Policy* (New York: NYU Press, 1975), pp. 28–45.

9. Robert Gilpin, *U.S. Power,* pp. 33–43.

10. Klauss Knorr distinguishes between potential power and actual power by defining the former as capabilities and the latter as those capabilities plus a state's *willingness* to use them. See his *Military Power and Potential* (New York: Heath, Lexington Books, 1970).

11. The best account of these consequences is to be found in Richard Cooper, *The Economics of Interdependence* (New York: McGraw-Hill, 1968). See also Raymond Vernon, *Sovereignty at Bay* (New York: Basic Books, 1971); and George Ball, "Cosmocorp: The Importance of Being Stateless," *Atlantic Community Quarterly* 6 (Summer 1960): 163–70.

12. Robert Gilpin, whose argument draws from the liberal analysis but is not wholly compatible with it, documents the negative impact that the American multinational firm has had on the performance of the U.S. domestic economy. See Gilpin, *U.S. Power.* A particularly instructive idea has been Raymond Vernon's "product cycle," which argues that the multinational's ability to produce and market abroad those products newly developed at home reduces the advantage of innovation to the home state. See Vernon, *Sovereignty at Bay.*

13. For work on the changing international division of labor, see Folker Frobel et al., *The New International Division of Labor* (New York: Cambridge University Press, 1980); OECD, *Facing the Future* (Paris: OECD, 1979); Bela Belassa, *The Changing International Division of Labour in Manufactured Goods* (World Bank, 1979; mimeo); *La Division Internationale du Travail,* Etude de Politique Industrielle, 2 vols. (Paris: La Documentation Française, 1976).

14. Richard Cooper, *The Economics of Interdependence,* Chaps. 6 and 7.

15. In the late 1960s, Charles P. Kindleberger argued that in the face of the multinational firm, "the nation-state is just about through as an economic unit." See his *American Business Abroad: Six Lectures on Direct Investment* (New Haven: Yale University Press, 1969), p. 207. Probably the most-notable leftist treatment of the multinational firm was by Richard J. Barnet and Ronald E. Muller, *Global Reach: The Power of the Multinational Corporations* (New York: Simon & Schuster, 1974).

16. The most-notable work is collected in Peter J. Katzenstein's *Between Power and Plenty.* For treatment of the United States, see the articles by Charles S. Maier and Stephen D. Krasner. The works in Katzenstein draw on work comparing the historical development of modern industrialized economies, such as Alexander Gerschenkron, *Economic Backwardness in Historical Perspective* (Cambridge: Harvard University Press, Belknap Press, 1962); Andrew Shonfield, *Modern Capitalism: The Changing Balance of Public and Private Power* (New York: Oxford University Press, 1962); Raymond Vernon, *Big Business and the State* (Cambridge: Harvard University Press, 1974). For a critique of this view, see Peter Gourevitch, "The Second Image Reversed: International Sources of Domestic Politics," *International Organizations* 32 (Autumn 1978): pp. 881–912. For an interesting variant

combining public choice findings and the importance of domestic groups in economic performance, see Olson, *The Rise and Decline of Nations.*

17. See, for example, Robert L. Paarlberg, "Domesticating Global Management," *Foreign Affairs* 54, no. 3 (April 1976): 563–76; and Wolfram F. Hanreider, "Dissolving International Politics: Reflections on the Nation-State," *American Political Science Review* 72 (December 1978): 1276–87.

18. Robert Reich identifies, in the fabric of American life, a civic culture and a business culture that presently work at cross-purposes. See his *The Next American Frontier,* Chap. 1.

19. See T. J. Pempel, "Japanese Foreign Economic Policy: The Domestic Bases for International Behavior," in Katzenstein, *Between Power and Plenty,* pp. 139–90; High Patrick and Henry Rosovsky, eds., *Asia's New Giant* (Washington: Brookings Institution, 1976); and Ezra Vogel, *Japan as Number 1: Lessons for America* (Cambridge: Harvard University Press, 1979).

20. See Alexander Gerschenkron, *Bread and Democracy in Germany* (New York: Fertig, 1966); Michael Kreile, "West Germany: The Dynamics of Expansion," in Katzenstein, *Between Power and Plenty,* pp. 191–224; Edwin Hartrich, *The Fourth and Richest Reich* (New York: Macmillan, 1980); Karl Hardach, *The Political Economy of Germany in the Twentieth Century* (Berkeley: University of California Press, 1976); and Andrew Spindler, *The Politics of International Credit: Private Finance and Foreign Policy in Germany and Japan* (Washington: Brookings Institution, 1984), Chap. 2.

21. On France, see Charles P. Kindleberger, "The Postwar Resurgence of the French Economy," in Stanley Hoffmann, ed., *In Search of France* (New York: Harper & Row, 1963), pp. 118–58; John Zysman, "The French State in the International Economy," in Peter Katzenstein, *Between Power and Plenty,* pp. 255–93; and John Zysman, *Political Strategies for Industrial Order* (Berkeley: University of California Press, 1977).

22. For a compelling defense of this position, see Katzenstein, "Conclusion: Domestic Structures and Strategies of Foreign Economic Policy," in Katzenstein, *Between Power and Plenty,* pp. 295–336.

23. John Ruggie argues that the content of an international regime may be as important a factor of regime stability or change as its form. See his "International Regimes, Transactions and Change," p. 382. Robert Keohane demonstrates that the predictability of the hegemonic stability theory varies by regime—oil, money, or trade. See Keohane, "The Theory of Hegemonic Stability." John Odell argues that it explains only some changes in the postwar monetary regime: see *U.S. International Monetary Policy* (Princeton: Princeton University Press, 1982).

24. For a critique on these grounds, see Peter Gourevitch, "The Second Image Reversed."

25. Robert Keohane and Joseph Nye make the useful distinction between what they call sensitivity interdependence and vulnerability interdependence. See their *Power and Interdependence,* pp. 11–19.

26. There have been many recent attempts to define and characterize interdependence. The sense used here is closest to that given by Richard Cooper in *The Economics of Interdependence.* For a good account distinguishing the systemic from the bilateral approach to economic interdependence, see Mary Ann Tetreault, "Measuring Interdependence," *International Organization* 34 (Summer 1980): 429–43. For attempts by political scientists to define and refine the concept, see Joseph Nye, "Independence and Interdependence," *Foreign Policy* 22 (Spring 1976): 129–61; Kenneth N. Waltz, *Theory of International Politics* (Reading, MA: Addison-Wesley, 1979), pp. 138–45; and Richard Rosecrance, Alan Alexandroff, Wallace Koehler, John Kroll, Schlomit Lacqueur, and John Stocker, "Whither Interdependence?" *International Organization* 31 (Summer 1977). For a conceptual treatment of interdependence and a good review of the definitional debate, see David A. Baldwin, "Interdependence and Power: A Conceptual Analysis," *International Organization* 34 (Autumn 1980): 471–506.

27. Several recent accounts have stressed the importance of domestic policy constraints on the making of foreign economic policy. See David P. Calleo, *The Imperious Economy;* Jeanne Gowa, *Closing the Gold Window: Domestic Politics and the End of Bretton Woods* (Ithaca: Cornell University Press, 1983); John Odell, *U.S. International Monetary Policy;* and Robert Pastor, *Congress and the Politics of U.S. Foreign Economic Policy, 1929–1976* (Berkeley: University of California Press, 1980).

28. Daniel Bell called this the "double bind" of advanced industrialized states. See his "The Future World Disorder," *Foreign Policy* 27 (Summer 1977): 16.

29. On Britain's postwar fortunes, see Stephen Blank, "Britain: The Politics of Foreign Economic Policy, the Domestic Economy and the Problem of Pluralist Stagnation," in Peter Katzenstein, *Between Power and Plenty*, pp. 89–137; Susan Strange, *Sterling and British Power* (London: Oxford University Press, 1971); Benjamin J. Cohen, *The Future of Sterling as an International Currency* (London: Macmillan and Co., 1971); and Robert Gilpin, *U.S. Power*, Chap. 3.

30. For contrasting positions on this point, see Richard Rosecrance, ed., *America as an Ordinary Country: U.S. Foreign Policy and the Future* (Ithaca: Cornell University Press, 1976); and Susan Strange, "Still an Extraordinary Power," in Ray Lombra and Bill Witte, eds., *The Political Economy of International and Domestic Monetary Relations* (Ames: Iowa State University Press, 1980).

31. There are many accounts of the origins of the Bretton Woods system. See, for example, Alfred E. Eckes, *A Search for Solvency: Bretton Woods and the International Monetary System* (Austin: University of Texas Press, 1975); Richard N. Gardner, *Sterling-Dollar Diplomacy in Current Perspective* (New York: Columbia University Press, 1980); Fred Block, *The Origins of International Monetary Disorder*; Armand Van Dormand, *Bretton Woods: Birth of a Monetary System* (London: Macmillan, 1978); and Sidney E. Rolfe and James Burtle, *The Great Wheel: The World Monetary System: A Reinterpretation* (New York: Quadrangle, 1973).

32. The failure of the ITO and the origins of the GATT have also been the subjects of considerable scholarly attention. See, for example, William Diebold, Jr., *The End of the ITO* (Princeton: International Finance Section, Princeton University, 1952); Gardner Patterson, *Discrimination in International Trade: The Policy Issues, 1945–1965* (Princeton: Princeton University Press, 1966); and Karin Kock, *International Trade Policy in the GATT, 1947–1967* (Stockholm: Almquist and Wiksell, 1969).

33. For an account focusing much more on the politics of domestic policy, see David P. Calleo, *The Imperious Economy*. See also Herbert Stein, *The Fiscal Revolution in America* (Chicago: University of Chicago Press, 1969).

34. The role of the dollar as a reserve currency and its evolution by the early 1970s as by far the most-important international reserve asset is the key to the U.S. ability to retain autonomy at home. The literature on the role of the dollar is overwhelming. See, in particular, Robert Triffin, *Gold and the Dollar Crisis: The Future of Convertibility* (New Haven: Yale University Press, 1960); Robert Z. Aliber, *The Future of the Dollar as the International Currency* (New York: Praeger, 1966); C. Fred Bergsten, *The Dilemmas of the Dollar*; Susan Strange, "The Dollar Crisis 1971," *International Affairs* 48 (April 1972): 191–215; Richard Cooper, "The Future of the Dollar," *Foreign Policy* 11 (Summer 1973): 3–23; Martin Mayer, *The Fate of the Dollar* (New York: Time Books, 1980); and Ernest Mandel, *Decline of the Dollar: A Marxist View of the Monetary Crisis* (New York: Monad Press, 1972).

35. Arthur Stein argues that concessions such as these are necessary for the leading power to secure economic followers and solidify its hegemonic position over the long term. See his "The Hegemon's Dilemma."

36. Benjamin J. Cohen, "The Revolution in Atlantic Economic Relations."

37. The author owes a significant debt to Wolfram F. Hanrieder for making clear the importance of this theme.

38. See Richard N. Cooper, *The Economics of Interdependence*, Part II.

39. On foreign direct investment, see Robert Gilpin, *U.S. Power*; Raymond Vernon, *Sovereignty at Bay*; and Richard Barnet and Ronald Muller, *Global Reach*. On the Euro-dollar market, see Jane Snedden Little, *Euro-Dollars: The Money Market Gypsies* (New York: Harper & Row, 1975); and Wayne F. Clendenning, *The Euro-Dollar Market* (Oxford: Clarendon Press, 1970). On interest rate sensitivity, see Eric Chalmers, *International Interest Rate War* (New York: St. Martin's Press, 1972).

40. John Odell persuasively argues that the power of ideas was an important factor in reshaping U.S. Monetary policy in this period. See his *U. S. International Monetary Policy*, pp. 362–67. See also Lawrence B. Krause, "A Passive Balance of Payments Strategy," *Brookings Papers on Economic Activity* no. 3 (1970); and Gottfried Haberler and Thomas E. Willet, *A Strategy for U.S. Balance of Payments Policies* (Washington, D.C.: American Enterprise Institute, 1971).

41. The continuing importance of domestic considerations is demonstrated by Joanne Gowa, *Closing the Gold Window*.

42. On the role of American banks abroad, see Janet Kelly, *Bankers and Borders* (Cambridge, MA: Ballinger, 1976); and Jonathan D. Aronson, *Money and Power: Banks and the World Monetary System* (Beverly Hills: Sage Publications, 1977).

43. See Wolfram F. Hanrieder, *The Stable Crisis: Two Decades of German Foreign Policy* (New York: Harper & Row, 1970), Chap. 2.

44. The growth of interest in industrial policy is one indication of this thinking. See Robert Reich, *The Next American Frontier*; John Zysman and Laura Tyson, eds., *American Industry in International Competition* (Ithaca: Cornell University Press, 1983); William Diebold, Jr., *Industrial Policy as an International Issue* (New York: McGraw-Hill, 1980).

45. For an excellent treatment of the economic summits, see Robert D. Putnam and Nicholas Bayne, *Hanging Together: The Seven Power Summits* (Cambridge: Harvard University Press, 1984).

46. Cf. Melvyn B. Krauss, *The New Protectionism: The Welfare State in International Trade* (New York: New York University Press, 1978).

CHAPTER 2

1. For treatment of economic policy in the Eisenhower years, see Burton I. Kaufman, *Trade and Aid: Eisenhower's Foreign Economic Policy, 1953–1961* (Baltimore: Johns Hopkins University Press, 1982); Herbert Stein, *The Fiscal Revolution in America* (Chicago: University of Chicago Press, 1969), Chaps. 11–14; and Dwight D. Eisenhower, *Waging Peace, 1956–1961* (Garden City, N.Y.: Doubleday, 1965).

2. Herbert Stein, *The Fiscal Revolution*, pp. 319–45.

3. Dwight D. Eisenhower, *Waging Peace*, p. 460.

4. Quoted in *The New York Times*, 17 November 1960, p. 10.

5. *New York Times*, November 1967, Sect. IV, p. 11. Some evidence also suggests that the U.S. sought to convince certain European central banks to lower their interest rates to slow American capital outflows as American interest rates declined. Britain, in particular, had kept interest rates high to attract foreign capital and aid its balance of payments. See Eric Chalmers, *International Interest Rate War* (New York: St. Martin's, 1972).

6. The cuts were to be made in the following areas: (a) the State Department was to place primary emphasis on purchases of goods and services of U.S. origin in economic and technical aid abroad; (b) purchases of military equipment abroad by the Defense Department would be reduced; (c) civilian operations abroad would reduce employees; (d) the Agriculture Department's disposal of surplus products should not interfere with cash sales of U.S. products; (e) the Development Loan Fund would hold to a minimum any credit advances that did not finance direct procurement of U.S. goods and services.

7. The huge surplus in 1957 was due, first, to greatly expanded U.S. oil exports to Western Europe that replaced dwindling supplies from the Middle East in the aftermath of the 1956 Suez crisis. Large-scale "dumping" of U.S. cotton and grain supplies on world markets also contributed to the inflated trade surplus, sales that were not to be repeated in 1958 and 1959. Although these unusual circumstances were duly noted at the end of 1957, they were quickly forgotten when trade balances deteriorated in 1958 and 1959.

8. While the French were later eager to unload their glut of dollars and buy gold, the British were the first to initiate large-scale conversions, purchasing $400 million of gold in 1958 and another $350 million in 1959.

9. For discussions of the early years of the Euro-dollar market, see Jane Snedden Little, *Euro-Dollars*; and Wayne E. Clendenning, *The Euro-Dollar Market*.

10. Charles de Gaulle, *Memoirs of Hope: Renewal and Endeavor* (New York: Simon & Schuster, 1970), pp. 137–38. See also Antoine Pinay, "Economic Revolution in France," *Foreign Affairs* 37 (July 1959): 587–97; and Herbert Tint, *French Foreign Policy Since the Second World War* (New York: St. Martin's, 1972).

11. Among the best accounts of French foreign policy under de Gaulle are Edward Kolodziej, *French International Policy Under De Gaulle and Pompidou: The Politics of Grandeur* (Ithaca: Cornell University Press, 1974); Edward L. Morse, *Foreign Policy and Interdependence in Gaullist France*; Alfred Grosser, *French Foreign Policy Under De Gaulle* (Boston: Little, Brown, 1965); Roy Macridis, *De Gaulle—Implacable Ally* (New York: Harper & Row, 1966);

and W. W. Kulski, *De Gaulle and the World System* (Syracuse, N.Y.: Syracuse University Press, 1967).

12. The most-thorough accounts of French foreign economic policy are Kolodziej, *French International Policy*, Chap. 4; and Morse, *Foreign Policy and Interdependence*, Chaps. 5–7.

13. Quoted in *The New York Times*, 29 December 1958, p. 1.

14. As de Gaulle himself stated, "Politics and economics are as closely linked as action and life" (*Memoirs of Hope*, p. 131).

15. It was sometimes said that de Gaulle loved France but disliked the French.

16. The growth and modernization of the French economy in the 1960s amazed those who had long attempted to explain its weakness. For a good review of the old weaknesses and an attempt to account for the postwar strength, see Charles P. Kindleberger, "The French Economy," in Stanley Hoffmann, ed., *In Search of France*, pp. 118–58. Much of the credit for French successes is given to the role played by the state, in general, and the unique form of French planning, in particular. See, for example, Stephen Cohen, *Modern Capitalist Planning* (Cambridge: Harvard University Press, 1969); John H. McArthur and Bruce R. Scott, *Industrial Planning in France* (Boston: Harvard University Division of Research, Graduate School of Business Admnistration, 1969); John Sheahan, *Promotion and Control of Industry in France* (Berkeley: University of California Press, 1977); Charles-Albert Michalet, "France," in Raymond Vernon, *Big Business and the State*, pp. 105–25; Robert Gilpin, *France in the Age of the Scientific State* (Princeton: Princeton University Press, 1968); and John Zysman, *Political Strategies for Industrial Order*.

17. For a good discussion of the external and internal constraints on British foreign economic policy, see Stephen Blank, "Britain: The Politics of Foreign Economic Policy," in Katzenstein, *Between Power and Plenty*, pp. 89–137. The constraints imposed by contending domestic groups would seem to support Mancur Olson's theory of economic decline. See his *The Rise and Decline of Nations*.

18. There is an abundance of literature seeking to explain Britain's economic troubles. The best discussions of long-term problems are E. J. Hobsbaum, *Industry and Empire* (London: Penguin, 1968) and Robert Gilpin, *U.S. Power and the Multinational Corporation*, Chap. 3. On the postwar period, see Andrew Shonfield, *British Economic Policy Since the War* (London: Penguin, 1958); Richard Caves et al., *Britain's Economic Prospects* (Washington: Brookings, 1968); Samuel Britton, *Steering the Economy* (London: Penguin, 1971); and Isaac Kramnick, ed., *Is Britain Dying? Perspectives on the Current Crisis* (Ithaca, N.Y.: Cornell University Press, 1979). On the role of sterling, see Susan Strange, *Sterling and British Policy*; and Benjamin J. Cohen, *The Future of Sterling as an International Currency*.

19. Certainly, other political and economic reasons also made British labor and industrial leadership shy away from the European movement. Labor leaders were fearful that full employment commitments made by the British government after the war would be sacrificed in a common European venture. Corporate interests worried that a European industrial policy would be unsympathetic to the task of modernizing British industries. All British citizens were uneasy about the political aspects of European integration that threatened to undermine national sovereignty and place British welfare in the hands of an untried and potentially unreliable European coalition.

20. See Robert Gilpin, *U.S. Power*, Chapter 3.

21. See Susan Strange, *Sterling and British Policy*, and Benjamin J. Cohen, *The Future of Sterling*.

22. The best account of the German economic recovery is Henry Wallich, *Mainsprings of the German Revival* (New Haven: Yale University Press, 1955). See also Karl Hardach, *The Political Economy of Germany in the Twentieth Century*, Chap. 5; and Edwin Hartrich, *The Fourth and Richest Reich*, Book I.

23. See Hartrich, *Fourth and Richest Reich*, Chapter 7; Karl Hardach, *The Political Economy*, Chapter 7.

24. Compare Michael Kreile, "West Germany," in Katzenstein, *Between Power and Plenty*, pp. 191–95, and Charles P. Kindleberger, "Germany's Persistent Balance of Payments Disequilibrium," in Robert E. Baldwin et al., *Trade, Growth and the Balance of Payments, Essays in Honor of Gottfried Haberler* (Chicago: Rand McNally, 1965), pp. 230–48. Kreile argues that policy choices by Erhard and others played an important part in trade successes; Kindleberger attributes success more to structural features of the German economy and to

other social factors. See also Christian Deubner, "Industry and Politics in West Germany," *International Organization* 38 (Summer 1984): 501–35.

25. Wolfram Hanrieder makes this point in *The Stable Crisis*, Chap. 2. Nevertheless, as economic issues become more important on foreign policy agendas in the 1960s and 1970s, the German cultivation of economic strength did begin to bear political fruit. See Wolfram F. Hanrieder, "Germany as Number 2?" *International Studies Quarterly* 27 (March 1982): 57–86.

26. On French views about the EEC, see Edward Kolodziej, *French International Policy*, Chap. 5; Alfred Grosser, *French Foreign Policy Under De Gaulle*, Chap. 6; and W. W. Kulski, *De Gaulle and the World*, Chap. 5.

27. See Wolfram Hanrieder, *The Stable Crisis*, pp. 53–60.

28. The tension between German political and economic interests in the late 1950s can be shown by the conflicting positions held by Adenauer and his Economics Minister, Ludwig Erhard. Erhard unsuccessfully battled for the economic priorities in foreign policy—a less-restrictive trading community, an unchanged parity for the mark, and minimal assistance to developing countries. Adenauer stressed the importance of good relations with France and the United States, which required acceptance of the French view of Europe and the need to placate Washington on defense costs.

29. On British commercial policy in the late 1950s, see Miriam Camps, *Britain and the European Community, 1955–1963* (Princeton: Princeton University Press, 1964); Uwe Kitzinger, *Diplomacy and Persuasion: How Britain Joined the Common Market* (London: Thames & Hudson, 1973); and David P. Calleo, *Britain's Future* (New York: Horizon Press, 1968).

30. For the British view of French fortunes, see *The Times*, 1 January 1958, p. 7d.

31. The 10 percent tariff cut made by the EEC members on 1 January 1959 was also extended to all other GATT members, and the quota increases were offered to all OEEC members. These concessions were, in part, an attempt to keep the United States and Britain close to the European position, making adjustments easier should Britain decide to join later. This attitude of accommodation changed considerably when de Gaulle began to direct the progress of the EEC.

32. In a joint communiqué following a meeting between Eisenhower and Erhard in March 1960, the two leaders criticized EFTA for its contribution to trade divisions in Europe. Text reprinted in *The New York Times*, 20 March 1960. See also Walter Lippman, *Western Unity and the Common Market* (Boston: Little Brown, 1962).

33. By May 1960, such diverse sources as the Liberal Party, *The Economist*, *The Observer*, the *Manchester Guardian*, prominent Conservatives and leading businessmen were all recommending British membership.

34. In 1959, German trade with the "outer seven" was 27 percent of its total trade.

35. As quoted in *The New York Times*, 12 May 1959, p. 49.

36. For treatment of the round of trade negotiations, see Gardner Patterson, *Discrimination in International Trade*; Karin Kock, *International Trade Policy and the GATT*; and Robert Hudec, *The GATT Legal System and World Trade Diplomacy* (New York: Praeger, 1975).

37. The return to convertibility is discussed by Brian Tew, *The Evolution of the International Monetary System, 1945–1977* (London: Hutchinson, 1977), pp. 51–63.

CHAPTER 3

1. As Arthur Schlesinger quotes Kennedy, "I don't want to be tagged as a big spender early in this administration. If I do I won't get my programs through later on." See his *A Thousand Days* (Greenwich, Conn.: Fawcett Publications, 1967), p. 570. See also Herbert Stein, *The Fiscal Revolution in America*, Chap. 15.

2. For fuller comment on these choices, see Arthur Schlesinger, *A Thousand Days*, p. 573.

3. Herbert Stein discusses this period in detail. See *The Fiscal Revolution*, Chaps. 16 and 17. See also Jacob Viner, "Economic Foreign Policy in the New Frontier," *Foreign Affairs* 39 (July 1961): 560–77.

4. The Trade Expansion Act was written as if British membership were a certainty, empowering the President to eliminate tariffs on items for which the United States and the EEC together accounted for 80 percent of world trade. With British membership this list totaled

26; without Britain only two items (oleomargarine and jet airplanes) qualified for tariff elimination.

5. For a thorough treatment of protectionism in textiles, see Vinod K. Aggarwal, "Hanging by a Thread: International Regime Change in the Textile/Apparel System, 1950-1979," (Ph.D. dissertation, Stanford University, 1981). See also I. M. Destler, Haruhiro Fukui, and Hideo Sato, *The Textile Wrangle: Conflict in Japanese-American Relations, 1969-1971* (Ithaca: Cornell University Press, 1979); and David Yoffie, *Power and Protectionism* (New York: Columbia University Press, 1983), Chaps. 2-4.

6. Yoffie, *Power and Protectionism*, pp. 116-21.

7. See Gus Tyler, "Labor's Multinational Pains," *Foreign Policy* 12 (Fall 1973): 113-32.

8. Lawrence Krause, "Why Exports Are Becoming Irrelevant," in Richard Cooper, *A Reordered World* (Washington: Potomac Associates, 1973), pp. 92-99.

9. David Yoffie, *Power and Protectionism*, pp. 116-21.

10. Robert W. Stevens, *A Primer on the Dollar in the World Economy* (New York: Random House, 1972), p. 153. The currency swaps depended upon cooperation and collegiality among Western central bankers. For some sense of this environment, see Charles A. Coombs, *The Arena of International Finance* (New York: John Wiley & Sons, 1976), Chap. 5.

11. Coombs, *Arena of International Finance*, Chapter 6.

12. The members were the United States, Britain, France, West Germany, Italy, Switzerland, Belgium, and The Netherlands. See ibid., Chap. 4.

13. The term "ad-hocery" is used by David P. Calleo, *The Imperious Economy*, pp. 20-21. Calleo's view of the contradictions between American foreign and domestic economic policy is similar to the view I offer in this section. (See Chapter 1.) Gordon Weil and Ian Davidson refer to American policy as "tinkering" and "fire-fighting." See their *The Gold War* (New York: Holt, Rinehart & Winston, 1970), pp. 48-57.

14. The approach was reported to have been a composite of many points of view — Treasury, Federal Reserve, Council of Economic Advisors. The Fed and Treasury would have liked to have tightened money policy. But the CEA resisted, and Johnson liked the idea of a "voluntary" policy because it protected the easy money policy at home and avoided the stigma of exchange controls.

15. As quoted in *The New York Times*, 19 May 1966, p. 65.

16. For a broader perspective on French foreign policy in the Gaullist years and the place of economic policy in that period, see Edward Kolodziej, *French Foreign Policy Under de Gaulle and Pompidou*, Chap. 4; and Edward L. Morse, *Foreign Policy and Interdependence in Gaullist France*.

17. See Waverly Root, "De Gaulle and the Dollar," *American Scholar* 37 (Summer 1968): 469-81.

18. The views of Rueff appear to have made a deep impression on de Gaulle and influenced both his analysis of the American challenge and his view of an appropriate French response. Among the relevant writings of Rueff are *The Balance of Payments* (New York: Macmillan, 1967) and *The Monetary Sin of the West* (New York: Macmillan, 1972).

19. The economic and technological challenge of American firms generated considerable concern in France and stimulated policies of adjustment and adaptation. See Jean Jacques Servan-Schreiber, *The American Challenge* (New York: Atheneum, 1968); and John Zysman, *Political Strategies for Industrial Order*.

20. See John Newhouse, *Collision in Brussels: The Common Market Crisis of 30 June 1965* (New York: W. W. Norton, 1967).

21. This view is elaborated in Jean Jacques Servan-Schreiber, *The American Challenge*.

22. The roots of British postwar commitments are identified by Richard N. Cooper, "The Balance of Payments," in Richard Caves et al., *Britain's Economic Prospects* (Washington, D.C.: Brookings Institution, 1968). See also Stephen Blank, "Britain: The Politics of Foreign Economic Policy," in Katzenstein, *Between Power and Plenty*, pp. 89-137.

23. See Susan Strange, *Sterling and British Policy*.

24. For a good account of Britain's policy through the decade, see C. D. Cohen, *British Economic Policy, 1960-1969* (London: Butterworths, 1971).

25. As quoted in *The New York Times*, 25 July 1964, p. 24.

26. Understandably, the Germans were reluctant. Bonn was already paying for 60 per-

cent of the costs of British troops in Germany, as well as $150 million in military purchases and $675 million per year in offset purchases to keep U.S. troops in Germany. These negotiations were carried out in utmost secrecy in Munich. See *Dusseldorf Handelsblatt*, 19 September 1966, p. 4.

27. Britain's troubles in the 1960s produced a number of analyses seeking both to explain the emerging weaknesses and to point to viable remedies. See, for example, Max Beloff, *Imperial Sunset* (New York: Alfred A. Knopf, 1975); David Black and K. W. Watkins, *Can Britain Survive?* (London: Joseph, 1971); and Richard Caves, ed., *Britain's Economic Prospects*.

28. For a good discussion of the interest rate tool in German monetary management, see Eric Chalmers, *International Interest Rate War*, pp. 202–17.

29. See Miriam Camps, *Britain and the European Community*; Uwe Kitzinger, *Diplomacy and Persuasion*; and Emile Benoit, *Europe at Sixes and Sevens* (New York: Columbia University Press, 1961).

30. See Nora Beloff, *The General Says No* (Baltimore: Penguin Books, 1963).

31. On Labor's position, see R. H. S. Crossman, "British Labor Looks at Europe," *Foreign Affairs* 41 (July 1963): 732–43; and Robert Pfaltzgraff, "Britain and the European Community, 1963–1967," *Orbis* 12 (January 1968): 87–120.

32. See Donald Puchala, "Integration and Disintegration in Franco-German Relations, 1954–1965," *International Organization* 24 (Spring 1970): 183–208.

33. See Edward Kolodziej, *French International Policy*, Chap. 7.

34. For an excellent analysis of Franco-German relations see F. Roy Willis, *France, Germany and the New Europe, 1945–1967* (London: Oxford University Press, 1968).

35. If there is one area where the theme of American control over regime change does not hold up, it would have to be agricultural trade. The French are masters at making progress on all sorts of negotiations conditional on concessions to French agriculture. Such leverage was exercised against the Germans in the early 1960s, against the Americans in the Kennedy Round, and later with the British when the terms of EEC membership were negotiated in the early 1970s. For a good review of commercial negotiations on farm products, see T. K. Warley, "Western Trade in Agricultural Products," in Andrew Shonfield, *International Economic Relations of the Western World, 1959–1971* (London: Oxford University Press, 1976), pp. 287–402.

36. Here, German and American interests coincided. By bringing the French along, the Germans were assisting American commercial interests at the same time they were assisting their own.

37. See John Newhouse, *Collision in Brussels*.

38. The Dillon Round is treated by Gerard and Victoria Curzon, "The Management of Trade Relations in the GATT," in Andrew Shonfield, *International Economic Relations*, pp. 168–75; Karin Kock, *International Trade Policy and the GATT*; and Robert Hudec, *The GATT Legal System and World Trade Diplomacy*.

39. On agriculture, see T. K. Warley, "Western Trade."

40. There is a large literature treating the Kennedy Round. See, in particular, Ernest H. Preeg, *Traders and Diplomats* (Washington, D.C.: The Brookings Institution, 1970); John N. Evans, *The Kennedy Round in American Trade Policy: The Twilight of GATT?* (Cambridge: Harvard University Press, 1979); Kenneth W. Dam, *The GATT: Law and International Organization* (Chicago: University of Chicago Press, 1970); Thomas B. Curtis and John R. Vastine, Jr., *The Kennedy Round and the Future of American Trade*; Karin Kock, *International Trade Policy*; Robert Hudec, *The Gatt Legal System*; and Gerard and Victoria Curzon, "The Management of Trade Relations."

41. See Ernest H. Preeg, *Traders and Diplomats*, Chap. 4.

42. The debate over a common European exceptions list resulted in a predictable split between the French and the Italians, on the one hand, who insisted on a long list to protect domestic industries, and the more-competitive Germans, on the other, who argued for a short list that would stimulate German exports and encourage modernization and development of European industry as a whole. All Community members agreed that chemicals should be included on the common list unless the United States were willing to alter its discriminatory American Selling Price of valuing imports of certain organic chemicals.

43. The United States later criticized the method that the EEC used to calculate its percentage of exceptions that gave them an advantage. The U.S. percentage was derived by

measuring its exceptions list against industrial dutiable imports, while the Common Market percentage was figured by comparing exceptions with all dutiable imports.

44. Ernest Preeg, *Traders and Diplomats*, Chaps. 6 and 8.

45. Ibid., Chap. 11.

46. Such a rough estimate obscures many of the particular nuances of the agreement sector by sector. For some of the problems of measurement, see ibid., Chap. 14.

47. Ibid., p. 261.

48. Cf. Robert O. Keohane, "The Theory of Hegemonic Stability," in Holsti et al., ed. *Change in the International System*, pp. 152–54.

49. Ernest Preeg, *Traders and Diplomats*, p. 262.

50. At the IMF meeting in the fall of 1960, the Unites States expressed opposition to any change: "We are not confronted with any immediate need to consider changes in the system as a whole or in the International Monetary Fund." See the International Monetary Fund, *Summary Proceedings, Annual Meeting* (1960), p. 5. For an account of the rethinking of American policy see Susan Strange, "International Monetary Relations," in Shonfield, *International Economic Relations*, pp. 79–82. For a personal account of this changed American attitude, see Charles A. Coombs, *The Arena of International Finance*, pp. 15–23. See also Robert Solomon, *The International Monetary System* (New York: Harper & Row, 1977), pp. 35–37.

51. Belgium, Britain, Canada, West Germany, France, Italy, Japan, The Netherlands, Sweden, and the United States made up the Group of Ten.

52. Confidence in monetary arrangements was expressed by IMF Executive Director Per Jacobsson, who cited the monetary calm that prevailed during the Cuban Missile Crisis and concluded: "For the longer term, the proven stability of the dollar and the Central Banker's support of the price of gold together hint that the day may be approaching when the international monetary speculation may join the dodo in the ranks of extinct species. And the proponents of dollar devaluation may suffer the same fate." Quoted in *The New York Times*, 4 November 1962, Sec. III, p. 14.

53. British Labor Party leader Harold Wilson also submitted a plan similar to Maulding's in May 1963. Wilson's plan called for the IMF to issue credit-creating certificates that would permit national expansion to make use of unemployed resources. Wilson claimed that the "nuclear citadel" of the West was in danger of being undermined by "economic dry rot" unless the West's monetary base was expanded. He concluded colorfully in a speech before the American Chamber of Commerce: "In international affairs we are living in the age of Charles II, with gold-laden stage coaches foundering through the mud, the prey of marauding highwaymen." Quoted in *The New York Times*, 16 May 1963, p. 49.

54. The disagreement between Roosa and Maulding was particularly heated and has generated considerable discussion. See Stephen D. Cohen, *International Monetary Reform, 1964–1969* (New York: Praeger, 1970), p. 31; Robert Solomon, *The International Monetary System*, pp. 63–64; and Susan Strange, *International Monetary Relations*, pp. 209–12.

55. A Brookings Institution study under the direction of Walter S. Salant advocated an overhaul of international monetary machinery. The Atlantic Institute recommended the formation of a committee of three "wise men" to explore opportunities for improving Atlantic monetary cooperation. Federal Reserve officials generally opposed creation of any new mechanisms to expand international credit, preferring instead the reduction of American payments deficits and more monetary discipline at home. The Council of Economic Advisors viewed new deficit financing arrangements with more enthusiasm, since they generally permitted policies of continuing expansion at home.

56. Robert Roosa, "Reforming the International Monetary System," *Foreign Affairs* 42 (September 1963). The *Journal of Commerce* (25 September 1963, p. 3) explained the changed position by suggesting that in 1962 the dollar was under attack, adequate defense arrangements had not yet been completed, and the Americans would therefore be at a significant bargaining disadvantage. In late 1963, when the dollar defenses were in order and the American currency had survived the pressures of the preceding year, the time was right to get reform studies under way.

57. See the *International Monetary Fund, Summary Proceedings. Annual Meeting* (1963).

58. An interesting footnote to these studies was the role, or rather non-role, played by academic economists. After serving as important catalysts in the whole debate over international monetary reform in the early 1960s, government leaders of leading states made it clear

that they would not involve academic economists in actual negotiations. Upset by this re-buff, the economists, led by Fritz Machlup of Princeton, joined together in what was to be called the Ballagio Group and conducted their own study of the needs of the international monetary system. Other than providing some useful technical information, the group had little impact on the actual conduct of negotiations. See Susan Strange, "International Mone-tary Relations," p. 217; and Robert Solomon, *The International Monetary System*, pp. 70–71.

59. See the *Ministerial Statement of the Group of Ten*, 1 August 1966, pp. 1–2.

60. Ibid., p. 1.

61. For a discussion of the Group of Ten report as a compromise between the U.S. and French positions, see *Le Monde*, 12 August 1964.

62. *International Monetary Fund, Summary Proceedings. Annual Meeting* (1964), p. 205.

63. For an analysis of these competing national positions, see Oscar L. Altman, "The Management of International Liquidity," *IMF Staff Papers*, vol. XI (July 1964), pp. 216–45.

64. *Report of the Study Group on the Creation of Reserve Assets* (Rome: Bank of Italy Press, 1965). For a discussion of the group's deliberations, see Robert Solomon, *The International Monetary System*, pp. 74–79.

65. For an excellent discussion of American policy and policy-making on monetary re-form, see John Odell, *U.S. International Monetary Policy*, Chap. 3.

66. Robert Roosa, *Monetary Reform for the World Economy* (New York: Harper & Row, 1965). See especially Part III, "Agenda for the Future," in which Roosa recommends the cre-ation of a new reserve asset. See also Robert Solomon, *The International Monetary System*, Chap. 8.

67. Solomon, *International Monetary System*, pp. 75–100.

68. Ibid. A minority view on the U.S. position was articulated by the economists Emile Depres, Charles P. Kindleberger, and Walter S. Salant. See "The Dollar and World Liquidity—A Minority View," *The Economist*, 5 February 1966, pp. 526–29.

69. *International Monetary Fund, Summary Proceedings. Annual Meeting* (1965), p. 2.

70. Ibid., p. 117.

71. This lack of growth can be traced to three related factors: (a) the small U.S. balance-of-payments deficit; (b) the French conversions of dollars into gold; and (c) the unusually high level of gold hoarding, i.e., newly mined gold sold to private holders rather than retained as part of official reserves.

72. As French monetary expert Roger Auboin concluded, the United States should aban-don its "regrettably neo-isolationist attitude" and adapt its internal policies to international needs instead of seeking artificial solutions. *Le Monde*, 13/14 March 1966, p. 12.

73. For a comprehensive discussion of the role of the "Emminger Group" and the subse-quent Emminger Report, see Susan Strange, "International Monetary Relations," pp. 229–41. See also Robert Solomon, *International Monetary System*, pp. 129–31.

74. The Group of Ten, *Communique of Ministers and Governors and Report of Deputies* (The Hague, July 1966).

75. Statements by French leaders indicated this unwillingness to cut themselves off from the process of monetary reform. Debré stated, after the vote on The Hague Agreement, "to be put in a minority is not to be put in exile," *Washington Post*, 27 July 1966, p. D7. Other French government statements emphasized the continued French willingness to be part of the reform process: "Reform of the international monetary system is a necessary undertak-ing to which France wishes to contribute positively" (*Le Monde*, 26 August 1966, p. 12). See also *Le Monde*, 28 July 1966, p. 13, which argues that France also realized that gold would "probably" be an insufficient source of liquidity.

76. *Financial Times*, 31 December 1966, p. 1.

77. Stephen Cohen, *International Monetary Reform*, p. 125.

78. For assessments of the reform process and the final agreement, see Fritz Machlup, *Remaking the International Monetary System: The Rio Agreement and Beyond* (Baltimore: Johns Hopkins University Press, 1968); C. Fred Bergstein, "Taking the Monetary Initiative," *For-eign Affairs* 46 (July 1968): 713–32; Francis Bator, "The Political Economics of International Money," *Foreign Affairs* 47 (October 1968): 51–67; and Henry Aubrey, "Behind the Veil of In-ternational Money," *Essays in International Finance*, No. 71 (Princeton: Princeton University Press, 1969).

79. These conclusions would appear to be consistent with Robert Keohane's judgments about the monetary and trade regimes. See his "The Theory of Hegemonic Stability." His position is also restated in *After Hegemony: Cooperation and Discord in International Politics,* Chap. 9.

CHAPTER 4

1. Robert O. Keohane and Joseph S. Nye, *Power and Interdependence,* p. 23.

2. See Daniel Bell, *The Coming of the Post Industrial Society: A Venture in Social Forecasting* (New York: Basic Books, 1973).

3. Concerned about the perception among Europeans that they were being neglected, the Nixon administration proclaimed 1973 as the "Year of Europe." In fact, relations in the Atlantic Alliance hit an all-time low on a number of issues in 1973. For a European reaction, see Z, "The Year of Europe," *Foreign Affairs* 52 (January 1974): 237–48.

4. The origins of the "benign neglect" strategy are discussed by John Odell, *U.S. International Monetary Policy,* pp. 191–99. The intellectual rationale for the strategy is to be found in Gottried Haberler and Thomas D. Willett, *A Strategy for U.S. Balance of Payments Policy.*

5. John Odell, *U.S. International Monetary Policy,* Chaps. 4 and 5.

6. The mandatory controls on foreign lending were the core of a comprehensive program in January 1968 to produce a $3 billion improvement in the balance of payments, which had deteriorated so precipitously in the second half of 1967. The strict regulations placed a moratorium on all new direct investment outflows to continental Western Europe and required banks to reduce short-term loans by 40 percent from the amount outstanding at the end of 1967, cut off all long-term loans, not renew existing loans, and not relend the proceeds of repayments on existing loans.

7. The appeal of the Euro-dollar market for American banks is discussed by Jane Snedden Little, *Euro-Dollars,* p. 227. For a fuller discussion of American banks abroad, see Janet Kelly, *Bankers and Borders: The Case of American Banks in Britain;* and Jonathan Aronson, *Money and Power: Banks and the World Monetary System.*

8. The heavy demand for dollars in the Euro-dollar market drove interest rates up precipitously (above 11 percent) and created a heavy demand for dollars held in European central banks. To slow the outflow of dollar reserves, bankers chose to keep domestic interest rates close to Euro-dollar levels, which coincidently undermined European efforts to promote domestic expansion. By mid-April, European central bankers agreed unanimously to impress upon Washington the need to curb American bank borrowing in the Euro-dollar market. Euro-dollar borrowing by American banks, which had the effect of reducing dollar balances in European central bank reserves, also protected the dollar from speculative attack by keeping it in high demand and short supply. This was the case despite the fact that dollar inflows undercut Washington's tight money policies and the efforts to fight inflation. The expectation that dollars would continue to flow out of European central banks also underlined the need for new international reserves at the same time the United States was arguing for a sizable initial distribution of Special Drawing Rights. For these reasons, the U.S. was not eager to cut Euro-dollar borrowing or to lower domestic interest rates when both brought a measure of stability to American internal and external accounts. Continuing European pressure for lending controls did prompt the Federal Reserve to impose minimum reserve requirements in July on American banks' Euro-dollar borrowing. The action was designed more to placate the Europeans than to restrain U.S. banks, but it did moderate Euro-dollar borrowing for the remainder of the year.

9. As quoted in *The New York Times,* 16 May 1971, Sect. IV, p. 1.

10. Joanne Gowa, *Closing the Gold Window: Domestic Politics and the End of Bretton Woods,* p. 69.

11. Treasury Secretary John Connlly and Under Secretary Paul Volcker preferred a more-assertive response, while Paul McCracken, the Chairman of the Council of Economic Advisors, urged a constitution of the passive balance-of-payments policy.

12. For accounts of the Camp David meeting, see Joanne Gowa, *Closing the Gold Window,*

Chap. 6; John Odell, *U.S. International Monetary Policy*, pp. 257–63; and Robert Solomon, *The International Monetary System*, pp. 177–87.

13. George P. Shultz and Kenneth W. Dam, *Economic Policy Beyond the Headlines* (New York: W. W. Norton, 1977), p. 116. Shultz made his case at the IMF meeting in September. See International Monetary Fund, *Summary Proceedings, Annual Meeting* (1972).

14. The move to flexible rates is treated in detail by John Odell, *U.S. International Monetary Policy*, Chap. 5.

15. There is a growing literature on the "new protectionism." See, for example, Bela Belassa, "The 'New Protectionism' and the International Economy," *Journal of World Trade Law* 12 (1978); David Yoffie, *Power and Protectionism*. For a brief discussion of this protectionist thrust in domestic politics, see Benjamin J. Cohen, "The Revolution in Atlantic Economic Relations: A Bargain Comes Unstuck" in Hanrieder, *The United States and Western Europe*, pp. 123–26; and William Diebold, Jr., "U.S. Trade Policy: The New Political Dimensions," *Foreign Affairs* 52 (April 1974): 475–78.

16. See Destler, Fukui, and Sato, *The Textile Wrangle*; Hazama Genzo, "Behind the U.S.–Japanese Textile War," *The Japan Interpreter* 7 (Spring 1971): 111–14; and David Yoffie, *Power and Protectionism*, pp. 123–58.

17. Yoffie, *Power and Protectionism*, Chapters 5 and 6.

18. For a discussion of the international effort to assist the franc, see Charles Coombs, *The Arena of International Finance*, pp. 176–81. The French also resorted to exchange controls to slow the outflow of capital. See the comments of Paul Fabra in *Le Monde*, 4 June 1968, p. 9.

19. The speculative outflow of funds was aggravated by French companies betting on a devaluation of the French currency. There were stories of these companies using government funds to speculate against the franc and of suitcases full of francs crossing into Switzerland in defiance of the exchange controls. See *The Economist*, 1 June 1968, p. 67.

20. Edward Morse points to a curious new convergence of monetary interests at the Group of Ten meeting in Bonn: "The monetary meeting was noteworthy for the rebirth of an economic alliance of Britain, France and the United States against Germany and the undervalued mark. Germany had then replaced France as the prime interlocutor of the United States on monetary affairs, and the rebirth of this tripartite accord was based, in part, on the need of France to have support against the German negotiators, who had become the strongest in Europe. In addition, Nixon's more orthodox economic policies seemed amenable to de Gaulle. The United Kingdom, for its part, was aligned with de Gaulle for fear that a devaluation of the franc would lead to another run on sterling" (*Foreign Policy and Interdependence in Gaullist France*, p. 248).

21. Wolfram F. Hanrieder argues that de Gaulle's decision was made primarily for reasons of prestige. There was a growing resentment of German economic strength and the ability of Bonn to translate that strength into political power. See his *The Stable Crisis*, p. 81.

22. Some pointed out that the relatively small size of the devaluation was an indication of French willingness to play by the rules of international cooperation, seeking not to hurt seriously the competitive position of any of its partners. The timing of the move was also interesting. In August, the time of vacations in France, many of those most likely to speculate against a publicized move were far from their portfolios. It was reported that Giscard and Pompidou had agreed upon the devaluation as early as July 16 but preferred to wait for the August calm. The announcement was kept secret in France by allowing only a small group (eight) to know of the plans, by working on the proposal after hours, and even by disguising the work as budgetary considerations. French domestic reaction from the left was predictably unfavorable. George Seguy argued that France's monetary troubles were being treated at the expense of French workers. Jacques Fauvet, editor of *Le Monde*, reflected some other domestic skepticism over the move: "The logicians who govern us have already answered: things are getting better but not enough to prevent them from going from bad to worse." Quoted in *The New York Times*, 17 August 1969, Sec. IV, p. 4.

23. Because it exceeded France's automatic drawing rights in the Fund, the IMF obligated the French to submit to surveillance of their recovery program. Of the $1.6 billion in additional assistance, $1 billion came from a new "swap" arrangement with the U.S. Federal Reserve. The final post-devaluation challenge was how to adjust the Common Market's CAP with its common pricing system to the altered French exchange rate. The problem arose be-

cause the calculation of farm prices was not made on the value of member currencies, but on a standard unit of account based on the U.S. dollar. The French devaluation would have thus raised French farm prices by 11.1 percent, benefiting French farmers but damaging the government's fight against inflation. In EEC meetings in Brussels, the French proposed a devaluation of the unit of account that would have offset the inflationary impact of the franc devaluation in France, but would have raised the price of farm exports from France to other Common Market members. In an 18-hour meeting of Finance Ministers in Brussels, the six hammered out a compromise agreement. They decided to suspend uniform support levels for farm prices, in effect isolating French farm goods for 28 months until the end of 1971. During that period, French prices would be permitted to rise slowly. The French market was to be sealed off from other European markets by a system of export taxes and import subsidies. Although the arrangement effectively served the government's battle against inflation, it was particularly ironic since the French, who had been most insistent about the construction of a common agricultural policy, were the first to encounter circumstances requiring its suspension. Moreover, French troubles with the CAP indirectly enhanced the prospects for British membership into the EEC. By demonstrating that even a major actor like France could require special treatment on farm issues under an arrangement designed particularly to suit their purposes, the British were able to argue more persuasively for special treatment of their own during the transition to full membership.

24. Edward Kolodziej points out how this two-tiered scheme had the additional effect of tying the franc to the American dollar: "Considerations of parity advantage led the Pompidou regime to tie the franc to the dollar by creating a double market for the franc. The commercial market was keyed to the official rate of 5.5 francs to the dollar. Government pronouncements, justifying the double market as a way of escaping American dominance, barely hid the umbilical cord uniting the two currencies. Paris had no wish to give too great a trade advantage to the United States (OR its partners) or to permit market forces to push the franc to levels that would decrease the competitiveness of French goods in world trade" (*French International Policy Under de Gaulle and Pompidou*, p. 227).

25. See Stephen Blank in his article, "Britain: The Politics of Foreign Economic Policy," in Katzenstein, *Between Power and Plenty*, pp. 92–93.

26. Wilson announced the closing of British military bases east of Suez, the withdrawal of British forces from those bases by the end of 1971, and the cancellation of plans to purchase fifty F-111 swing-wing planes from the United States. The moves were designed to cut government expenditures by $720 million in the fiscal year beginning 1 April 1969 and $1 billion the following year. Economic adjustments had telling military-strategic consequences. As Wilson concluded about this new defense policy, Britain's "security lies fundamentally in Europe."

27. France was not included in this group because of her own monetary difficulties at the time. The British program to protect sterling was threatened in November 1968 by French problems with the franc and a growing confrontation between France and West Germany over proposed exchange-rate changes. With the franc and the pound both in a weakened state, the French and the British became involved in a moderate deflationary competition to assure that the next inevitable speculation into marks would come at the expense of the other state's currency.

28. See Wolfram Hanrieder, *The Stable Crisis*, p. 82.

29. For insight into Schiller's views, see the interviews published in *Die Welt*, 6 June 1969, p. 6; and *The Times*, 4 June 1969, p. 21, and 6 June 1969, p. 26.

30. See John Odell, *U.S. International Monetary Policy*, pp. 322–26.

31. Another consequence of the revaluation was that the new SPD government had to face angry German farmers, a confrontation the CDU had long avoided. In the course of the float, the government had asked the EEC to permit border taxes of 5.5 percent on agricultural imports to protect German farmers from lower prices from abroad as the mark appreciated in value. The revaluation lowered the government's guaranteed minimum prices for farm goods, since they were denominated in dollars. Schiller's tack was to ask the EEC for $50 million in additional direct farm subsidies for each percentage of revaluation. The agreement reached was a combination of these direct farm subsidies to be paid to German farmers from the Common Agricultural Fund through 1973 (though at a rate lower than Schiller had

requested) and a supplemental domestic subsidy to farmers. German farmers complained bitterly that this compensation was less than the advantages won by French farmers after the devaluation of the franc.

32. The measures included a 10 percent advance payment on self-employed and corporate income taxes and a temporary 10 percent increase of withholding taxes on workers' income.

33. Monetary exchange controls were a sensitive issue in postwar West Germany because of their association with the policies of Hitler's lieutenant Hjalmar Schacht.

34. Extremely unhappy with the German unilateral action, Paris charged Bonn with breaking the Common Market Treaty and seeking an economic and monetary domination of Europe. See Le Monde, 11 May 1971, p. 1. The Dutch decided to float with the mark, and the Swiss and the Austrians revalued their currencies.

35. See Uwe Kitzinger, Diplomacy and Persuasion: How Britain Joined the Common Market.

36. The prospects for monetary union and its impact have received wide treatment. See, for example, Fred Hirsch, "The Politics of European Monetary Integration," The World Today 28 (October 1972): 424–33; Giovanni Magnifico, European Monetary Unification (New York: John Wiley, 1973); Peter Coffey and John Presley, European Monetary Integration (London: Macmillan & Co., 1971). For its implications for the United States, see Lawrence B. Krause and Walter Salant, eds., European Monetary Union and Its Meaning for the United States (Washington, D.C.: Brookings Institution, 1973).

37. See, for example, Ian Davidson, "Monetary Union: The Emperor's Clothes," International Currency Review 4 (July–August 1972): 26–29; and Richard N. Cooper, "Monetary Unification in Europe: When and How?" The Morgan Guaranty Survey, May 1972.

38. See Edward L. Morse, "European Monetary Union and American Foreign Economic Policy," in Wolfram F. Hanrieder, The United States and Western Europe, pp. 187–210.

39. See Gus Tyler, "Labor's Multinational Pains," pp. 113–32.

40. See Robert Pastor, Congress and the Politics of U.S. Foreign Economic Policy, 1929–1976. This sectoral protectionism amid an otherwise liberal scheme is discussed by Charles Lipson, "The Transformation of Trade: The Sources and Effects of Regime Change," International Organization 36 (Spring 1982): 417–55.

41. The French, in particular, have been attracted to orderly marketing arrangements and advanced proposals for such schemes in the 1970s.

42. For an excellent discussion of these negotiations, see Benjamin Cohen, "The Revolution in Atlantic Economic Relations."

43. The so-called Peterson report that appeared in late 1971, authored by Nixon's chief advisor on international economic affairs, stated the view that national power and economic well-being were a function of the trade surplus and that the U.S. would act aggressively, if necessary, to protect and enlarge it. See Peter G. Peterson, The United States in the Changing World Economy (Washington: U.S. Government Printing Office, 1971).

44. See Jane Snedden Little, Euro-Dollars.

45. See, for example, John Odell, U.S. International Monetary Policy, Chap. 5.

46. American policy-makers were concerned that the resolution of sterling's problems would result in an attack on the dollar. Robert Solomon reports that contingency planning for just such an eventuality had been under way for two years. (See his The International Monetary System, p. 96.) Immediately after the British move, President Johnson made a pledge to defend the fixed gold price of $35 an ounce, in effect denying any consideration of a dollar devaluation. The Federal Reserve also negotiated strengthened lines of defense for the American dollar most notably by increasing its reciprocal "swap" facilities with other European states by over $2 billion.

47. For an insider's account of the growing problems of the London gold pool see Charles Coombs, The Arena of International Finance, Chap. 9. See also Sherman J. Maisel, Managing the Dollar (New York: W. W. Norton, 1973).

48. For a more-thorough account of the role of South African gold, see Susan Strange, "International Monetary Relations," in Shonfield, ed., International Economic Relations of the Western World, 1959–1971, vol. 2, pp. 304–18.

49. As Susan Strange suggests, the agreement, in essence, permits "that sales of gold by South Africa to monetary authorities might be made on any day when both London fixing prices were $35 or less, in an amount reasonable and commensurate with one-fifth of weekly

sales of new production required to be marketed to meet balance of payments needs." Ibid., p. 312.

50. See Robert Triffin, "De Gaulle at Stockholm: Villain, Hero or Sphinx?" *Interplay* 1 (1968): 15–17; and Edward Morse, *Foreign Policy and Interdependence*, pp. 243–45.

51. For an account of the Stockholm meeting, see Robert Solomon, *The International Monetary System*, pp. 143–48.

52. The agreement to expand IMF quotas included an understanding that these member payments, 2.5 percent of which were to be paid in gold, would not deplete the U.S. gold supply.

53. See, for example, George N. Halm, ed., *Approaches to Greater Flexibility of Exchange Rates* (Princeton: Princeton University Press, 1970); John Williamson, *The Crawling Peg*, Essays in International Finance, no. 50 (Princeton: International Finance Section, 1965); and Fred Hirsch, *Money International* (London: Penguin, 1967).

54. At the 1969 annual meeting of the IMF, Treasury Secretary Kennedy informally suggested that a study of the "crawling peg" be undertaken. In December, the flexibility position was strengthened by Hendrik Houthakker, a leading Nixon advisor, when he called for smaller and more-frequent changes in exchange rates. See also Harry G. Johnson, "The Case for Flexible Exchange Rates, 1969," *Review of the Federal Reserve Bank of St. Louis* 51 (May 1969): 12–24. For British and French views on exchange-rate flexibility, see the *London Financial Times*, 3 October 1969, p. 18. The French refusal to participate in any studies of greater exchange-rate flexibility was given by Finance Minister Giscard d'Estaing, who referred to them as a "sort of monetary LSD." See the International Monetary Fund, *Summary Proceedings. Annual Meeting* (1969), p. 60.

55. The domestic politics of the Nixon decision are ably discussed by Joanne Gowa, *Closing the Gold Window*; and John Odell, *U.S. International Monetary Policy*, Chap. 4. See also Glen R. Shear, "The International Aspects of President Nixon's New Economic Policy, 1971," (Senior honors thesis, Brandeis University, 1981).

56. Nixon's appointment of John Connolly in December 1970 has invited considerable comment. He was, in many respects, the right man for the time—an outspoken advocate of American economic interests and a tough negotiator. With time, however, his toughness proved a liability in reaching an agreement, and his influence declined toward the end of negotiations. See, for example, Henry Kissinger, *White House Years* (Boston: Little, Brown, 1979), pp. 951–58; John Odell, *U.S. International Monetary Policy*, pp. 243–63; Joanne Gowa, *Closing the Gold Window*, pp. 155–58; and Robert Solomon, *The International Monetary System*, pp. 190–91.

57. Henry Kissinger, *White House Years*, pp. 957–59.

58. Robert Solomon, *The International Monetary System*, p. 198.

59. Ibid.

60. The communiqué from the Smithsonian Agreement is reprinted in the *Department of State Bulletin*, 10 January 1972. See also Marc J. Schneider, "The Smithsonian Monetary Accord of 1971: An Analysis of Failure in the International Monetary System," (Senior honors thesis, Brandeis University, 1981).

61. As quoted in *The New York Times*, 19 December 1971, p. 1.

62. This decline in cooperation among international financial officials is lamented by Charles A. Coombs, who blames the Nixon administration for this new environment. See his *The Arena of International Finance*, Chap. 12.

63. For the text of Shultz's statement, see *The New York Times*, 13 February 1973, p. 56.

64. John Odell argues that the appointment of George Shultz as Treasury Secretary, replacing John Connolly, gave influence to those in Washington favoring greater exchange-rate flexibility. Shultz made his support clear to the IMF annual meeting in 1972. Odell suggested that the abrupt devaluation in February 1973 was not warranted by market conditions, that the U.S. trade account was on the road to recovery, and that the Smithsonian parities could have been preserved. See his *U.S. International Monetary Policy*, pp. 292–313. While acknowledging his support for exchange-rate reform, Shultz suggests that the pressure of events carried greater weight. See George P. Shultz and Kenneth W. Dam, *Economic Policy Beyond the Headlines*, pp. 126–31.

65. Odell suggests that the top American leadership on international monetary affairs, with the exception of Arthur Burns, was inclined toward a floating regime. This group in-

cluded Shultz, Paul Volcker, Peter Flanigan (the new head of the Council on International Economic Policy), and Herbert Stein (the new Chairman of the Council of Economic Advisors). See his *U.S. International Monetary Policy*, pp. 307–13.

66. The French wanted the items to be presented as "demands" rather than "suggestions."

67. The reform effort is treated by John Williamson, *The Failure of World Monetary Reform, 1971–1974* (New York: New York University Press, 1977); Robert Solomon, *The International Monetary System*, Chapter 14; Edward M. Bernstein et al., *Reflections on Jamaica: Essays in International Finance*, No. 115 (Princeton: International Finance Section, 1976); and Tom de Vries, "Jamaica, or the Non-Reform of the International Monetary System," *Foreign Affairs* 54 (April 1976): 577–605. There is also a large literature analyzing the problems of the international monetary system after 1971 and making suggestions for reform. See, for example, Benjamin J. Cohen, *Organizing the World's Money* (New York: Basic Books, 1977); C. Fred Bergstein, *The Dilemmas of the Dollar: The Economics and Politics of United States International Monetary Policy*, Chaps. 14–16; Fred Hirsch, Michael Doyle, and Edward L. Morse, *Alternatives to Monetary Disorder* (New York: McGraw-Hill, 1977); J. Marcus Fleming, *Reflections on International Monetary Reform, Essays in International Finance*, No. 107 (Princeton: International Finance Section, 1974); Lawrence B. Krause, "Sequel to Bretton Woods: A Proposal to Reform the World Monetary System; A Staff Paper," (Washington, D.C.: The Brookings Institute, 1971).

68. The communiqué included the following suggestions: "It was agreed that attention should be directed to the appropriate monetary means and division of responsibilities for defending stable exchange rates and for insuring a proper degree of convertibility of the system; to the proper role of gold, of reserve currencies, and of Special Drawing Rights in the operation of the system; to the appropriate volume of liquidity; to reexamination of the permissible margins of fluctuation around established exchange rates and other means of establishing a suitable degree of flexibility; and to other measures dealing with movements of liquid capital. It is recognized that decisions in each of these areas are closely linked." (Reprinted in the *Department of State Bulletin*, 10 January 1972.)

69. The work of the Committee of Twenty is summarized in IMF, *International Monetary Reform: Documents of the Committee of Twenty* (Washington, 1974).

70. Robert Solomon points to the ironic similarities of the Volcker Plan with the Keynes Plan for a Clearing Union in 1943. What the United States had opposed as a creditor nation in 1943, it was now sponsoring as a debtor state thirty years later. See his *The International Monetary System*, pp. 242–43.

71. For the text of the meeting's communiqué, see *The New York Times*, 28 March 1973, p. 65.

72. See, for example, Jack Bennett, "A Free Dollar Makes Sense," *Foreign Policy* 21 (Winter 1975–1976): 63–75.

73. Cf. Benjamin J. Cohen, *Organizing the World's Money*, Chaps. 7–8.

74. Peter G. Peterson, *The United States in the Changing World Economy*.

CHAPTER 5

1. Albert Bressand, "Mastering the 'Worldeconomy'," *Foreign Affairs* 61 (Spring 1983): 745–72.

2. For one example of the impact of regulatory policies on American industry compared with their competitors in Britain, France, and West Germany, see Ronald Brickman, Sheila Jasanoff, and Thomas Ilgen, *Controlling Chemicals: Regulatory Politics in Europe and the United States* (Ithaca: Cornell University Press, forthcoming 1985), Chap. 9.

3. Robert Keohane made this point clear to me.

4. Albert Bressand, "Mastering," p. 745.

5. William Diebold, "The United States in the World Economy: A Fifty Year Perspective," *Foreign Affairs* 62 (Fall 1983): 97.

6. Robert D. Putnam and Nicholas Bayne, *Hanging Together: The Seven-Power Summits* (Cambridge: Harvard University Press, 1984), p. 101.

7. Albert Bressand, "Mastering," p. 745.

8. See IMF, *International Monetary Reform. Documents of the Committee of Twenty* (Washington: IMF, 1974).

9. The work of the Interim Committee is treated by Robert Solomon, *The International Monetary System,* Chap. 17, Brian Tew, *The Evolution of the International Monetary System,* pp. 203–209; and Kenneth W. Dam, *The Rules of the Game,* Chap. 8.

10. The role of multinational banks is treated by Jonathan Aronson in *Money and Power.*

11. See, for example, Jack Bennett, "A Free Dollar Makes Sense," pp. 63–75.

12. See, for example, Otmar Emminger, "Exchange Rate Policy Reconsidered," Occasional Papers No. 10 (New York: Group of Thirty, 1982); and Richard M. Levich, " 'Overshooting' in the Foreign Exchange Market," Occasional Papers No. 5 (New York: Group of Thirty, 1981).

13. See, for example, Henry C. Wallich, Otmar Emminger, Robert V. Roosa, and Peter B. Kenen, "World Money and National Policies," Occasional Papers No. 12 (New York: Group of Thirty, 1983). See especially the article by Robert Roosa, "Economic Instability and Flexible Exchange Rates," pp. 35–62.

14. See Robert Solomon, *The International Monetary System,* pp. 312–17.

15. The Jamaica meeting invited considerable comment. See, for example, Tom de Vries, "Jamaica or the Non-Reform of the International Monetary System," pp. 577–605; Edward M. Bernstein, et al., *Reflections on Jamaica;* and George H. Halm, *Jamaica and the Par-Value System,* Essays in International Finance, No. 170 (Princeton: International Finance Section, 1977).

16. For a recent call for a return to the gold standard, see Jack Kemp, "Why the G.O.P. Needs a Heart of Gold," *The New York Times,* 12 August 1984, Sect. III, p. 2.

17. See David Yoffie, *Power and Protectionism;* and Louis Turner and Neil McMullen with Colin I. Bradford, *The Newly Industrializing Countries: Trade and Adjustment* (London: George Allen and Unwin, 1982).

18. For a detailed look at the Tokyo Round Agreement, see GATT, *The Tokyo Round of Multilateral Trade Negotiations* (Geneva, 1979). See also William R. Cline, Noburo Kawanade, T.O.M. Kronsjö, and Thomas Williams, *Trade Negotiations in the Tokyo Round: A Qualitative Assessment* (Washington, D.C.: Brookings Institution, 1978) and Stephen D. Krasner, "The Tokyo Round: Particularistic Interests and Prospects for Stability in the Global Trading System," *International Studies Quarterly* 23 (December 1979): 491–531.

19. See Thomas R. Graham, "Revolution in Trade Politics," *Foreign Policy* 36 (Fall 1979): 49–63. See also Hans O. Schmitt, "Mercentilism: A Modern Argument," *The Manchester School* 47 (June 1979): 93–111; and W. M. Gordon, "The Revival of Protectionism," Occasional Papers No. 14 (New York: Group of Thirty, 1984).

20. Robert Keohane, *After Hegemony: Cooperation and Discord in the World Political Economy,* p. 190.

21. The role of surplus capacity is emphasized as an explanation of growing protectionism by Susan Strange, "The Management of Surplus Capacity: Or How Does Theory Stand Up To Protectionism 1970s Style?" *International Organization* 33 (Summer 1979): 303–34. For a view generally supportive of this argument focusing on the automobile sector, see Peter F. Cowhey and Edward Long, "Testing Theories of Regime Change: Hegemonic Decline or Surplus Capacity?" *International Organization* 37 (Spring 1983): 157–83.

22. Cowhey and Long, "Testing Theories of Regime Change."

23. Interview with *L'Aurore,* 25 March 1977. See also the address by Louis de Guiringuad, 8 November 1977, reprinted by the French embassy in Washington, Press and Information Division.

24. Speech by Foreign Minister Hans-Dietrich Genscher before the OECD, Paris, 19 June 1978. Reprinted by the German Press and Information Division.

25. For a discussion of chemicals, see Thomas L. Ilgen, "Better Living Through Chemistry: The Chemical Industry in the World Economy," *International Organization* 37 (Autumn 1983): 647–80.

26. See GATT, *The Tokyo Round.*

27. For treatment of the economic summits, see George de Menil and Anthony M. Solomon, *Economic Summitry* (New York: Council on Foreign Relations, 1983); and Robert D. Putnam and Nicholas Bayne, *Hanging Together.*

28. Putnam and Bayne, *Hanging Together,* pp. 11–17.

29. This point is raised by Henry C. Wallich, "Evolution of the International Monetary System," *Challenge* (January–February 1979): 13–31.

30. The most influential study was done by Alexander Crockett and Morris Goldstein, "Inflation Under Fixed and Flexible Exchange Rates," *IMF Staff Papers* 23 (1976): 509–44. Another study examining the roots of inflation in the 1970s was the so-called McCracken Report. See Paul McCracken et al. *Towards Full Employment and Price Stability* (Paris: OECD, 1977). For a critical review of the McCracken Report see Robert O. Keohane, "Economics, Inflation and the Role of the State," *World Politics* 31 (October 1978): 108–28.

31. Speech before the subcomittee on foreign economic policy of the Senate Foreign Relations Committee, 19 March 1977.

32. For a good defense of the German position, see Helmut Schmidt's address to an IISS meeting, 28 October 1977, reproduced by the German Information Center, New York, New York.

33. On the European Monetary System, see Tom de Vries, *On the Meaning and Future of the European Monetary System*, Essays in International Finance, No. 138 (Princeton: International Finance Section, 1980); P. H. Trezise, ed., *The European Monetary System: Its Promise and Prospects* (Washington: Brookings Institution, 1979); and Benjamin J. Cohen, *The European Monetary System: An Outsider's View*, Essays in International Finance, No. 142 (Princeton: International Finance Section, 1981).

34. Reproduced by the German Information Center, New York, New York, 1978.

35. See Henry Wallich, "Evolution of the International."

36. Address before the Iowa State Bar Association, 22 June 1978. Reproduced by the Bureau of Public Affairs, U.S. Department of State.

37. For a full text of the Bonn summit communiqué, see *The New York Times*, 18 July 1978, p. D12.

38. Robert D. Putnam and Nicholas Bayne, *Hanging Together*, pp. 94–99.

39. For an account of the politics and economics of this decision, see *The New York Times*, 13 November 1978, p. D3.

40. Ibid.

41. For Putnam and Bayne, the Tokyo summit represents a turning point in the legacy of the seven-power summits. The early summits address the problems of recovery; those beginning with Tokyo focus on inflation and economic slowdown (see *Hanging Together*, Chap. 7). For another group of reflections on the summit process, see C. Fred Bergsten et al., *From Rambouillet to Versailles: A Symposium*, Essays in International Finance, No. 149 (Princeton: International Finance Section, 1982).

42. The critique of regulation is often based on an approximation of its costs. See *The Cost of Federal Government Regulation of Economic Activity* (Washington, D.C.: American Enterprise Institute, 1978), and *Cost of Regulation: Study for the Business Roundtable* (New York: Arthur Anderson & Co., 1979). For critiques of the American approach to regulation, see Ronald Brickman, Sheila Jasanoff, and Thomas Ilgen, *Controlling Chemicals;* Steven Kelman, *Regulating America, Regulating Sweden: A Comparative Study of Occupational Safety and Health Regulations* (Cambridge: MIT Press, 1981); and Eugene Bardach and Robert A. Kagan, *Going by the Book: The Problem of Regulatory Unreasonableness* (Philadelphia: Temple University Press, 1982).

43. For support of recourse to market incentives, see Allen V. Kneese and Charles L. Schultze, *Pollution, Prices and Public Policy* (Washington: Brookings Institution, 1975); and Robert Dorfman and Nancy S. Dorfman, eds., *Economics of the Environment* (New York: W. W. Norton, 1972). For a critique of this approach, see Steven Kelman, *What Price Incentives?* (Boston: Auburn House, 1981).

44. This is a prominent theme in Peter J. Katzenstein, *Between Power and Plenty*. See particularly the contributions by Kreile on West Germany, Pempel on Japan, and Krasner on the United States. See also Ezra Vogel, *Japan As Number ONE: Lessons for America* (New York: Harper & Row, 1980).

45. Corporatism is the term frequently used by students of comparative politics to describe this pattern of cooperation among business, government, and labor. See, for example, Philippe C. Schmitter, "Still the Century of Corporatism?" *Review of Politics* 36 (1974): 85–131; and Philippe C. Schmitter and G. Lehmbruch, eds., *Trends Toward Corporatist Intermediation* (London: Sage Publications, 1979).

46. Industrial policy became a politically attractive option in the early 1980s for Democrats opposed to Reaganomics. The literature on industrial policy is extensive. See, for example, Robert Reich, *The Next American Frontier;* and John Zysman and Laura Tyson, *American Industry in International Competition.* The international consequences of industrial policy are treated by William Diebold, *Industrial Policy as an International Issue* (New York: McGraw-Hill, 1980); and John Pinder, Takashi Hosomi, and William Diebold, "Industrial Poicy and the International Economy," *The Triangle Papers* No. 19 (New York: The Trilateral Commission, 1979).

47. For thorough treatment of these two summits, see Robert Putnam and Nicholas Bayne, *Hanging Together,* Chap. 10.

48. Ibid., p. 104.

49. A recent study by William C. Freund and other economists at the New York Stock Exchange, "U.S. International Competitiveness: Perception and Reality," argues that American competitiveness has at least held its own over the last decade, and in important areas it has improved. See Freund's comments on this report in *The New York Times,* 5 August 1984, Section III, p. 2.

CHAPTER 6

1. The "demand for such rules and dependable behavior is explored by Robert O. Keohane, "The Demand for International Regimes," *International Organization* 36 (Spring 1982): 325–55. Theoretical explanations for such cooperation are treated in Robert O. Keohane, *After Hegemony,* Chaps. 4–7.

2. See Stephen D. Krasner, *International Regimes* (Ithaca: Cornell University Press, 1983); Robert O. Keohane and Joseph S. Nye, *Power and Interdependence;* and Seyom Brown, Nina W. Cornell, Larry L. Fabian, and Edith Brown Weiss, *Regimes for the Ocean, Outer Space and Weather* (Washington, D.C.: Brookings Institution, 1977).

3. The need for such cooperation is convincingly argued in Robert J. Gordon and Jacques Pelkmans, *Challenges to Interdependent Economies: The Industrial West in the Coming Decade* (New York: McGraw-Hill, 1979).

4. Daniel Bell, "The Future World Disorder," *Foreign Policy* 27 (Summer 1977): 16.

5. Cf. Robert Gilpin, *War and Change in World Politics* (Cambridge: Cambridge University Press, 1980).

6. This view is supported by Albert O. Hirschman, *National Power and the Structure of Foreign Trade* (Berkeley: University of California Press, 1945); Stephen D. Krasner, "State Power and the Structure of International Trade," pp. 317–43; and Charles P. Kindleberger, *The World in Depression.*

7. The argument is not that hegemonic economic powers will inevitably support liberal rules; rather, that their economic interests will suggest this choice. Foreign policies, economic and otherwise, are a product of many considerations, among them important political calculations that may run contrary to economic interests. The "content" of economic regimes is explored by John G. Ruggie, "International Regimes, Transactions and Change," in Stephen D. Krasner, *International Regimes,* pp. 195–232. It should be noted, however, that in the two relevant historical cases of hegemonic powers with market economies, Britain in the 19th century and the United States after World War II, liberal international rules have been followed.

8. See Robert Gilpin, *U.S. Power and the Multinational Corporation.*

9. For literature on the hegemonic stability thesis, see Chapter 1, note 2.

Index

Adenauer, Conrad, 36
Agnew, Spiro, 81
Agriculture, in trade negotiations, 65–66. *See also* Common Agricultural Policy
Atlantic relations: and commercial interdependence, 66–67; and coordination of economies, 128–29; French vision of, 59; 1950s transition in, 42–43
Automobiles, voluntary trade restraints, 122
Autonomy, 14; contradiction with interdependence, 9–10; 22, 113–15; in domestic economy, 8–9; maintenance of, 138; strategies for, 12

Balance of payments: deficits, 13, 22, 25; and flexible exchange rates, 115; U.S. management of, 23, 80, 101
Ball, George, 48
Barre, Raymond, 122
Bell, Daniel, 139
Benign neglect, 78, 79–80, 98–99, 133; and interdependence, 114; and 1972 election, 81; as policy, 15–16; shift away from, 124
Blumenthal, Michael, 127
Bonn summit, 129–30
Brandt, Willy, 91
Bretton Woods regime: basic principles from, 10–11; death of, 101; and interdependence, 100; major changes in, 93; "Pauper's Oath," 71. *See also* GATT-Bretton Woods regime
Britain: commercial ties with Commonwealth, 32; currency devaluation, 57; and EEC, 36, 89; in late 1950s, 31–32; in 1960s, 55–57; policy failures of, 37. *See also* Pound sterling
Burns, Arthur, 105
"Buy American" policy, 26

Callaghan, James, 56
Capital markets: European restrictions on, 40; internationalization of, 27, 49–50, 79
Carter, Jimmy: anti-inflation program, 130; election of, 126
Chemicals, in trade negotiations, 66
Christopher, Warren, 129
Cold War, 41; and American economic policy, 28
Common Agricultural Policy, 36, 60–61, 63, 94; and U.S. trade, 99–100. *See also* European Economic Community
Common Market. *See* European Economic Community

Connolly, John, 105
Currency: central bank swaps, 50; convertibility of, 10, 13, 27, 30, 40–41, 100–101, 109–10; European joint float of, 92; markets, 108, 118–20; speculation, 41, 44, 50, 58, 102; stabilization, 70; values, 110

Debré, Michel, 73, 74
Defense, European contribution to, 26
DeGaulle, Charles: and British EEC membership, 60; challenge to American privileges, 52–55; economic authority of, 29–30; and Free Trade Area, 37; and French independence, 85; meeting with Macmillan, 60
Dillon, Douglas, 38, 45–46, 71
Division of labor, international, 3–4, 6–7, 49, 77
Dollar: central role of, 11, 53–54, 76; convertibility with gold, 82, 105; devaluation of, 106–7, 108; and liquidity gap, 12; as reserve currency, 71; and speculation, 15, 69, 81, 92, 127; as standard, 79; strength of, 135; weakness of, 41–42
Domestic policy, and foreign economic policy, 23, 30

Economic growth, and Kennedy presidency, 46
Economic interdependence. *See* Interdependence
Economic power: American use of, 16; concept of, 2; interstate distribution of, 7; and wealth, 2–3. *See also* Political power; Wealth
Economic summits, 124–25
Economies, internationalization of, 141
EEC. *See* European Economic Community
Eisenhower, Dwight: free trade commitment, 25–26; and payments balances, 24–25
EMS. *See* European Monetary System
Erhard, Ludwig, 32; and Free Trade Area, 37
Europe: commercial divisions in, 28–29, 35–38, 59–63; economic friction with U.S., 44–45; economic relations in, 94–97; elusive common strategy, 139; and foreign economic policy, 28–34, 52–59, 85–93; and interdependence, 9–10; political unity, 62; postwar recovery of, 1, 12–13; and trade advantages, 13; undervalued currencies of, 93; and U.S. foreign policy, 78
Euro-dollar market, 14, 27; growth of, 100; and U.S. interest rates, 80
European Commission, increased authority to, 62
European Economic Community (EEC), 13, 28, 35; British membership in, 54, 59–60, 89–90, 94–95;